MW00948370

# STORMS AND GRACE

# STORMS AND GRACE

Robert A. Gardner

Copyright © 2008 by Robert A. Gardner.

ISBN:           Hardcover            978-1-4257-8478-2
                Softcover            978-1-4257-8447-8

All rights reserved. No part of this book may be reproduced or transmitted
in any form or by any means, electronic or mechanical, including photocopying,
recording, or by any information storage and retrieval system,
without permission in writing from the copyright owner.

This book was printed in the United States of America.

**To order additional copies of this book, contact:**
Xlibris Corporation
1-888-795-4274
www.Xlibris.com
Orders@Xlibris.com
42469

On many occasions' people ask, "Tell us about yourself. Have you always been so quiet and calm? How is it that you have such spiritual insight and maturity about life?" Sometimes I smile and say there's not much to talk about. Then there are times I feel the urge to thank God publicly as loud as I can for His saving grace in my life. In hearing my stories, many have asked me to write them down so others can know that the providence of God is real and full of hope for all.

*(This) fallen world is the battlefield for the greatest conflict the heavenly universe and earthly powers have ever witnessed. It was appointed as the theater on which would be fought out the grand struggle between good and evil, between heaven and hell. Every human being acts a part in this conflict. NO ONE CAN STAND ON NEUTRAL GROUND. Men must either accept or reject the world's Redeemer. All are witnesses, either for or against Christ. Christ calls upon those who stand under His banner to engage in the conflict with Him as faithful soldiers, that they may inherit the crown of life. They have been adopted as sons and daughters of God. Christ has left them His assured promise that great will be the reward in the kingdom of heaven of those who partake of His humiliation and suffering for the truth's sake.*

—Ellen G. White, *Sons and Daughters of God*

# INTRODUCTION

I call to remembrance my song in the night . . . . Oh that men
would praise the Lord for His goodness, and for His wonderful
works to the children of men! . . . . He maketh the storm a calm
so that the waves thereof are still.

*Psalms 77:6; 107:21, 29, KJV*

The autumn forest was quiet, stirred only by the occasional wind that rustled dry leaves and bare branches. I stood in line with others facing the forest, holding the small Military Armament Model 10 or MAC-10 machine gun. I breathed deeply the cool air and squeezed the trigger. The recoil, like a giant hand, pushed me back as the MAC exploded to life. Cords of angry orange fire sputtered from the short barrel, chasing ghostly bullets that ripped the ancient and young trees with shedding vengeance they didn't deserve. Bullets that missed the trees tore great clumps of hard-packed dirt, twisting the jagged pieces wildly into the mournful air. The acrid gun smoke drifted upward in lazy spirals, filling my nose with the perfume of war and chaos I knew so well. Round after round, the bullets poured from the barrel as my body shivered and swayed in rhythmic dance with the MAC. *Zooot, zooot, zooot,* the vibrations and cadenced of death raced up my arms in waves of excitement and down my spine like demon fingers, a masseur from hell or a lover gone mad in the heat of passion. When the last empty shell spun hot from the chamber, silence once again fell across the forest. Likewise, an emptiness and silence fell across me. In the cool forest morn, the mist hovers above low spots in the autumn woods and so was the mist of shrouded reason, the detached numbness, the trance of the hopelessness that settled in to the low spots of my wounded conscience. No amount of distractions, like this day in the forest, could erase the fact that all seemed lost. I was a hapless prisoner inside myself, always calling for help, calling for release and realizing in the end there was no one to hear.

Sometimes it's hard to know why you do things, why you make such bad, unexplainable choices like this one. Not so long ago, I was a Christian, a conscientious objector. I suffered like so many others the terror and hell of Vietnam's jungles and rice paddies. I was a medic, a lifesaver, and I never carried or fired a weapon until now. But now, here I was, in America, training with soldiers from every country, mercenaries, and imitators. Some were as mixed up and confused as I was. Some worst, they were beyond confused they were predators and scavengers on the fringe of humanity. They were frozen in glacial pain, claiming hearts that beat but were lifeless, claiming dreams that were as nightmarish as merchants of death could be. In Nam, you could look at people and tell they were going to die; all of us looked like those people. Chiseled into our dirty bearded faces were two black holes that stared expressionless. Our eyes were like rat eyes—black, dark, and deep as time itself. We mastered the art of death, and we valued nothing innocent or sacred. Even among us there was a predatory caution toward each other that was unspoken but deadly clear.

In the stillness of the forest night, like in Nam, like now, I try to figure it all out—something left over from thirty years ago. Phantom fears, untested courage, a lost innocence and a struggle for identity in my own family. I want so much to scan the universe for understanding and unravel the darkness I feel inside, this sense that I am an imitation of nothing special—common, fragile, and eternally cursed in life's journey. From the past, my dreams flood with torrent memories of suffocating jungles, rice-paddies, searing heat, diesel fuel, AK47s, M16s, mangled bodies and vicious bugs. My heart race in rhythm with thumping chopper blades, thudding mortar rounds, and distant bombs that rumbled like earthen thunder. Then I shiver as my skin remembers the bone-chilling monsoon rains, and the stinking, rotting mud that clung as tightly as a desperate lover. Vietnam, over and over again, a scratched record nobody wanted to hear. On quiet star-filled nights, the noise within beckons louder then the stillness outside. Glimmers of lighting spark the horizon of my memory and summon long ago storms of childhood. Early years of pain that never healed, the curse of being the second child, the hand-me-down one. The ugly one with nappy brown hair, and for all intense and purpose, I was considered a mistake.

The brightness and hopefulness of the new day, like the night, fail to rescue me from sorrow. It's always there; it's soul pain that hurt deeper than flesh. It was this pain that brought me to this wooded nightmare, in America.

More then life itself, I long to breathe the air of freedom once again—to be free to love, free to trust, and free to hope. But for now, I remain a prisoner inside myself. I thirst as one in the desert for my best friend, my only true friend, Jesus. I've never seen Him, but I've heard Him and felt Him a thousand times. I'm still lost in a far country, alone, hardwired in "neutral," and resisting no evil, inviting no good; whatever happens, happens. At times, I am a child at heart, innocent and hopeful; yet at other times, I am more afraid of myself than any man living and know in my innermost soul that, if angered, any man living should be afraid of me.

I am not sure when my life began, but I am told that in the dreariness of a Michigan winter, I was born. The bright lights and rush of cold air that welcomed me came Wednesday, December 11. Harry Truman was president, a loaf of bread cost ten cents, and a gallon of gas was a nickel more. The weather page of the *Detroit News* scrawled in faded black print says, "Increasing cloudiness, mild, with showers on Thursday, changing to snow flurries and colder Thursday night"—a winter storm. It seems that at each phase of my life or fork in the road of experience, I am reborn into the winter of change or into the turbulent storm of some life's event. My uneven paths knew days of gentle winds, sunshine, and the sweet fragrance of spring, but it was the storms from which I grew. Fearful, and yet divine, the storms nurtured in me the best and, at times, the worst. Here is my story. I begin in the middle. I begin in a storm.

# PART I

## VIETNAM

# CHAPTER ONE

*"A perfect day . . ."*

The summer sky in 1962 was ocean blue with armadas of delicate clouds sailing high gentle winds. Throughout the neighborhood, annoying cicadae fresh from their seven-year sleep chirped, piercing concerts among old two-story homes and tall maple trees. I was fifteen, and it was a perfect day—hot and lazy.

Eastern High School, an old four story gray brick building a block from where I lived was out for the summer. Summer recess meant there was little to do for nearly three months, but I was rarely bored, thanks to an active imagination and a knack for being accident pone. I was a student in the Junior ROTC, the Reserve Officer Training Course, and that became my source of pride, the one place where I felt important and alive. Nevertheless, I knew in my heart that in spite of pride and importance my academic abilities bordered on extinction, and that bothered me greatly because it seemed I always struggled with things other students found easy. But, even then, I was learning how to compensate for my deficiencies, doing things differently and in my own way. For example, unlike other cadets who scribbled or sketched class notes and drawings with pen and pencil, I actually painted pictures of weapons in brilliant watercolors and meticulously printed all my class notes in neat block letters. Admittedly, that became a bit obsessive, yet it made me focus on details others overlooked. The best thing to happen from my artistry was that I stood out from the crowd in a way that brought notice from the ROTC instructors who eyed me suspiciously for medical competency or brilliancy.

I virtually lived and breathed ROTC day and night. It was my third year as a cadet, but the memory of my disastrous first year and how it nearly changed the course of my life stood out with painful clarity.

My first year in ROTC was really bad—grade wise, that is; I got a D. All I ever wanted to be was a soldier, a United States Marine ultimately. The D was a spear through my heart. It was like a horse kick in the stomach. My pulse raced wildly, and my head swirled with disbelief, shame, and anger when I torn open the report card. I wanted to disappear from the face of the earth and probably would have were it not for one man. Six feet tall, gritty, broad shouldered and sporting a short brown, crew cut, Sgt. Richard Flynn, my instructor, became my best friend and hero. His raspy drill sergeant's voice poured out machine-gun diatribes, words that crushed and molded young minds at the same time. Between trashcan-tobacco spits, creative and colorful profanity, interrupted only by long draws on his cigarette, the students knew he really cared about them. At times, he smiled like Jackie Gleason; and at other times, he was more demonic, terrifying, and the unchallenged master of controlled rage. Like I said, Sergeant Flynn could totally crush or totally inspire. For me, it was the latter. By the third year of ROTC, I rose like the mythical Phoenix from the ashes of my morbid freshman dejection, ready to die, to the fastest-rising cadet in school history. Miraculously, my grades managed to rise with me. For the first time, I began to see Bs and a rare A or two. Sergeant Flynn and I knew I was not the smartest or most polished cadet at first, but I was the most dedicated, most enthusiastic, hardest working, most loyal and determined student he ever saw. In three semesters, I went from a buck-private to lieutenant colonel and brigade commander for all of the Eastside High School Districts of Detroit. He invested in me, and I didn't let him down.

It was that intense fascination with the military, the tentacles of curiosity that made war and its weapons such an enticing way to rid the summer of its boredom. I had imagined and actually made many improvised bombs in the past. From smoky ash can missiles to bombs made from dry ice, I made them, revised them, and looked for new ways to explode them.

As I said, it was a perfect day. I stood in our backyard along with my reluctant younger brother Darrell who was my assistant. Darrell struck a match and was holding it when the back screen door creaked and my baby brother Lester peeked his head out to see what we were doing. "Get back into the house", I shouted at him. I turned back around just in time to see my outstretched left hand and the hissing gray smoke billowing from the top of the homemade bottle bomb disappeared. Darrell had lit the bomb. As the day was perfect so was the absolute silence and darkness that followed. Time stopped and then started again in slow motion. Flickering bits of light filtered through my eyelashes as I tried to open them. I could see red, lots of red. My outstretched hand reappeared in ragged crimson and curled pieces of flesh. Squirting fountains of blood leaped from my face like a garden hose, and my ears swayed with a high-pitched ring. A scream froze in my throat and fought for escape, warbling, it raised in staccato shivers, exploding into Ma, Ma! Ma, Ma! I ran toward the wooden steps of the back porch with arms reaching out for help, reaching for life. The screen door flung open, then snapped closed behind me and I stood paralyzed in the middle of the kitchen floor.

"My God! My God, sonny!" Mom screamed.

"What did you do?"

Mr. Brown, a family friend grabbed dish towels and slammed one to my face and the other to my hands. I looked down at my legs,

"Oh shoot, my new pants!"

The polyesters were full of holes, and each one seeped with shards of glass and blood. A crimson pool gathered around my shoes and spread across the flood like a rising river.

In Detroit, and in most of America there was no 911 or emergency medical service (EMS). This was painfully true especially in the black neighborhoods; it took nearly an hour and a half for the police to show up. The police walked straight into our house, hardly asked any questions, offered no additional help, and casually pointed out they were there to drive me to the hospital. My father was at work, so we had no transportation. I sat in the back seat of the patrol car on cold dirty plastic covers that smelled of old blood, vomit, and urine transfixed in anger staring at the ragged floor. My tongue was numb, it was split down the middle, and so talking was difficult. I didn't want to talk anyway. Though the sun shown brightly that afternoon, darkness filled my mind. I mumbled to myself and partly to anyone listening, "It should have killed me! I wished it would have killed me!" The key turned, and the patrol car engine sputtered to life, drowning out my dirge of self-hatred. The policemen briefly glanced at me, then nonchalantly turned forward and said nothing else the whole trip to the hospital. Tears filled my eyes as passing trees and buildings reflected off the car windows. I knew things were changing in my life, and I knew I would not see a perfect day again for a long time.

# CHAPTER TWO

*Search me, O God, and know my heart: try me, and know*
*my thoughts: and see if there be any wicked way in me,*
*and lead me in the way everlasting.*
—Psalms 139:23, 24

That summer of change was drawing to a close. The bright scars along my left cheek and across my lip could not compare to the scars inside. How could I deal with people, with school, with ROTC? I was disfigured and a fool. Why didn't I just die! Why was I always doing dumb, stupid things! Many nights, I sat on my bed looking out the window. The moon and stars sparkled and swayed gently through teary eyes and muffled inner cries. At times those moments of mental angst were overshadowed by physical pain. In the emergency room, chattering, playful medical students had hurriedly sewed up my face and a small wound in my right upper chest. Although the chest wound was now healed, a sharp pain would unexpectedly rip across my chest from time to time, causing me to grunt loudly and clutch my chest with both hands. Dr. Hill, our longtime family doctor, shook his head as he reopened the wound and pulled out a long sliver of glass just in front of my right lung. "Boy, this thing almost killed you!" Of course, a saged lecture poured from his freckled brown face; but as always, it ended with a broad smile of perfect teeth through a haze of cigarette smoke. I really liked Dr. Hill; he died of lung cancer years later. Many more years were to follow before I learned that that same explosion had nearly blinded me. I would discover I had a serious left retinal injury from a glass shard that tore through my cornea and into the delicate retina. Amazed, many doctors queried why I wasn't blinded or suffered bad vision in that eye. All would shake their heads in disbelief but none was more amazed than I was.

I often think of Billy, my older brother. He was my tormentor, mentor, and hero. He was born on December 10 and I on December 11 the following year. Except for the get-lost-little-brother that plagued my teenage years, we have always been close. Right after that explosion, my face and hands in bandages, he attempted to cheer me in his usual what-the-hell attitude. He said, "Bobby, that was the best one yet! Man, it was loud! Everybody in the neighborhood heard it!" Then he started to grin and laugh uncontrollably like a hyena. I tried not to laugh but couldn't help myself. Oh, how it hurt to laugh. I loved Billy for that bit of psychology. He knew I was hurting inside. Usually, his playfulness and jokes were continuous and ever annoying; but that day, he limited his fun to that one moment.

Not long after that Billy joined the Marine Corps and went away. He did what I always dreamed of doing. I wanted to be a John Wayne marine, a marine whose chest bulged with shiny medals and colorful ribbons of valor. A marine with large steel-like muscles, a confident, seductive smile, and a paralyzing stare that demanded respect, but Billy did it first! The moment I found out, I was breathless with excitement, wild with visions of Billy and I dressed in bright red, white, and blue uniforms. My thoughts were a torrid of racing words and phases of how to ask Mom "the question." I begged and pleaded for her to let me drop out of high school and sign for me to join the marines. I envisioned Billy and me in the same combat unit, looking out for each other. But Mom's reply was sharp and final—no! Looking back now, she probably saved my life. The distant war in a place called Vietnam was just starting, and the young marines who served there would eventually pay a high price. Many would die, all would be changed forever, and I would have been among them.

I was nearly seventeen, and it was my last year in ROTC. It was the year I was to make the cadet corps' highest rank—full colonel. I was already the brigade commander for the east side of Detroit in 1963, but now I was in a position to be citywide cadet commander. I was to be honored to lead a large parade and receive several awards at graduation the next June. But over that summer, the explosion happening, Billy leaving, Mom saying no, and my almost nonexistent self-esteem further disappearing, I could not have felt worst or more hopeless. The fire for life and adventure was on permanent hold. I began to think about life and death, but more about death since I considered visiting its domain more than once. Then this thing about religion, God and the devil kept coming to mind. I was not a church person by any means. As far back as I could remember, the Baptist Church we attended every Sunday was long and boring except for the pageantry of funny people Billy and I observed. "Mother," that's what we called my grandmother, always made sure we had clean skull-scraping haircuts from my father. Billy and I were then ceremoniously dosed with strong cheap perfume, our faces and shoes greased with Vaseline petroleum jelly, given a dime or quarter for the offering, which usually ended up at the local corner store instead, and told the well-recited lecture to not start anything foolish at church. That last warning was justified because the things to laugh about in church were endless. There were the powdered fat ladies with watermelon heads, oversized feathered hats cocked to one side, and dead beady-eyed foxes draped across their shoulders. Then there were the deacons in black suits, white socks and brown shoes that sang miles out of tune and the audience who either grimaced or laughed but said amen anyway. Of course, Sunday afternoon was much better. There was always freshly killed chicken fried golden brown from our backyard, hot buttered biscuits, streaming rice, and the query by my father of why Billy and I acted a fool in church.

But anyway, there in my emptiness, with no foreseeable future of my choosing, I found myself picking up and reading "religious stuff." I listened to choral music and radio evangelist night after night; I even took a Bible correspondence course from one of them. Still, the emptiness continued; nothing seemed right in my life. Then one day, I saw a silver-headed man with a kind mellow voice on television; his name was George Vanderman. His program was called *It Is Written*. The program's slogan was, "Man shall not live by bread alone, but by every word that proceedth out of the mouth of God." What captivated my attention more than all the other religious programs was his series on the vastness of the universe and the god of the universe who personally cared about sinners, even me. The book *Planet in Rebellion* along with a free Bible correspondence course was offered; I accepted it, and my life was forever changed. Eventually, I met two Bible workers sent from *It Is Written*—David and Hattie Fulton. They belonged to a strange group of people called Seventh-day Adventist. They invited me to go to church with them on Saturday, or Sabbath, as they called it. Mom was suspicious, so was Dad; but they had noticed my depression was less, and I appeared to be a little happier, so they cautioned, "Just be careful." Over the weeks that followed, I attended nightly revival meetings at the church. I felt a strong battle raging inside. What will everybody think if I joined these people, if I got religious? What about ROTC? What about the marines? What about my parents? Little by little, the resistance weakened, and I gave my heart to God. I determined to read everything I could get my hands on, Seventh-day Adventist literature, Jehovah's Witnesses, Baptist, Catholics, Holiness, Church of God, Muslims, and many others. I wanted to know what "truth" was for myself. My father called me hard rock because I was so stubborn and strong willed; I was determined to be sure of what I was going to believe. No one was going to tell me what he or she thought was right or wrong; I was going to search God's word for myself. Of all the churches and beliefs, this one, the Adventist appeared to follow the Bible most consistently. They seemed to have a purpose, a prophetic future rooted in Biblical history. After much prayer and fasting, I joined the Adventist Church.

Sergeant Flynn, my ROTC instructor, was outraged by my decision. "What to you mean you joined a church and can't drill on Saturday! What the hell! They don't believe in killing for your country either, huh?" Clearly, he was devastated.

He'd groomed me for leadership and excellence, a model for other cadets. Now I had "gotten religious!" My real father had even less to say then Sergeant Flynn, as if he didn't care what I did. We didn't speak much anyway. We had this mutual love-couldn't-stand-each-other relation that spanned years. I hated his rampages of fussing punctuated by an occasional "dammit!" Mom didn't say much either, only for me to be careful. Years later my Mother would attend the Adventist Church more then the Baptist Church she was a member of. Billy, on the other hand was himself. He scoffed and laughed in his usual mule-bantering way. So did most of my friends and not a few of my enemies who preferred the old me. It became the best of times and the worst of times. The question that gnawed most was, "Would I stand true to God or give up under pressure?" I didn't know. All I knew was that for the first time in my life I had real value—I was worth something. The Jesus of the Bible became my Savior and my friend. All the "stuff" that muddled my life was forgiven, and inside, I felt free and clean! The outer scars and inner wounds didn't matter any longer. Despite my newfound happiness and peace, a chill wind stirred my subconscious. At the edge of hearing, I sensed an inner rumbling. Ominous mental flashes caused a restlessness I could not explain. I knew a change was coming as certain as summer faded to fall and fall to winter. For me, the summer of joy and new discovery was passing into a season of storms and darkness. I wondered what was next. I think, in all of life, sometimes the future is best left unknown.

# CHAPTER THREE

*Though He slay me, yet will I trust in Him.*

—Job 13:15

Swiftly, the currents of time pass like moving clouds; and as from an eagle's view, scenes of early long-forgotten years reappear on memories landscape. There were scenes of singing in the choir, Bible studies, leading out in church programs, even preaching, witnessing door to door, selling magazines for college, being thrilled by the miracle of answered prayers, enduring the uncertainty of job firings for keeping Sabbath, rejoicing in trials, and totally aflame for the love of God. I had an eternal restlessness for the lost I could not reach. More than anything else in life, I wanted to be a champion for God, like David, Daniel and Paul! But in all my enthusiasm, there was one dilemma—even champions had to eat and make a living. What was I going do between earthly now and heavenly later? I had graduated from high school and was clueless as to what to do next. Should I go to art school and be a sign painter? What about the ministry? Definitely no, there were still too many cracks in my life. Besides, it was too strict, too sacred, and too perfect a job for me. What about medicine? That whimsical thought lasted all of a few seconds. Being a doctor was for people much smarted than me, it was a momentary fantasy of the poor and a delusion of the overly optimistic. Then the idea of a laboratory technologist popped up, mostly because it sounded pretty good and kind of important. Brother David Fulton, the first Adventist I every met in person, helped me make up my mind. "Robert," he said, "it doesn't matter what you do in life. If you dedicate your talents and life to God's service, He will bless you. Always make Him first, and you will never be last." So there it was, I would be a laboratory technologist.

After a summer of odd jobs—selling magazines, working as a grocery store stock boy, picking up trash and garbage, painting houses, washing dishes, doing janitorial work, cleaning windows, and whatever I could do—I earned enough money along with some savings to start college.

The trip to Berrien Springs, Michigan, about three hours east of Detroit, was exciting and scary. I was the first in my family to go away to college and really wanted to succeed. I'm not sure how my parents felt about my leaving, but for one brief moment, I thought I saw sadness in my father's eyes. The beautiful well-manicured Seventh-day Adventist campus of Andrews University was located in a rural community; it was alive with hundreds of freshmen from all over the world. The crisp fall air was fresh, clean, and filled with the scent of flowers. The atmosphere was electric and charged with excited conversations of students just as eager as I was to get started. Yes, it was the fall of 1965—the start of my becoming a medical technologist even though I wasn't quite sure what that was, but it sounded important, and I could earn a living.

My first year bought me new lifelong friends, like JT Smith, from Seattle, Washington, and David Henry, from Chicago. JT became my best friend and spiritual sidekick. He was short—five feet eight—but very muscular from years of weight training and bodybuilding. He was quick to laugh and just as quick to inflict the wrath of God. JT was studying for the ministry, and it was rare to see him without his Bible or singing an old-time gospel or spiritual. His favorites were "Ride on King Jesus" and "Come Thou Font of Every Blessing." A verse in that last song, "Prone to wander Lord, I feel it, prone to leave the God I love," would hold prophetic meaning for both of us in years to come.

JT and I experienced many adventures on and off campus, from preaching and leading out in local churches, like the Dowagiac church and prison ministry in Benton Harbor; we even managed to get into a fight together at the College Wood Products shop where we both worked. That latter event, though not the first, sparked by racial remarks, stained my impression of the campus and awaken in me the sense that all those in Zion weren't converted. But before the fight, one moment of pride stands tall in my memory at Andrews. It was Afro American week on campus, but as usual, the only people aware or interested in recognizing it were Afro Americans. The highlight of the week was the worship service on Sabbath in the Seminary Hall. There was a mixture of undergraduate students, graduate students, seminary students of color from all over the world, and a couple of white visitors; every seat was taken in the small building. The university president, Dr. Richard Hammil, was the keynote speaker. He was a white-haired, slightly balding, tight-faced thin white gentleman. He rarely smiled and seemed always distant and artificial in the presence of blacks. He certainly reflected the sentiment of much of America in the 1960s. But that Sabbath was his day, his day to put us in our place, his opportunity to show the unimportance of blacks in the prosperity of the "great university" at Berrien Springs, if not in America itself. Without much introduction or warm platitudes, his remarks never crested a positive note during the mudslide of ethnic scolding. A faint smile, a snide hint of satisfaction spread like acne across his face as he quoted statistics about paltry money contributions, unreliable and menial participation, and an overall parasitism from the Afro American and nonwhite constituency in the Lake Region

Conference. The audience was stunned, some mumbled, others were clearly angry, but as a whole sat depressed like a child being upbraided by a parent. "And you people" his tirade was interrupted by heavy footstep pounding the carpeted wooden floor. *Thump, thump, thump*, a short but large shadow passed by. "Mr. President, Mr. President, I would like to make some corrections to your figures." It was Elder Charles E. Bradford, president of the Lake Region Conference. Elder Bradford was a dynamic, down-home-style preacher and world evangelist who would in later years serve as one of the great general conference presidents of the North America Division. Very spiritual, he never held his peace when it came to the things of God, and everybody knew that. A wave of electricity immediately filled the room. A sickening pallor enveloped Dr. Hammil as blood drained from his face, and in a flash, he seemed to have aged ten years. "Mr. President, may I have a word with these brethren?" and politely, Elder Bradford nudged Dr. Hammil aside, grasped the small wooden podium, and began to set the record straight. "Brother Hammil, I am not sure where you found those figures, but I am certain you will be enlightened and overjoyed to know that Lake Region per capita gave more money, supported more programs, conducted more evangelism, won more souls than all the predominantly white conferences in North America." With his classic smile and booming voice, he quoted statistic after statistic from memory and showed how the Lake Region Conference members had rescued the great university from financial embarrassment time and time again. Further, in the spirit of the occasion and the Sabbath, he preached with clear eloquence how God is no respecter of persons, religions, or institutional affiliations. "We all must be born again and live, treat and respect each other like brethren, if we are going to be in God's kingdom!" He looked squarely at the embarrassed and trembling president. The small room erupted into the loudest amen ever heard on the campus. God had sent His champion to rescue our embattled souls at just the right moment as He always does.

Back to the fight, the event started one ordinary morning in the college furniture factory where JT and I worked. We met a kid who had one leg shorter than the other, and he walked with a pronounced up-and-down limp. The freckled-faced skinny, gaunt white kid with red hair lived in the area; and like many others, some non-Adventist, he worked at the College Wood Products. He was dressed in a studded black leather jacket, tight blue jeans, thick scruffy black motorcycle boots, and a "what's your problem" attitude to match. His problem began when he called JT the N word. As I said, JT was short, but built like a bull and like a bull, short-tempered about some things, especially the N word. Seconds after waving the red-flagged insult, JT charged the kid, and both of them crashed into boxes and furniture in the warehouse packing room, JT was on top. In one quick move JT spun to his feet, stepped back, and snapped a powerful karate front kick to the kid's chest, and he flew back several feet, landing hard against the floor. I didn't know what to do; everything happened so fast. I was just as mad because the *N* word applied to me too, and deep down, I was waiting my turn to give a knuckle sandwich. My chance never came; the foreman showed up, pulled JT off the kid, and within five minutes, we were fired and threatened with expulsion from school for beating up this innocent cripple.

Later, when the adrenaline rush and the avenging dragon of ethnic rage returned to its cave, JT and I actually felt bad. We prayed and asked God to forgive us and awaited our fate. When the truth came out some days later, we were reinstated, and in the spirit of Christ, we apologized to the redhead kid and he to us with reluctance. Nevertheless, the atmosphere in the shop had permanently changed, and we weren't too popular for beating up a white kid. It didn't matter because we were genuinely sorry and wished things had happened differently. Ironically, life is sometime like a movie that keeps on running, and almost a year later, I met this same kid—still cripple, still skinny, still scruffy looking—in Vietnam. He had been wounded in a Vietcong ambush. Amazingly, we were so glad to see each other. I bandaged his wounds, gave him a hug, and wished him well as he was evacuated. I never saw him again but knew since his wounds were not serious; he would be sent back into the jungles. I prayed that God would take care of him. This thought brings me back to Andrews and how my life was about to change forever.

Further disappointment came some weeks later when I applied for a 1-A student deferment from military service. The college administrators denied my pleadings. I was told because I had a C average and one hour short of full-time status I had to be reported to the draft board as military eligible. I tried to explain how hard I worked to get there, how financially poor my family was, and how I got up every day before daybreak and worked six hours before going to class. I explained that's why I had to take fewer classes and was desperately tired all the time, but all appeals and reasoning were coldly rejected. I was drafted and left campus in May 1966.

Fort Wayne was built on a military campus in 1796 and named after the famed revolutionary war general Anthony "Mad" Wayne. He was famous for his unorthodox combat tactics against the British and their Indian allies. The area on Detroit's southwest side along the Detroit River facing Canada was further expanded in 1844-47 during a time when tensions were high between Canada and the United States over border territories. During WWII, it was renovated and used as the United States' largest motor vehicle and parts depot. In the 1960s, it was an army recruitment and induction center. The main army induction facility was a long three-story, dilapidated gray building with about sixty to seventy windows and old weather-beaten doors.

The muggy July morning seemed overcast in memory although it actually was sunny. Clouds of anxiety, numbness, and apprehension weighed heavily in my thoughts. I felt like a condemned prisoner but, strangely, a happy one because I was back where I started—in the military. I understood order and discipline and welcomed the structured lifestyle of the soldier. I felt comfortable—not ready for anything, just comfortable.

Of all the things that happened that day, two are remembered most clearly. First, the long line of nervous inductees draped in multicolored under shorts, mostly white, waiting for their physical exams. The noisy wooden floors were littered with the last vestige of civilian life, gym shoes, polyester jump suits, and crumpled T-shirts. Like a beehive, the large windowed room bristled with medical and administrative types, both men and women. Someone dressed in white—a doctor, I think—methodically came behind each man, ordered him to lower his shorts and be examined front and back. Bending over, I too grimaced at the jabbing finger, rough and rhythmic plodding that each man received. When my ordeal painfully passed, I was happy that my newfound faith modified the words I said. Apparently, the whole event of doing physical exams was done in record time because muffled laughter in the room's corners signaled that betting was afoot. The wager was to see how fast the procedure could be done. Modesty was lost in the business, and pleasure for some, of processing men and boys for war. The other memorable event was standing in a much-smaller room with my right hand raised. All, but one, in unison repeated the pledge of allegiance to the United States, its president, and the military. I closed my eyes and gave my allegiance and heart to God.

# CHAPTER FOUR

*The greatest want of the world is the want of men,*
*men who in their inmost souls are true and honest,*
*men who do not fear to call sin by its right name,*
*men whose conscience is as true to duty as the needle*
*to the pole, men who will stand for the right though*
*the heavens fall.*

—E. G. White, *Education*

Fort Leonard Wood, Missouri, was like waking up from anesthesia 680 miles from home. I don't remember much of the long dark train ride from the Army Induction Center in Detroit. The monotonous squeal of the chugging steel wheels cluttering over wooden tracks was familiar and hypnotizing. It seemed most of my childhood with Mom, Billy, Beverly (my sister), and me was on a train between Detroit and Philadelphia. The Bibbs' side of the family lived in Philadelphia, and memories are rich with characters and stories of clanging trolley cars, smoky wood stoves, coin-fed televisions, and on cold nights five giggly kids stuffed tightly in bed. They were fun times brimming with harmless pranks, daring escapes across the slanted roof during nap-time, and sumptuous food cooked with lots of love. Grandma Bibbs—Ms. Ada, the neighbors called her—was the jewel of the household. She was in charge; all things centered on her. It seemed that everybody in Germantown area knew Ms Ada. Her birthroots stemmed from the Blackfoot Indian tribe of Montana and Alberta, Canada. The Blackfoot traded, made war and intermarried with tribes like the Shoshone, Crow, Cree, and other tribes in the Northern Plains. She was thin, neatly dressed, slightly grayed and her high cheekbone smile was delightfully infectious and warm. Her joy was her family of some thirteen children and her church. Most of what I pictured God and angels were like, I got from her. She was full of common wisdom, stories of trials and faith, a wink of assurance, and always a song or Bible verse to encourage. To all of us she would sing her soft melody, "If I can help somebody as I travel alone, then my living will not be in vain". The last time I hugged her it was long and filled with emotion as the curtain of her life came to a close. I miss her.

"Everybody, off the train!" bellowed a voice from somewhere. The cool morning air was deceptive. By 9:00 a.m., Missouri was on fire. Fingers of dancing heat waves spiraled up, catching all in its mesmerizing trance of exhaustion. Fort Leonard Wood Army Reception Center was stuck in the middle of one of the many Mark Twain National Forest that were scattered south along Interstate 40 between St. Louis and Springfield. The buses stopped, and off came the half sleepy, wide-eyed recruits. The next several hours was a blur of shouting, pushing, cursing, melee of fast-paced lines through clothing issue, haircuts, and filling out forms and wondering how we got into all of this. Eating should have been a time of rest and enjoyment—not a chance. No assembly line at Jefferson Chrysler auto plant, where I worked after high school, could equal the synchrony of the line in; eat-fast, line-out rhythm of the chow hall. Some thought the drill sergeants were "rough, tough bastards" until the real terror appeared in the mess hall door like an apparition amid billowing clouds of stream. Six feet tall, green T-shirt covered by a dingy white apron, the sweaty black mess sergeant expertly gripped a baseball bat tightly in his right hand. "Eat and get out of my mess hall! You got three minutes, and no talking!" With that, the dented metal trays were slammed with lumpy grits, runny eggs, and drowning stripes of bacon whether you wanted it or not. True to the warning, no one dared talk. Shuffling feet, chairs, clinging trays on tables, and suddenly, *bam, bam.* "Three minutes up, get out of my mess hall" ended the possibility of going to sleep without tears and regret because tomorrow the mess sergeant would be at his post.

As the first day was hot, the next was even hotter. Although heads still sore from the unceremonious haircuts the day before, we stood in ragged formation waiting to find out what would happen next. It was test day. Every recruit had to take a military job aptitude test. This would decide what kind of training the army would give us. If you had some college and scored high, you could be a warrant officer (fly helicopters, etc.) or attend regular army officer candidate school. For others, the choices mostly were infantry, cooks, clerks, radio operators, truck drivers, and medics. I think the testing was really a joke because I scored above average, had college, and found my test paper stamped Infantry. I quickly told the officer I was 1-A-O, a conscientious objector (CO). "A what?" he shouted. I repeated, "I'm a Seventh-day Adventist. I can't be an infantryman. I want to be a medic." Rising tension in his voice, matched his crimson face, he shot back, "We don't need no damn medics, we need killers! Get the hell out of here!" From that time on, the cadre's attitude toward me and the other COs went from hostile to contempt. We were given extra duties to include barracks night-fire watch, trash pick up, latrine duty, and worst, KP (kitchen patrol) with the mess sergeant. Surprisingly, I didn't hear much complaining from the other COs. The ecumenical brotherhood of suffering erased, for a while at least, lines of our differing religions and faiths.

Friday night, the Sabbath, finally came, and so did the tension of what I was going to do now. This was not the first time a showdown of conscience placed me at a point of decision. ROTC was but one. After high school I worked at the Jefferson Chrysler Auto Assembly plant in Detroit. That crisis caused me to choose between working on Sabbath or getting fired; I was fired. Two months later I was rehired. But four months later I was again fired for the same reason. Later, I worked as a night stock boy at an Atlantic & Pacific Food store in the suburbs of Detroit and eventually lost that job too because of shift changes. I worked as a magazine salesman, garbage man, junk collector, house painter, window cleaner, and dishwasher, all trying to make a living and be faithful to my beliefs. "Sarge, I'm a Seventh-day Adventist. I don't work on Saturday. I'd like to go to worship tomorrow". The Sarge started at me like I had just talked about his mother. "I don't care what you'd like or what you believe, you better be out in formation tomorrow like everybody else!" he snarled. I remembered seeing pictures in magazines and books of Christians resting peacefully amide crisis, but for me, that night, it was an illusion and far from the reality of the moment. It was not a matter of losing my job but of going to jail. During war, it meant for a long time. In the quietness of the barracks, I knelt and prayed for courage to be true. It was an uneasy, restless night that ended too soon. As others rustled out to formation for chow, I ducked behind the barracks and took off in a half walk-run to who knows where. Moments later, I saw a small military chapel with its one tall pointed steeple affixed with a cross at the top. The little white building was to be my fortress. I would hide in there until I am found no matter how many days it took. I spent the day reading my Bible, humming hymns, and praying. I closed my eyes for what seemed a few minutes, but looking outside, the sun had set, Sabbath was over, but my troubles, I feared, were just starting. As I crept back to the barracks, my biggest surprise was that no one said anything. The next morning, however, the cadre sergeant asked where I was and that I was going to be charged with being AWOL (absent without leave). But on Monday, before anything could be done, the loud speaker called for all COs to assemble. A dozen or so of us were being shipped out to a place called Fort Sam Houston Texas for medic training. As the days had been hot, that afternoon was different. A sudden wind arose, followed by a cold rain shower that seemed to chill to the bone. In a matter of minutes, Missouri's summer had turned to fall. I shivered inside, but my heart was filled with joy. I was afraid and, at the same time, excited. A change was coming, and I knew my adventure was starting.

# CHAPTER FIVE

*Let me live out my years in heat of blood!*
*Let me die drunken with the dreamer's wine!*
*Let me not see this soul-house built of mud*
*go toppling to the dust a vacant shrine!*
*GIVE ME HIGH NOON! . . . then, let it be night.*
— John Gneisenau Neihardt, 1881

They were the biggest horse flies I every saw. I knew flies, and these were huge, thumb-sized germ carriers. I cringed and ducked in the small wooden building next to the airstrip. We waited for the airplane to arrive to take us to Texas. *Zooom*, another germ carrier flew by. I winched. *Ten years ago,* I thought to myself, *and this fly would have been just a smear on the wall.* I laughed as I remembered the nothing-to-do-afternoon, the day after Dad had painted the house in Detroit with a fresh coat of white. The paint was almost dry and reflected brightly in the hot August sun. Then I saw them, hundreds of black specks sunbathing on my dad's newly painted house. Apparently, they were oblivious to my approaching with a long flat stick. *Whack, whack, whack,* they splattered. Tens, then hundreds, the slaughter went on all afternoon. A couple of times, Mom called out, "Bobby, what are you doing?" "Nothing" was my standard answer. Had she come out to see the carnage, I may have been spared the "what the hell!" and fierce whipping I got when my dad came home. The two-tone house—sparkling white above the reach of my stick, dark and crimson below—was a testimony to my persistence and determination to ride the earth of flies.

A buzzing sound different from the flies grew louder. *Ploop, ploop, ploop,* the whirling propellers on either side of the gray airplane came to a stop. Looking out the screen window, excitement grew with each moment; this would be my first airplane ride. To me, it was a frightening beauty; it reminded me of the large cargo plane in the movie *Casablanca.* Unfortunately, it rode like a cargo plane too. Bumpy and noisy, the deafening roar of the engines could not drown out the sheer joy of leaving the earth and flying like an angel. I did wonder, however, why it flew seemingly just above the ground all the way from Missouri to Texas. I'm sure birds and other low-flying animals also wondered.

The plane ride lasted few hours but passed like minutes as we arrived in San Antonio, Texas. The moments seemed to blur before the bus pulled into the basic training area of historic Fort Sam Houston military medical training center. I had never seen real palm trees in their natural state, and I was amazed. The sand-colored building topped with roofs of classic southwest red ceramic tile was simply magnificent. The grandeur from inside the air-conditioned bus quickly evaporated once we stepped outside into merciless heat and humidity of Texas. If Missouri was the furnace of the Midwest, then San Antonio, in July, was where the devil lived. It was hot and suffocating all the time. Instantly, from the moment I stepped off the plane, my wrinkled kaki uniform was soaked; and a deep suntan spread slowly and evenly across my face, arms, and hands.

With my heavy duffle bag at my side, I stood looking at my new home. Heat waves shimmered above the long sidewalk that ran between the one-level brick buildings of the training cadre and the two-story, circa World War II wooden buildings of the trainees. A few sprawling pecan trees near the parking area were the only shade anywhere. What little grass that dared to grow was well manicured by hundreds of trainees that had come and gone before. Considering that basic training was going to last eight weeks, I sighed and wondered if I would last eight days.

To my delight, unlike Fort Leonard Wood, Fort Sam had many COs (conscientious objector/1-A-O), and most of them were SDA. The best thing to happen that first day was to see an old friend from the Burns Avenue church in Detroit, Andrew Shroppshire. Andrew, an SDA, had only two weeks left in basic training. Seeing his big eyes and forty-two-teeth smile almost made me run and hug him as we did in church each Sabbath, but it wasn't the time or place. Eventually, he went to Fort Polk Louisiana for training in communications. There, he had to stand up for his faith. Writing to me later, he lamented the constant harassment and maltreatment he experienced and was hoping they would discharge him sooner then later. But for a few days, in the training area, it was good having him around. On Sabbath, we went to church on post and sat around talking about old times. To this day, Andrew is one of my dearest friends.

As I mentioned, there were many Adventist in our basic training class of forty to fifty soldiers at first. The class would expand to nearly a hundred before the teaching actually started, so in the meantime, the first arrivals had to practice cleaning latrines, do KP (kitchen patrol) duties, cut grass, sweep sidewalks, and learn to march in formation. It was during the marching and drilling that I meet the son of the WWII Adventist Medal of Honor recipient; Desmond Doss Sr. Desmond Doss Jr. was stout, broad shouldered, and tough looking. That's why he was chosen to drill us around the cement training area. The blistering heat, humidity, and nagging sweat flies paled in annoyance to the dull, monotonous "hut one, hut two, hut three . . . left, right, left" marching commands of Doss Jr.

Everyone groaned and murmured to the point of faking death. I couldn't take it any more either, so during a rest break, I went up to one of the trainers and told him I had ROTC drill experience and could do better. Immediately, I was put in charge of the formation, and Doss Jr. was out of a job and the power he so relished. In the smooth, melodious cadence I'd learned at Eastern High School, we marched and sang until other groups showed up to watch us. From that experience, I was made the commander of the training class—Sergeant Gardner. Needless to say, Doss never got over the loss of prestige and seemed to dislike me from then on. Nevertheless, he was my brother in Christ, and I tried many times to befriend him. The most memorable thing to happen between Doss Jr. and I was to meet his father, Desmond T. Doss Sr. and to shake his hand while admiring the warm, gentle, and quiet spirit that flowed from him.

In 1944, Desmond T. Doss Sr. was a twenty-three-year-old medic, conscientious objector from Lynchburg, Virginia. He was a devout, Bible-reading-and-praying-Sabbath keeper. He was often mocked and ridiculed for his beliefs and at one point was going to be separated from the army with a section 8, signifying that he was unfit for military duty. But after insisting that he wanted to serve his country but refuse to kill, the army decided to keep him. He was assigned to 307th Infantry, 77th Infantry Division in the Pacific theater during WWII. In July 1944 on the island of Guam, he began to prove his courage and devotion to his men, saving many lives while under direct enemy fire. In October, while in combat at Leyte in the Philippines, he braved enemy fire over and over to rescue wounded soldiers. At one point, a Japanese machine gunner trained his weapon on Doss while he bandaged a wounded soldier. Doss's fellow soldiers saw the Japanese gunner but couldn't help Doss. Amazingly, bullets and explosions filled the air but none cut him down. Years later during an evangelistic meeting in Japan, a missionary recounted the story of that day; and after the meeting, a Japanese man walked up to him and said he was the Japanese gunner. He said, "I was there and remember having a soldier in my gun site but couldn't pull the trigger."

The following year, April 29, 1945, the battle in the Pacific had shifted to Okinawa at a place called the Maeda Escarpment. This was a four-hundred-foot cliff that separated the island. Private First Class Doss assigned to Company B and along with Company A was to climb the cliff and secure the top. The whole area was honeycombed with enemy gun positions, tunnels, caves, booby traps, and well-camouflaged snipers. Before the attack, Doss asked the officer in charge if he could have the company pray. They knew he was a man of prayer, and so they prayed. As Company A and B reached the top, both were pinned down by heavy enemy fire. Five men were killed, and numerous casualties were in Company A. But in Company B, not one single man was killed none injured by the enemy. Word spread all the way back to Washington DC that prayer saved Company B.

On May 5, the Japanese counter attacked, and almost immediately, about seventy-five or more men of Company B fell wounded. The rest of the company retreated back down the cliff, leaving Doss and the wounded. For nearly five hours, amid exploding shells and gunfire, one by one he lowered to safety over fifty wounded soldiers; later, estimates were seventy-five men. During those terrible hours, he prayed, "Lord, help me get one more, just one more." Miraculously, Desmond's prayers for protection and courage were answered even as the Japanese were closing in on him and he lowered the last man. A few weeks later, during an attack by the Americans on May 21, Desmond was severely wounded by a hand grenade and bullets but continued to aid other wounded soldiers. He was evacuated and underwent numerous operations. On October 12, 1945, Pres. Harry S. Truman presented the Congressional Medal of Honor to Corporal Desmond Thomas Doss, being the first and only such award given to a noncombatant during WWII.

The eight weeks of training passed quickly. I worked extremely hard to be a good and effective training commander, and I was. I felt good because I was the one Adventist all the other Adventist could count on to be there for them. I would pray with them, study the Bible, have discussions, encourage them to stand up for principles, attend church, and look out for each other. But I showed them no favoritism when it came to training and duty because there were other beliefs and denominations for which I had to be a leader for as well. I made sure all work assignments were fair and equal. My troops who were Baptist, Methodist, Catholic, or other Protestant faiths were not assigned duties on Sunday—their day of worship—and I fought to maintain the Sabbath for the Adventist. Unfortunately, a number of the Adventist were seen downtown or elsewhere doing all sorts of non-Sabbath, non-Christian things on the Sabbath, which made defending some very hard. To crack down on those who abused God's privilege, I threatened to give them extra duty on the weekends; revoke passes, and makes their life miserable. The senior training cadre watched how I dealt with all the troops and was pleased. They gave me a free hand to do just about what ever I wanted to because we were the best training class they had seen to date. Doss Jr. was my big problem and got on the nerves of not a few of the other guys. One day, one of the troops whispered in my ear that a blanket party was being planned for me and Doss. A blanket party is when a person is not liked or is a troublemaker in the platoon, a group will sneak up while that person is sleeping, throw a blanket over them, and beat them with any object hard enough to hurt. The rebels were only six to ten in number; several were disguntled Adventist I had disciplined. The bunk bed sleeping area was quiet as the moon shown through the open window. I lay on the bottom bunk with my arms across my chest, inwardly daring any of the rebels to touch me. Across the room, shadows crept slowly toward my bed, then just as the attack yell broke the silence about fifteen loyal troops surrounded my bed and dared the rebels to touch me. At that moment, another group of rebels had a blanket over Doss, beating him mercilessly and were attempting to throw him out the window to the pavement below. The loyal troops considered joining the rebels when it came to Doss. Doss was scared and pleaded for them to stop. Some of the loyalist and I managed to snatch Doss out of his predicament. In the minutes following the melee, I gained control, and everyone went back to bed. Next day, hardly anyone spoke of what happened. Doss was bruised, shaken, and quiet. I thanked God that He watched over me as always with His unseen angels. I prayed that Doss would one day really let God in to his heart.

Several other events happened that were thunderclouds in my life at Fort Sam, but thankfully, there was also much sunshine. In San Antonio, I stayed at the servicemen center near downtown on Ashby and San Pedro streets a few times. There I met Elwood Clay—missionary, entrepreneur, handyman, fiery street preacher, friend, and much-loved brother in Christ. In San Antonio, I also met my treasured brother, Albert Marks, who became my prayer partner in Vietnam. I became acquainted with many of the members of the Ephesus SDA church—the Miltons, Shannons, and others who to this day are written on my heart. And finally, my dear friend and counselor, Dr. Leonard Johnson who's thirst for life and service in Christ was my greatest inspiration.

As I left the San Antonio airport, I was excited to be going home—excited to see my family, to see my church, and above all, to tell the wonderful things God had done for me. After another eight weeks of advance training, I would leave this same airport, going home less joyful to tell my family I was going to Vietnam. I would sit reading a copy of the *New Yorker* magazine about an article "The Lost Platoon." It was a story of the last moments captured in pictures of soldiers carelessly milling around in a jungle clearing. A frozen piece of time immortalizing young lives bound for eternity, unaware that their lives, hopes, and dreams would end. The picture came from a captured enemy who had the camera of one of the soldiers. That article stayed with me as I thought about my future. "God," I remembered praying, "help me never to be careless in my duties as a soldier and never let me be careless with any soul."

# CHAPTER SIX

*By the rivers of Babylon, there we sat down, yea, we wept, when we remembered Zion . . . . How shall we sing the lord's song in a strange land.*
*—Psalms 137:1,4*

A thick gray fog smothered the chilled early San Francisco morning as the yellow-and-white Continental jet rose gently into the sky. I sat with other solemn seventeen, eighteen, nineteen, and twenty year olds staring out the tiny airplane windows. The Golden Gate Bridge's red spans flickered briefly, caught in the rays of the morning sun, before disappearing into the rolling mist like a ghost. Each of us had our own thoughts, our own heartaches, and our own way of dealing with the intense sadness we felt. This was the first time I was so far from home, leaving America with the real prospect of never coming back again. I had already cried leaving Detroit New Year's Eve, and so I sat with waves of memories and emotions lapping back and forth.

No one knew I had orders for Vietnam, except the Fultons, the Adventist couple I stayed with after joining the church. They were deeply saddened and did the best they could to assured me of God's providence and protection. Mrs. Fulton's tears mingled with mine as we hugged our good-byes. Years later, David Fulton would die from diabetic complications and Mrs. Fulton, my mother in Israel, would basically died of loneliness in a secluded nursing home in Alabama. I miss them so much.

Coming back to Detroit on military leave or from being away for other reasons was always a joyous event. This was especially true in my family; there was plenty of hugs, kisses, old stories, and jokes that were classic. We had lots of fun as a family, lots and lots of love and tolerance. People at church were also glad to see me. I wore my dress green uniform shape, crisp and proud. My shoulders were always straight and squared. John Tolson, a very dark-skinned heavyset new member of the Adventist church became my best friend. He too had been recently drafted and was home on leave from basic training. John still had the advance medical training course to complete at Ft. Sam Houston before he would also receive his orders for Vietnam. John's girlfriend was Travis Daniels, and he introduced me to her sister Genora. Though our acquaintance started casual, it blossomed. She was my shoulder height with smooth brown skin, silky black hair, penetrating dark eyes, and a curvaceous figure. What was even more captivating was her singing voice; it was rich, pure and angelic. We dated a couple of times during my leave, but I avoided getting too close to her or anybody; future happiness and Vietnam just didn't seem to mix. I actually did have another girlfriend, Sharon Jowers, whom I asked to marry before being drafted but who said no. Then, while I was away in Texas, she started dating other guys mostly because my future as a soldier was so uncertain. In Texas, I had changed, and so did she. We grew apart but remained friends.

Neither Mom nor Dad knew I was home for possibly the last time. I wanted to have a good time with them and not spoil it with bad news. Just after Christmas 1966, the time came for me to leave and to figure out how to tell my family good-bye. I decided to tell Dad first. My relationship with my father had always been strained. I was never sure if I loved him. Resentment, respect, admiration, and fear, but never love or even like. He seemed to resent my strong self-will, stubbornness, and at times, defiance. His frustration was born out with my getting punishments and whippings that seemed harsher, longer, and more painful than with my siblings. Nevertheless, I felt I owed it to him to tell him first. "Dad, can I talk with you?" We went into my parent's bedroom. I stood by the door; Dad sat on the other side of the bed turned toward me. "What's up, Dodiha?" That was his nonsense name he called me at times when he was in a good mood, or Hardrock when talking to others about me. "Dammit, boy!" was what he called me when he was mad at me about something, and that was most of the time. "Dad, I'm getting ready to go to Vietnam." "Yeah," he said, softly turning his head toward the windows. There was a long silence. He stood up, turned to me, tears in his eyes, and said, "Why do they always want to take my best boys!" His voice wavered; he turned back to the window. I wanted to hug him or say something more to him, but I left the room with moisture filling my eyes. *Dad really does love me*—that was the strangest thought I even had about him, and it felt good.

Morning came too quickly. I was going to quietly leave the house without waking anybody, but Mom sprang from somewhere and held me tight almost choking me and cried. She was hurting, and so was I. She was everything to me then, now, and forever.

The hours on the jet passed in slow and uncomfortably time. The narrow cloth seats gnawed at our butts and painfully wrinkled both clothing and skin. The brilliant and irritating sun kept pace with the jet traveling at three hundred miles per hour. And the day, it seemed to stand still as did the solid gray ocean forty thousand feet below us; naps were fitful and timeless. As it has been for thousands of years, the ancient sun, like a silent guardian, watched other warriors even as these young warriors go to war. If the sun had feeling and thought, I wondered if it was sad, if beyond its brilliance, there were rivers of lava like tears like those mothers and fathers and wives and sweethearts would shed for us. Or could the sun simply not care from its distant haunt far from human cruelties and foolishness? I wonder.

Hawaii's Diamond Head volcano loomed up from the coral blue Pacific Ocean. We landed and had thirty minutes inside the airport to make phone calls, buy souvenirs, stretch our legs, and wiggle back into truly painful seats. Somewhere after passing over Guam, a pimple on the ocean expanse the sun passed us, and darkness slowly folded around us like a stranger's embrace. Suddenly, the plane decelerated and began to descend through layers of clouds. Unexpectedly, below us, a million lights from Manila Bay, Philippines, shown up at us like sparkling diamonds. It was simply beautiful beyond words. Our ears popped as the landing gears growled opened and we landed. It had been nearly sixteen hours flying time so far, and we were exhausted. Corralled into a small building at Clark Airfield, most of us found a spot in chairs or on the floor to sleep stretched out. Forty-five minutes later, we reboarded, sleepy and more somber than ever. Now Vietnam, and our uncertain futures were only hours away. Someone whispered it was safer to go in at night than during the day. For us, we didn't have a clue to why this was true, but it sounded reasonable. Later, it proved true. Everyone was awake, everyone was still, and everyone looked tensely out the window as the inside cabin lights went black. The plane itself drifted quietly down as if sneaking into a house late at night. The blackness inside the plane melted into the blackness outside. We were suspended in space like a bottomless pit. A billion stars hovered over us in reverent vigil while below; white embers flickered upward from tiny campfires. As the jet's slow decent continued, my heart sped up. "What are you doing here? What are you doing here?" it rhythmically thumped to my quickened pulse. In unison, other parts of me wanted nothing more than to spout wings and fly away from this nightmare. Turning to look inside the blackened aircraft cabin I sensed the prayers of everyone was as thick; even more than the dense fear that pulsated to the engine's droning. Wishing it would all go away ended as the blue runway lights of Tan Son Nhut airbase sentenced our landing. The plane gently touched down and rowed smoothly to a dimly lit corner of the runway. From the darkened cabin, we saw ten to twenty nervous-looking soldiers with M16 rifles and .45-caliber weapons at the ready surround the plane even before it stopped. There were two olive green jeeps with mounted M-60 machine guns and two black-colored buses lined up close to the mobile air-stairs. "Everyone get out!" a voice said with authority from the blackness. I have never felt such oven heat and humidity in my life as I entered the doorway. It was after 2:00 a.m., January 4, and even Texas would have felt better then here. In a flash, we were on the buses and racing through the slums and strange smells of Bien Hoa, a small section near Saigon the capital of South Vietnam. The headlights shamefully spotlighted the ragged shacks of weathered gray wood, twisted barbed-wire fences, hard-packed dirt floors, and garbage-littered streets. Diesel exhaust fumes from the buses mercifully blunted some of the sickening smells, but not all. Finally stopping in a pitch-dark open field, we piled off the buses. I picked up my duffle bag filled with fifty pounds or more of books, Bibles, magazines, filmstrip projector, and who knows what else. I was sorry I had packed so much junk because I had to drag and carry it plus two other fully loaded duffle bags. I fell, stumbled, and fell over and over again, trying to keep up with the others whom were also half running in the dark. From the humidity, straining, bruising, and fear, I found myself wishing for a heart attack so I could end this misery right then. Relief came when I saw the in-processing tent where our names were checked off and we were assigned an open-sided tent with bunk beds. Latrines were out back of the tents a few yards. No one had to point them out; the pungent sickening smell left no one in doubt of the direction. Quick instruction was given that if anything happened, there was a trench and sandbag bunker just to the side of the tents. No one dared ask the chances of something happening; we felt just being here was "the happening," and sleeping in the bunker seemed far safer than the tents. We moved about in total darkness, talking in whispers, flinching every now and then to the sound of distant explosions miles away and gunfire much closer. Sometime between the plane landing and nearly 4:00 a.m., the night grew cold, very cold. I was soaked from the duffle bag run and actually started shivering. A mile or two away, flares popped open to flitter their eerie light and shadows across the base's perimeter. Above, "night guardians"—the stars—stood their post, silent and amazed, even as I was, for the heartache occurring in the jungles of this troubled land. Peering past galaxies, time, and endless blackness, I wondered if morning would ever come and this entire nightmare is but only a dream. In my heart, I wished, but the stars knew better. Sleep beckoned at last, and my eyes closed.

*Baah boom, boom, boom, baah, boom, boom, boom!* The earth shook! My sleep exploded like the last high plunge of a roller-coaster ride; muscles and reflexes snapped to action faster than my brain. All over the tent, blankets, covers, mattresses, and clothes flew everywhere as thirty or forty panicky newcomers raced wildly for the bunker. *Baah boom, boom, boom!* Sound and shock waves spit the air with such violence that everything shook as if the ground would open up and swallow us. In the millisecond following the explosions, someone shouted, "Outgoing! Outgoing! Settle down! It's ours, an artillery fire mission." All crept nervously back to our bunks, but no one slept. Within minutes, it seemed the darkness gave birth to my first Vietnamese morning; I had 365 to go. A brilliant, angry, and immensely hot sun rose to take charge of the day, and it would do so every day without compassion.

By 0630 hours, chow was over; but the memory of runny, off-colored eggs, bacon, soggy and limp toast, and watery orange juice with tiny-winged bugs fighting to keep afloat was hard to forget. The sun was up and so were an armada of airplanes and helicopters. Some were troop carriers; others were gunship escorts. It was exciting! The deep, resonant *wump, wump, wump* of the Huey helicopter would become a signature of the war itself.

It was January 5. We formed up for roll call and unit shipping orders. Rodger Hodge, from New York, a Seventh-day Adventist I met at Fort Sam Houston, was going to Pleiku, in the Central Highlands of Vietnam. Pleiku would be the scene of a fierce, desperate battle later in the year; but for now, for Rodger and me, it was a place with a funny name. The formation dispersed, and I was handed a shovel, pointed to a large mound of red dirt, and motioned to fill sandbags until told to stop. There was no time limit. In between bending grunts from shoveling, I noticed some Vietnamese women up close for the first time. They were short, slender, and rarely made eye contact. Most wore wide cone-shaped straw hats, silky black pants, and light-colored blouses that hung loosely outside the pants. Most were very attractive but later I would lean also that most were very deadly. Before long, sweat rivulets poured off my body like a leaky sieve. With T-shirt long since discarded, my natural ebony tan darkened to a deep rich chocolate that would last the whole year.

# CHAPTER SEVEN

*Abide with me, fast falls the eventide, the darkness deepens,*
*Lord with me abide; when other helpers fail and comfort flee,*
*Help of the helpless, O Lord, abide with me.*
                                                —Henry F. Lyte

Friday, January 6, began as every morning since I became a Christian with prayer. This morning, I didn't have much to say, just a short list of "thank you, Lords." The day was an encore of the day before. The sun was still hot; its rays lashing like a whip across the backs of slaves. My tan was still dark and getting darker by the minute. Humidity and sweat soaked every piece of clothing to capacity, and no one was spared the misery. Noon came none too soon. "Line up!" the loud speaker squealed. Names rolled off one after another, and then time froze. "Gardner! Cu Chi, Twenty-fifth Infantry!" *Ooh no!* I said to myself. *Infantry? I'm a hospital medic. I'm not suppose to be in the infantry!*

Within an hour, I was all packed and, with fifteen others, jammed in an overcrowded three-quarter-ton open bed truck, bouncing our way through the streets of Bien Hoa. The city was alive with thousands of tanned-faced Vietnamese, whizzing motor scooters, careening autos, lumbering water buffalo, and passing rickety horse carts. The smell of food cooking, wood fires, exhaust fumes, and smoke from who knows where were almost too much to take in at once. What an adventure! Before long, we were at the edge of town where we joined about ten other vehicles to form a convoy before going into the countryside. No one traveled the country roads without armed escort. Stretching our legs for a few minutes, I got the biggest kick discovering that monkeys loved beer. A small dusty gray monkey walked about on a lease. I don't remember anyone claiming the monkey. The little wino seemed a bit agitated until someone gave him a beer. He expertly held it with both hands, threw us a monkey wink, then gulped down half the bottle. I had to take his picture; no one would believe me. I aimed; he paused, looked directly into the Polaroid, raised both eyebrows, and smiled.

As we mounted the trucks again, I glanced down the road to see a column of green armored personnel carriers (APCs) parked along a fence. They looked so awesome and powerful with their .50-caliber machine guns atop a turret and two .30-caliber machine guns on each side behind the turret. I had no idea that I would spend the next eight months inside of them. I would discover they were not so awesome, so powerful, protective, or safe. I would see dust and death, fear and pain, hope and hopelessness, souls saved and souls lost. Our convoy started up; we passed slowly by the APCs. Young grim faces stared back, then faded into the dirt and smoke of our truck's exhaust. In my heart, I wished them well.

The trip to Cu Chi, some twenty odd miles northwest of Saigon, was just as exciting and scenic as Bien Hoa. People were everywhere. Smiling children with white shirts, dark pants, and skirts were playing in neatly trimmed schoolyards. There were colorful Buddhist shrines, glistening water-filled rice paddies, and the ever-present hoards of rickety-motored buses and scooters. The land seemed rich and green. Palm trees, grass, and beautiful flowers dressed the countryside with a quiet elegance I had never seen before. "How could there be a war going on in such a wonderful happy place?" The small crowded village of Cu Chi was chaotic and full of activity at every turn. It reminded me of shopping malls at Christmas back in the States. Ladies with clothe head wrappings and red-stained teeth from betel nuts-the astringent seed of the betel palm that was as addictive as tobacco huddled together discussing local gossip while other vendors haggled and sold everything imaginable—ducks, clothes, jewelry, tools, food, and hundreds of other curious whatnots. I wished people back home could see this.

Passing through the sandbagged, barbed-wired gates of the Twenty-fifth Infantry base at Cu Chi, the convoy trucks peeled off to go their separate ways. Cu Chi, sometimes called the Dust-Bowl of Vietnam for its fine powdery tan-colored soil, was also notorious for its over two hundred miles of Vietcong (VC) tunnels that snaked beneath the base and surrounding countryside. The tunnels stretched from the gates of Saigon to the Cambodian border and connected villages, districts and even provinces. They were originally dug as hiding places for the Viet Minh, the nationalist guerrillas who fought the colonial French in the 1940s and 1950s. These multi-level tunnels where used to launch attacks against American and South Vietnamese forces, hide large numbers of enemy troops, VC guerillas and served as operational command centers. It was an underground highway between villages, storage facilities, shelter from the powerful American B-52 bombing raids, and the casualty receiving area for enemy wounded. Later, I would enter these tunnels and find whole hospital complexes with surgeons, operating room, medical wards, and staff sleeping quarters. It was from these tunnels that twelve months later, on January 31, the North Vietnamese and VC, would launch the Tet Offensive to give the United States its most devastating combat wound of the war. A wound that would cause the death of American presence in Vietnam and the eventual lost of the war some eight years later.

We stopped in the reception area, got off the truck, and lined up in formation to listen to a brief welcome speech and be assigned to our night's quarters. The sun was setting; Sabbath was here. Several soldiers, Seventh-day Adventist whom I had been with since basic training, like me, were ordered to clean rifles before going to sleep. We huddled together, wondering what we should do. The others filed out to get rifles. I was determined not to dishonor God. What would happen caused me some fear, but as in Fort Leonard Wood, I made my decision; I went out the back door and hide in a ditch for about an hour. I realized I couldn't keep going "out the back door" all my life. I bowed my head and ask God to give me courage to be true and leave the consequences to Him. In the distant, the thunder of heavy artillery and explosions boomed louder then at Bien Hoa. The ground vibrated with each volley. The night sky glittered with billions of stars. My heavenly family was so far yet so close. I was glad they were there, and I was not alone.

Sabbath, January 7. I was assigned to the Fourth Battalion, Twenty-third Mechanized Infantry, Twenty-fifth Infantry Division. The division's symbol was the Tropic Lightning, a red Hawaiian palm with a streak of yellow lighting. The Twenty-third was also nicknamed the Tomahawks. I was introduced to several of the exhausted-looking medics at the battalion aid station. The sandbagged, wooden-famed, tent-covered sleeping quarters called hooches were lined up adjacent to the main three-room aid station. The medics greeted me enthusiastically; maybe because I was coming, and they were going. Inside the hooch, twelve canvass cots were lined up with six on each side. Everybody had their area jam-packed with stuff that made life comfortable for them. As hot and suffocating as the air was, a shiver ran down my spine as I looked at all the weapons these medics guys carried—M16 rifles, shot guns, .45 pistols, .38s, M79 grenade launchers, hand grenades, knives, signal flares, and claymore mines. After all the hellos, I was given an empty bunk draped with a mosquito net. Next to it was an empty ammunition box that served as a bookcase. Since there wasn't much else to do, I found my way to the little green chapel at the front entrance to the camp. There, I spent the rest of the afternoon praying, reading a devotional, and quietly singing to myself. The chapel really was a sleek, modern-looking wood structure. Its floor was concrete, the pews and podium wooden, and the sides opened to the air but protected from the sun by a roof that slanted nearly to the ground. The sun was setting, the Sabbath was ending, and the sky could not have been more beautiful. Clouds of gentle peach and crimson colors mixed with hints of blue velvet and purple slowly faded into the arms of night.

Six thirty, Sunday morning, January 8, exploded to life with ear-deafening volleys of 4.2 mm mortar and 105 mm artillery fire. Five helicopters had been shot down during an assault in a near by rubber tree plantation. A company of the Twenty-fifth had taken heavy casualties. Looking out over the barbed-wire perimeter, dark green F-4 Phantom jets swooped down over the distant trees with their bent wing tips ablaze with fury. Black smoke and fire rose noiselessly for a moment; then deep vibrating thuds shook the air and ground. My heart raced uncontrollably. This was a real firefight! The trembling I felt inside was not from the bombs but the fear and realization I was here and very much a part of this madness. People were dying, and before long, I would see them or be among them. I don't remember how long I stared at the distant battle, but as suddenly as it had started, the noise and motion stopped. Thin fingers of black smoke rose slowly into the hot morning air. I knew the dead were being collected and wounded cared for, and somewhere in America, a family's hopes and dreams would soon be shattered.

Later that day, I met Specialist 4 (Spec4) Baggett near the aid station. He was a slightly nervous, dark-haired, slim-built, tired-looking medic from Alabama. He was young—maybe eighteen or nineteen—but his eyes were much older, sadder, and wiser. Around his waist hung a holstered .45-caliber pistol. He smiled as I approached him. I instantly liked him. I soon discovered he was on his way home. More surprisingly, he told me he was a Seventh-day Adventist too. He said he made his mind up to carry a weapon because the VC (Vietcong) didn't care if you were a Noncom (noncombatant) or CO (conscientious objector); you died the same as everybody else in the boonies (jungle/field/countryside). "I carry a weapon to protect myself and my patients." I said nothing else about that but wondered if I too would change my mind. Only God knew.

Two days later, I moved out of the hooches (tents) near the aid station to Charlie Company, Second Platoon. C Company was just down the hot dusty road from the aid station in the same battalion area. A black panther on a faded blue sign was the emblem for C Company. I was introduced as the new medic. Most of the guys were cordial; some hardly looked up. The first sergeant—a heavyset, short, mean-spirited black soldier from "nobody better ask" where or suffer a butt kicking—goaded me around the area like a shepherd prodding a goat. I got jungle fatigues, canteen, and other field gear. Alone, I shuffled over to the supply hooch where the supply Sergeant slid a .45-caliber pistol down the counter toward me. "Sarge," I said evently, "I don't want a weapon." "What the hell you mean 'you don't want a weapon'? Son, you better take something. Charlie, don't give a sh—who you are!" I signed a receipt, took the other stuff, and left without saying anything else. I met up with the first sarge again, who was still real ticked off about me being a CO. "Just before you came, one of you CO medics got shot in the back of the head by a VC, walked right up on him. The gook [VC] shot the wounded troop he was taking care of too. He didn't want no weapon either. Dammit, boy, you better get some sense!" Angrily, he left me standing in the middle of the yard. A short time later, Medic Swanson, the Charlie Company medic I was replacing, met up with me. After finding out I had not received the three-day Twenty-fifth Infantry orientation class, he agreed to go out on the next day's mission in my place. Another medic, named

Thompson, gave me my first medic bag. Nervously, as he handed me my prized possession, I was beginning to feel like a real medic. My excitement was short lived, however, when Lieutenant DeWalt—the freckle-faced platoon leader, who reminded me of Alfalfa of the *Little Rascals*—pulled me aside and tried to get me to carry a weapon. Again, I politely said, "No, sir, I can't." Lieutenant DeWalt would prove to be a real warrior. He would get slightly wounded several times but would always be out front leading his men. I had a lot of respect for him. I don't know if he ever made it home; many of his platoon members didn't.

The orientation class was in an area with low bleachers, a facing table of all kinds of captured VC weapons, and a roaming trail amid bamboo thickets displaying various booby traps. There were feces-smeared punji stake pits—sharpened bamboo spears and arrows attached to swinging branches or shot from miniature crossbows. The classes consisted of Twenty-fifth Infantry history, the origin of the VC, their weapons and tactics, and dos and don'ts, like don't pick up object in the field or being aware of children carrying explosive packages. During the three days, we saw films of dead enemy soldiers, torturing, and other war carnage. This was terrible to watch. We trained on patrolling, radio calls for medical evacuation helicopters (medevac) and fire support, as well as self-aid and buddy care for wounds. Classes ended late Friday afternoon. The next day, the Sabbath, was to be graduation day. It consisted of going into the jungles on an actual patrol. As the sun disappeared, I prayed that God would make a way for me not go on a Sabbath patrol. Before leaving the training area, I was impressed to speak to the officer in charge. I explained that I was a Seventh-day Adventist Christian and wanted to honor God and attend worship tomorrow, on Sabbath. He said that this was a war zone and that I may not always get the Sabbath off. "Keep it quiet, you're excused from tomorrow's patrol exercise." My heart was overjoyed; I sang all the way back to Charlie company. Another thing good happened. Specialist 4 Baggett opened the Sabbath with me in prayer. That was the last time I saw him. He went home. God bless him wherever he is.

Charlie Company laid heavily on my mind that night. The short mission that Medic Swanson had volunteered for in my place had turned into a full-fledged battle at the base of the Black Virgin Mountain some twenty miles north of Cu Chi base camp. The top of the Black Virgin peaked above a ring of dirty campfire smoke and cordite smog that lingered from exploding artillery and small arms gunfire. There were always morning clouds, but like a magician's cloth trick, the sun wisped them away with cool morning winds; the heavy battle smog, however, seemed to remain most of the time. An Army Special Forces camp barely held on to a few meters of ground at its summit while veteran VC and North Vietnamese regular troops were everywhere—on and inside the mountain. Later, Special Forces soldiers would joke and talk of making deals with the VC about time off from fighting. But sniping opportunities from both sides and an occasional ground attack to break up the monotony was the routine. The fact of the matter was that the mountain belonged to the VC. Honeycombed with deep caves, giant rocks, and dense dark jungles, it had withstood a hundred assaults by the French and now the American forces. Aerial bombing, mortar and artillery fire had made little difference, yet young men were still sent up that mountain and died in great numbers. Eleven months later that year, I would see some of their faces, carry and stack their mangled bodies, then helplessly cry all night *why*.

The ground trembled and seized for hours. Invisible and silent, thirty thousand feet in the sky, B-52 bombers dropped five-hundred—and one-thousand-pound bombs into the Iron Triangle. The Iron Triangle, which included the infamous Ho Bo Woods and Fil Hol rubber plantation, was a heavily fortified VC stronghold in the Cu Chi district. It was a death trap of tangled jungle, thorny vines, thick bamboo, snakes, hundreds of booby traps, mines, miles of tunnels, and dark caves. The Black Virgin Mountain was a part of this complex to the north in Tay Nihn province. This Friday night, army and marines were engaged in heavy fighting. No one had ever conquered this area, not even the French during their long and bitter war with the North Vietnamese. They lost, and I feared we too would lose.

A chilly Saturday morning came, dew droplets dripping off the tent edges shown like diamonds glittering in the morning sun. Despite the restless night, praise filled my heart. But as quickly as joy came, it vanished, for there would be no Sabbath worship that day. "Gardner, get your stuff together, you're moving out!" I was going up north to Tay Nihn base camp. I was to join up with Charlie Company and relieve Medic Swanson.

The truck convoy sped along dust-choked roads lined by ragged, war-wearied villages, smiling Vietnamese children, suspicious and silent adults and lots of heat and humidity. Five hours later, we arrived in Tay Nihn City, the provincial capital of Tay Nihn province. Catholic and Buddhist shines and places of worship were everywhere, but the most beautiful temple was the Cao Dai Temple. The rapidly growing religion of Cao Dai was a mixture of Catholicism, Buddhism, Taoism, and several other religions. The main gate to the temple was a kaleidoscope of every color imaginable. The tall ornate pillars were rimmed and inlaid with gold and silver designs and figurines. Shave-headed, orange-robed monks and temple workers dressed in white were all about. It was an exciting place to see and a wonderful place to visit, if there weren't a war.

The convoy stopped a few miles outside the city at a Twenty-fifth Infantry base camp. Charlie Company was there; so was Medic Swanson who was more than glad to see me and to get out of there. He was going home, and I was happy for him. The base camp had been mortared the night before, and it was still on full alert; tension was high. A large number of olive-drab tents dotted the area as different combat units mingled in preparation for upcoming missions. After greeting platoon members again, I milled around most of the afternoon by myself. I found a quiet spot and sat reading the book *Now Is the Time*. The hours passed quickly as I read and sang quietly to myself. The sun began to set in its usual grace and reverence. From my seat on a log at the edge of a tent, I looked up at the telephone lines webbed above the tents. My eyes followed the wire to the poles, where there they paused. Against the background of the setting sun, the silhouetted telephone poles became a line of crosses as far as I could see. The thought rose to deep sadness, *Was this a sign of all those that would die this year? Was one of them mine?* The sadness lasted only a moment, for I also felt joy for all who would hear of God's mercy and love. I knew for many, I was God's last messenger of hope, and that some would accept Him as their Lord and Savior. I prayed that this was true, and then for myself, in the fading Sabbath light, I prayed for courage and faithfulness. "Lord, let me not die a coward in this place. I am yours, help me to be true and faithful, amen."

# CHAPTER EIGHT

*He that dwelleth in the secret place of the Most High shall abide under the*
*shadow of the Almighty . . . A thousand shall fall at thy side . . . but it shall*
*not come nigh thee . . . For he shall give his angels charge over thee.*
—Psalms 91

Sunday, January 15, was my first combat mission. At 0800 hours, Charlie Company's eighteen armored personnel carriers with six to ten men each roared out of Tay Nihn base camp. We were on a search and destroy mission. It meant killing the enemy on sight. The acrid diesel exhaust smoke mixed with the fine powdery Vietnamese dust clouds made the bumpy, jerky ride inside the APC almost unbearable. The heat and humidity even in the morning was ovenlike. I wore a filthy green caveat scarf over my nose to keep from suffocating. The walls of the APC were lined with extra weapons, ammunition, water, cans, C ration food, radios, sleeping bags, and some personal items. Within the hull of one side of the track was the fuel tank. The Twenty-third Mechanized, my unit, had diesel. The Fifth Mechanized, our sister unit and the armored Calvary (Cav) units had gasoline fuel tanks. The VC took advantage of this weakness with their devastating mines and RPGs (rocket-propelled grenade). Some tracks (APCs) had sandbags lining the floor. The bags helped a little for small mine explosions beneath them but were of no use against the large command-detonated mines that usually killed everybody inside. Most of the men preferred risking bullets or tree mines on top of the APC rather than the mangling carnage of an inside explosion. Noticing the habit of the veterans, after a while, I too rode up top. Nobody told me to, but like most things in Nam, if you lived long enough, you learn by experience.

Around twelve or one o'clock, our track stopped, and I was asked (ordered) by Lieutenant DeWalt to go with seven or eight other soldiers on a patrol into the jungle. It was exciting and scary. Everything I learned at Fort Sam and at the introduction course at Cu Chi came back to me. "Look out for booby traps, ambush setups, and snakes." The jungle area wasn't too thick, but there were some green banana bunches, cashew trees, and a lot of sharp thorn bushes. Amazingly, the VC could get through that "natural bared-wire" with ease while others were snagged, torn, and stuck in a hundred places. Fifteen minutes into the patrol, a hand grenade dropped from the belt of a soldier hunched over in front of me; it didn't explode. Thankfully, the firing pin was still attached; and my heart rate, which had increased by a thousand beats, slowly calmed down. Some months later, a similar grenade incident happened. It was night. A soldier on guard duty was bitten by a scorpion and carried into the aid station. As his friends placed him on a cot in the half-lit treatment room, I heard a thump hit the floor. Looking down, I saw a hand grenade. There was no pin! I couldn't see the safety handle either. Panic filled my mind! *Run*, I said to myself, *shout, or something*, but I knew there was no time. I just stood there, waiting the inevitable explosion. Once again, time froze. I closed my eyes and whispered, "Lord, have mercy". Nothing! Grenades detonate within ten seconds. Nothing happened! Slowly, I bent down turned the grenade over, and there was the pin hanging in the safety handle only by the tip! I grasped the handle, then slid the pin slowly back in place. Gently, I carried it outside. Looking up at the stars, I thanked God for sparing our lives. I knew only He kept that pin in place when it hit the floor.

Back to my patrol, after that bit of excitement, nothing much else happened that day. We returned to Tay Nihn by nightfall. Six soldiers sat around discussing Vietnam, the Bible, and creation. I entered the conversation and was able to give a clear testimony of why God was so real to me and so important for them to know. It was a good day. Nobody died.

Over the next five days, we went out on daily patrols. I was assigned to track 24. I still didn't know the other six soldiers well, so I kept to myself much of the time. We prodded through dense jungle perfumed by the pungent smells of broken trees and crushed vegetation. The humidity left everyone soaked and in a state of stupor. The grinding noise of the track column, crashing trees, and occasional reconnaissance machine-gun fire to check for ambushes announced our presence for miles around. We were not surprising or sneaking up on anyone. The trouble with breaking through thick brush and fallen trees was breakdowns. The rotating tracks attached to sets of wheels and sprockets frequently popped off their runners. The lumbering APC ground and shimmied to a halt. This caused us to stop for an hour or two to repair and reseat the broken track. This time passed slowly and insufferably; most of the time, I sat slouched inside the metal oven reading my Bible, the *Stars and Stripes* (newspaper), or just catnapping. The newspaper often carried stories of United States' victories, a few tragedies, and always how we were winning the war, hearts and minds of the Vietnamese people. There were reports of nearly four hundred VC being killed in the surrounding area by the nightly B-52 bombings. Vietcong deserters were turning to the Chu Hoi (amnesty program) and being repatronized. That may have been true for many other units, but the only action we had was hand-to-hand fights with thousands of large, red, and very vicious fire ants. Sometimes they lived in huge ten to twenty-foot-high termite mounds that were in the open clearings, but often the mounds were camouflaged by tangles of creeping vines or bushes. To run into one with the APC was like hitting a reinforced concrete building. Every bone in your body rattled from the jar. No one dared hit or bother the mounds on purpose. It was the tree ants though that caused the most problems. Like well-trained commandos, the irritated red warriors dropped from hanging branches, bobbing leaves, or on command poured from holes in the ground to totally engulf an APC in seconds! Immediately, the whole column halted, and nearly everyone rushed to the aid of the APC's crew. Instead of blazing guns, we charged with hissing insect spray cans, flailing rags, and torn ammo cartons. *Smash! Bam! Pow! Hiss! Hiss!* The firefight would not end until we killed enough of them to get the APC out of the area. To demonstrate how brave or pissed off the ant warrior was, a soldier would hold a burning cigarette in front of one of the little maniacs, and it would fearlessly charge into the flaming tip. Venomous jaws opened and closed with defiant rage until it burned to death. There were times during these minibattles that we actually took casualties too. The ant stings were so painful and widespread that on occasion we had to air evacuate soldiers by helicopter to a field hospital. In some units, I heard there were deaths.

January 23, 4:30 p.m., Charlie Company arrived back at Cu Chi base camp. Rumbling into the motor pool area to park the tracks, I noticed two destroyed APCs, one from Alpha and one from Bravo Company. Both had been totally mangled, burned, and gutted. It was the Fifth Mechanized Infantry, our brother unit across base faired worst. A 250-pound command-detonated bomb exploded beneath one of their tracks, killing everyone on board, except the track commander who was thrown clear by the horrific explosion. The ambush occurred in a place called Bo Loi Woods. Rumor had it Charlie Company was to go into Bo Loi Woods the next day.

Later that evening, I studied the Bible with four Pentecostal soldiers; afterward, I read some Vietnamese language books before going to bed. In the distance, the earthquake of B-52 bombs falling vibrated the wooden floor of the hooch. I stared through the mosquitoes net into dark space and wondered about my future—what would happen tomorrow, what would happen the day after tomorrow, and the next. I trembled and sensed something was going to happen; I didn't want to imagine what. Perhaps if I thought about home, no, that only increased my fear—fear that I would never see it again. I fell asleep somehow. Time stopped, and a moment later, morning and fear again came to greet me.

The groans, shuffling and rustling noise of guys struggling to wake up began at 0430 hours and painfully increased until we all were awake. By 0700, we had eaten and boarded our APCs headed for Bo Loi Woods. The windless air was humid, the ground wet and muddy. The grinding drone of diesel engines rising, falling, and sputtering was momentarily halted at 10:00 a.m. by enemy sniper fire at the lead track. No one was hit. We swept through a patch of dense jungle and did recon by fire but found no VC.

Shortly after that bit of excitement, one of our six APCs got stuck. It was about noon, after freeing the vehicle that we entered a grassy clearing, took up defensive positions like circled wagons around the clearing. Minutes later, we began opening C rations for lunch. The grass was the deepest, greenest grass I ever saw, and it smelled so fresh. It was almost like being on a picnic, I thought. The clearing was about 100-150 yards across. The grass was thigh high in the middle and browner. On the other side of the clearing, a group from one of the other squads and a few of our guys sat around a small fire cooking C rations. I could hear small talk and laughter in the quietness of the afternoon. I sat on the APC's lowered ramp door that was the back wall of the APC when raised. I was actually enjoying this "camping trip." My helmet was off and flake jacket and shirt open for a breeze. It was 1:00 p.m. I was looking for a something to read when *pow*! A single dull rifle shot split the silence. Sniper? My heart stopped! Across the clearing, the group scattered; one soldier slumped forward onto the ground. "Medic! Medic! Medic!" I was paralyzed with wild fear. I turned right, then left looking for my precious medic's aid bag. Seconds passed. "Medic! Medic!" Fumbling with my helmet and flak jacket, I scooped up my aid bag and started a crazed run across the open field. The thought flashed, *Sniper, I'm gonna get killed out in the open*. Immediately, my legs gave out and I fell headlong into the grass. "Medic!" some one shouted. "Doc, hurry!" another voice pleaded. Hunched over, I got to my feet again and ran to the downed soldier and his glaring terrified comrades. Sergeant John L was kneeing face down on the ground—right were his legs suddenly buckled. A thick pool of gelled blood fed by bright red spurts flowed freely from the missing top of his head. Chunks of shattered bone and ragged tissue tailed to pieces of smoking brain that lay a few feet away. I knew there was nothing I or anyone else could do. "Oh sh—t, oh sh—t!" one of John L's friends moaned. Someone said, "It wasn't a sniper, he was leaning on his rifle." Another said, "He shouldn't have been out here. He only had two more weeks to go!" "What the hell's wrong with you, Gardner!" Lieutenant DeWalt appeared from nowhere. Inches from my sullen face, he yelled, "Gardner, dammit, can't you run no faster than that!" Shock and unbelief made words useless. I stared in to his teary eyes and felt worst, if that was possible. My anguish gave way to nausea, fear, and uncontrollable trembling. I walked slowly back to my side of the clearing. John L was gently placed in a dark green body bag and flown away in a helicopter. It was 3:45 p.m. As the deep thud of the Huey vanished into silence, I wondered how John L's mother and family would take the news—the news of shattered dreams, a joyless homecoming and darkened tomorrows. Tears rose from my heart, filling my eyes, for John L and for my failure. I knew from that time on, I would always know where my medic bag and every piece of my equipment was. More importantly, I vowed never to miss a chance to tell these guys how much God loved them, died for them, and offered them the Blessed Hope, even in Vietnam.

Depressed and dazed, like everyone else, the rest of the day seemed surreal and vacant. Eventually, we broke camp and moved nosily through the lush green countryside to a dry open rice paddy where we set up defensive positions for the night. It was 1700 hours, and the sun was setting. The mortar teams started their night bracketing of our camp with test mortar rounds in case an attack occurred during the night. This allowed for fast response from the firing coordinates set during the day. They also could fire random shells around the perimeter to make the VC nervous. *Doomp!* a mortar shell left the tube. I watched it disappear, then reappear 180 degrees back toward the mortar tube. "Mortar! Mortar!" the mortar team shouted as they sprinted wildly in different directions. Everybody started running to get out of the way. Fortunately, the round curved as it was falling and exploded in a fiery, hot shower of white phosphorous just outside the perimeter. No one got hurt that time, but that wasn't always the case.

I slide comfortably into my sleeping bag unrolled along side a rice paddy dike. The ground was soft with dry straw from rice stems covering the rich dark soil. I knew the richness was due to water buffalo dung, but I was too tired to care. The moon rose full and brilliant. I thanked God for the light; it always made things less frightening. Orange sniper fire traced across the distant night sky several times, but like most things in Nam, if it ain't close, it doesn't matter.

Next morning, I awoke with a start to find a six-foot snakeskin in my sleeping bag. Perhaps its owner was too busy shedding, and I was too busy sleeping to care. Anyway, we both were happy with the outcome.

# CHAPTER NINE

*It is of the Lord's mercies that we are not consumed,*
*because His compassion fail not. They are new every*
*morning: great is thy faithfulness.*
—Lamentations 3:22-23

The week of February 3, a Friday, began with a dewless morning that gave birth in coolness—a gift—ever so temporary but always welcomed. The sun rose vengefully as it did each morning. It promised hotness, dryness, and death. Today, we were headed for the Cambodian border to intercept a North Vietnamese battalion crossing into South Vietnam. The operation was called Gadsden. It was a diversionary mission for a much-larger operation called Junction City. The end of Junction City would result in some two thousand seven hundred enemy killed. The rumbling column of armored vehicles included tanks, tank retrievers, APCs, jeeps towing artillery pieces, and helicopter gunships overhead. The fearsome force stretched for nearly a mile. Along the way, we passed through many villages. People lined the narrow asphalt and dirt roads, smiling children shouted and giggled like any you'd find on American streets, waving and begging for candy or food. The older leathered-faced men and women stared with glazed war-weary eyes, tear-filled eyes, eyes of fear, and eyes of hatred. Along the way, there were blown-up bridges, lifeless, dead brown areas sprayed by Agent Orange defoliants, groups of frightened South Vietnamese infantry, and dense green jungle. Alas, night came. We formed a huge wagon train circle in a clearing, dug foxholes, and settled in for the night. The night came quick and with it, the cold jungle darkness. It was Sabbath, and though I was miserable outside, my heart was joyous inside. The stars greeted me like angels with flashlights, and I smiled in return.

Sergeant Langsford, a black soldier from Kansas City, Kansas, was near by, so we started to talk. We spoke about the war, marriage, family, and finally, religion. The fact that I didn't carry a weapon wasn't popular with the field troops, but they all knew I would do my job. I spoke of how God had changed my life and how he gave me courage to be true to him. The what-if question always came up. "What if Charlie is coming at you, what are you gonna do?" "What if you were asked to shoot a gook or carry ammo?" or "What are you gonna do, Doc?" My answer was never pat, theoretical, or made-up. I really didn't know. I prayed that I would not be placed in a situation to make that decision. Every Adventist Christian had to make their own choice, like the several Adventist I saw carrying .45s and M16s. I was too afraid not to trust God. Though one of my early Sabbaths in Vietnam, during a fierce close gun battle, I had to make a choice. I was inside the APC. The driver was violently swirling the APC about to avoid direct hits. The ear splitting .50-caliber gun rained down hundreds of empty shell casings while two other soldiers wildly fired their M16 rifle and M60 machine gun. "Doc, Doc, I need ammo! Get me some ammo now!" My heart was in a panic and in a crisis. *Lord, what shall I do? I don't want anybody to die!* "Doc, get me some ammo!" In a moment, in a terrifying rush, I began tearing out belts of .50-caliber ammo and passing it to the gunner. Remorse and fear whaled up inside as the gunfire sputtered to single shots, then quiet. When the Sabbath ended that day, God read my heart and confusion. Had I betrayed Him? Had I lost my faith to cowardice? I wanted to cry, but a gentle breeze passed over me, and a peace seemed to fill my soul. From the starry blackness came the assurance that no matter what was to happen in the months ahead, my Heavenly Father would fight my battles. He would be my shield and my defense. Time seemed frozen. Sergeant Langford said little after that but was glad we talked.

# CHAPTER TEN

*To every thing there is a season, and a time to every purpose*
*under the sun ... A time to heal ... a time to kill ... a time to weep ...*
*and a time to laugh.*
                                                              —*Ecclesiastes 3:1-4*

February passed slowly and quickly. There were four kinds of time in Vietnam—fast, slow, fast slow, and out of time. "Fast time," was when you finally got back to base camp and paused before the next mission. It was time that could be just a deadly as the boonies (field) with sudden *shooowish ... boom* of incoming mortar or rocket fire; but as the expression went, "it didn't mean nothin'." It was a small price to pay to be in relatively safe time. This fast time meant a hot shower, a dusty trip to the PX (post exchange) in search of music tapes, camera film, magazines, and junk food. Fast time was also the R&R (rest and recuperation) trips to such places as Japan, Singapore, Hawaii, Bangkok, or Kuala Lumpur. Fast time could also be the hellish adrenaline filled seconds of an ambush, the time between a smile and the bullets exiting your chest. It was the time the click sounded in your ear, your heart stopped, and the world rose in thunderous swirls of red and black as the booby trap exploded fast time into no time.

The "slow time" was waiting time. Time waiting for mail, waiting to go home, or time waiting for urgent medical DUSTOFF helicopters, Phantom jets, or artillery to arrive to save your life. Slow time was long nights of stinging mosquitoes, moving bushes, rain, mud, heat, and monotony. February had a lot of slow time. Our rumbling tracks roamed the countryside and jungles slightly north and east of Tay Ninh and the area south toward Cu Chi. We found many enemy bunker complexes, hot food still cooking, tons of rice, clothing, and signs of recent enemy presence. There were many sniper firings, sporadic ambushes, brief firefights, injuries from landmines, and red ant attacks. Minor accidents took their toll and amazingly there were only a few deaths mostly in other units. Some of my slow time I spent reading a psychology text for my correspondence course. I read the spirit-filled books *Steps to Christ* and *Great Controversy* by E. G. White and enjoyed poems and other devotional books on occasion. I was grateful to have *Steps to Christ* because I gave it to Sergeant Langford before he left for home. He hugged me. "Doc, take care of yourself." I was glad, excited, and sad to see him go. Another sergeant left with Sergeant Langford—Sergeant Helmig, a wiry, leathered face white platoon sergeant from California, I think. He stayed on my case for one thing or another. He didn't like the idea of a CO (conscientious objector) in his platoon. One such run in was an impromptu order to dig a foxhole on the Sabbath (if there was an urgent need to do so, I would have done it), but this was more a "make yourself useful" order. The details of what I did were a little fuzzy, but no foxhole got dug, and Sergeant Helmig just looked at me in discuss. Oddly, one night, we had a religious talk around the campsite. He recounted that "wherever I am, that's what I am." He meant that for the moment, he was a Methodist but said if he hung around me long enough, he'd probable be an Adventist. Down deep in his heart he liked me, I think.

February 26 was a good day. A good day because I was leaving line track number 24 and going to the HQ (headquarters) track in the center of the column; I was elated! That meant I would not be on the lead track, the one that is blown up first or receives the brunt of an ambush. It was also good news because I met Private Mullen. I was thin as a cucumber, wiry, but Mullen was slightly shorter, stockier, crowned with short beady hair and had an easy smile. My replacement was a black medic fresh from St. Louis, Missouri. Mullen and I spoke as often as we could in the field. It was good to have a brother medic around. Mullen is remembered not so much for that day but for what happened months later. Our unit was on a search and destroy mission in a deadly VC stronghold called HoBo Woods. We'd spent long slow hours breaking trail through dense, hot, suffocating jungle. To this day, I am sickened by the smell of diesel fuel, broken trees, and cut vegetation. The arduous misery took its toll on several of the troops—one was Mullen; he collapsed from heat exhaustion and lack of sleep. I told him to take my place in the center track, and I would take his position on the lead track. After only a few hours on the track knocking down trees and clearing a path for the rest of the column, I too felt hot and sick. Riding atop the track was the safest place to be if a mine went off. Bullets were also a concern, but at least they wouldn't blow your body into a hundred unrecognizable pieces. The hours past in tedium, and I whispered a prayer over and over we wouldn't hit a mine or get ambushed. This was VC country, and we were noisy strangers. As the column mulled to a halt, my prayers were answered—nothing happened. The shadows of the tall palm trees stretched long to chase the fleeing daylight. The noise of grinding engines spluttered to silence, and night strolled into the camp like an unwelcome mistress. Mullen was still sick, so I told him to go back to his track for the night, and I would take his place tomorrow. The thought of another day doing point frightened me, but Mullen was my friend.

Darkness shrouded the tiny jungle clearing, soldiers talked in whispers, and the stillness settled in for the night. *Thud . . . thud . . . thud*, the sound of a helicopter grew louder and louder as a voice came over the radio, "Charlie-16, this is Lima-4 inbound, got a medic named Gardner, coming in for pickup." "Get your stuff, Gardner," the platoon sergeant barked. "Chopper ain't waiting." A panic rushed over me. Choppers didn't come in at night for routine pickups in the jungle, and they certainly didn't call out names over the radio! What was the emergency? Had someone in my family back home died ? I couldn't imagine why me.

Next morning, Mullen was still too sick to go back on point, so he stayed with my track in the center column. An hour in to the Search and Destroy patrol, *kabooom!* The earth shook, and the air filled with black smoke and thousands of bits of metal shrapnel, glass, tree bark, and human feces. The point track was hit by a command-detonated mine mounted in a tree; all the soldiers riding on top were blew off and severely wounded. One, a friend, was blinded.

The night ride to Cu Chi filled me with terror. What was this all about? The answer came and enraged me. A medic was needed to fill a slot at the "ambush academy," the school to learn how to conduct night ambushes and kill. "I'm a Seventh-day Adventist!" I reminded the company officer, half pleading. "So what? You will attend that school starting tomorrow!" The answer was short and blunt.

By morning, my rage turned to fear. Charlie Company's lead track had been hit; my heart sank. Was Mullen riding on top where I would have been? Was Mullen okay? When I asked about him, I found out that he was safe. I closed my eyes and lifted my heart to heaven in gratitude, but heaviness filled my soul for the others who were wounded.

Looking back from the future, the whole year was filled with such miraculous deliverance for such an unworthy sinner. As God was faithful and compassionate for the prayers of those who remembered me and for my own prayers, I tried to be faithful to His calling in Vietnam. At times, fearful, awkward, and even bone tired, I gave Bible studies in the hooches, in the mess halls, in the chapel, inside the tracks, or cramped in a foxhole. Whether I was ever successful, I don't know; I only tried to be faithful.

There are so many I remember. Among those whom I hope to meet in heaven were Sgt. Herbert Sherrill, from St. Albas, New York, and E-4 Robert Pendarvaris, from Orangeburg, South Carolina—two tall black soldiers who I grew to love as brothers and to whom at every opportunity talked with about the Lord. They were regular guys too. Full of fun, foolishness, wild stories, and adventures unique to being raised in the black inner city.

Pendarvis screamed and hobbled over to my track. He caught his foot in the ramp door of his armored personnel carrier (APC) while it was closing. Although his dusty grimace of pain captured the moment, behind those teary eyes was a kidlike face and boyish smile I grew to admire. After bandaging his foot and talking casually, the conversation easily settled on his personal relationship with

God. He was glad I spoke of such wonderful things and especially the Blessed Hope. We became instant friends. He was afraid, like most of us, but in his life, it was reassuring to see that even in that terrible place God was changing hearts and drawing his children to Him. Robert's eyes sparkled when he talked about his baby daughter—the joy of his life—and his beautiful wife.

Then I met Sherrill. It was during a running gun battle with some VC. Two of our tracks (APCs) had set out to patrol an area a mile or so from the other ten tracks. We had not yet broken camp in a grassy field. Suddenly, the radio snapped to life. "Charlie-16, Charlie-16, ambush! Ambush! We're hit!" Everybody scrambled, dropping everything the diesel engines roared to life like avenging lions. Swirling about, cascades of mud and grass flung skyward as we charged into the direction of the black smoke. As we approached, one track was disabled with the ramp door down. A couple of soldiers stood around in the grassy yellow green field. The sky above them was gray and overcast. I thought to myself what a bad day to die. Quickly, the situation became clear. A VC popped up from a spider hole in the ground and fired his RPG (rocket propelled grenade), then ducked back into his hole. The rocket burned its way through the side of the track and exploded inside, spraying thousands of deadly shards of hot metal. Other VC were seen racing in to the near by jungle or disappearing in to clumps of grass. My track pulled up next to the disabled track to let me off while the rest of the tracks continued on after the VC. The track commander's hand was blown off, and a small command helicopter in the area immediately evacuated him. I didn't see him. Two other soldiers sat mutely inside the track hit by the RPG, cradling a third soldier who lay between them. His name was George. "Hi, Doc! Guess Charlie finally got me, think I'll go home now?" He smiled. I managed a smile back but knew by the grim expressions on his friends' faces things were bad. George was covered from the chest down with a green poncho raincoat. "George, let me take a look, everything is gonna be all right." Hunched over, I squeezed in to the small compartment. The smell of cordite explosive, burnt flesh, sweat, and blood hung heavy in the air. I raised the poncho, George's intestines where blown out along with everything else. From his chest down, all was blackened, burned, and totally mutilated. I lowered the poncho, stroked his blond hair, and whispered, "George, God loves you. Everything will be all right." He smiled and then died.

Moments later, my track came back and picked me up to join the other tracks racing to find the VC. We approached a rubber tree plantation area with thick under brush. All the tracks got on an assault line. My track was on the far left, the last track. I was the only protection for an attack from the left, and I had no weapon. My heart raced with adrenaline and cold raw fear. The air exploded with heavy .50-caliber machine gun fire and grenade launchers. M60 machine guns ripped up the foliage in front. Our track gunner put out the rounds too, but being the only one in the track besides the driver and gunner, there was no protection from the flank or rear. "Please, God, don't let a VC pop up now!" Thoughts raced through my mind, *Pick up one of the extra weapons inside the track. Protect the track!* "No, God will protect me!" The wild ride through the trees finally broke out into a clearing. No VC.

"Medic! Medic! We got some casualties!" one of the other tracks yelled out as it swerved across the grassy clearing. Sergeant Sherrill hopped out grinning. "I almost got the VC SOB!" Steaming beads of sweat rolled down his charcoal skin like a diamond waterfall. Six feet one, he looked more like a tall Massi warrior hunting lions then a US soldier. His smiling face was covered with numerous small bleeding shrapnel wounds. "What happened?" I asked. "Saw this VC pop up out of his hole, my track ran over the hole, and I dropped a couple grenades. The SOB pulled a straw cover over the hole, and the damn grenades bounced up and exploded." Fortunately, most of the wounds were superficial and had already stopped bleeding. Sherrill rode the rest of the afternoon with me, and eventually, we returned to Cu Chi. Of course, there was a moment, as most times, when the conversation turned to issues of ordinary life, eternal life, and the Giver of life, my Lord and Savior. I wasn't a fanatic about religion, politics, the war—whatever; in fact, I wasn't overly zealous about anything other than giving hope whenever and wherever I could. And in that hellish place, God was the only hope, the only subject worth talking about.

Sherrill and Pendarvis both died on the same day. Standing at the barbed wire fence on the edge of the main Cu Chi base camp, I stood paralyzed one moment and frantically pacing another, hardly able to stand still as fast-moving Phantom jets swoop low over the jungle tree line some three to four miles away. Vibrations and shock waves from deadly bombs pulsed the air in saccadic symphony. Fiery black napalm (jellied gasoline) smoke boiled skyward like angry dancing snakes. The whispered sounds of small arms gunfire drifted faintly across the open field like popcorn crackling to the last kernel. Then silence, and smoke settled over the nightmare. It was frozen time—snapshots of moments heralded by chaos, frantic aid station radio wailing for help, "O God, ambush!" or "Jesus, help us!" Now silence.

Night fell; the field reports filtered back to the company. Over ten dead, some fifteen to twenty others wounded. My heart broke when I heard my two friends were dead. I cried forever then; I cry forever now.

In the future, I walk along Constitution Avenue in the shadow of Lincoln's gaze. The pulsating cacophony of familiar but strange and deadly sounds of that distant war is now silent. Reverently, in the company of others who come to Washington DC's Vietnam Memorial to view the terrible reminder of freedom's worth and sins cost—over sixty-five thousand names—I stand among this painful reality. The wall's angular black marble holds the glacial past of so many, all that's tangible and all that's left of a generation forever lost. As I run my fingers along the perfect letters and numbers, panel 22E, lines 84 and 85 quietly summon the names of my friends Robert Pendarvis and Herbert Sherrill. The smoke of that ancient day still rises in my memory, still shuttering from the smell, the sound, and the sorrow. The chiseled words "died 29 June 1967" still hurt with an eternal pain, yet I know with bowed head as the wind gently stirs the cherry blossoms, and birds sing their songs of hope, and the beautiful clouds pass silently above that a morning is coming—a glorious, endless morning when I shall see them again.

# CHAPTER ELEVEN

*The dusty concrete floor of the little green chapel was cold and hard. The stifling Vietnamese air hung still and humid. It was quiet. Tears rimmed my eyes. "Lord, I'm not gonna make it, I'm not gonna make the whole year . . . I . . . I need help." The rivulet of salted tears turned into a flood.*

It is said the month of March comes in like a lion and leaves like a lamb. That may be true in America, but in the Nam, every month had its lions; there were no lambs. They've all been eaten. The Lion of March carried in its teeth more ferocious fighting and death. The 1st Infantry Division and the 173rd Airborne bore heavy causalities during Operation Junction City. Seventeen miles east of the Twenty-fifth Infantry base camp at Tay Nihn was a small hamlet area called Sui Tre. I was in this area some weeks earlier.

Looking north, the Black Virgin Mountain loomed nearly a thousand feet above the rich green forest, jungles and rice paddies that ringed its base. A muddy, bomb-scared US Special Forces camp controlled the very top, but the rest of the mountain was Vietcong. It was honeycombed with miles of enemy tunnels, bunkers, mines, snipers, mortar positions, and booby traps. Later in the year, in December, just before Christmas, nearly a hundred young American and South Vietnamese would die attacking the mountain.

The area of Sui Tre was ominous from the start. Camped there one morning, I took a short walk to relieve myself. A little distance from my rest spot, I noticed the gnarled, bomb-scared trees all around. Some were burned with napalm; others had large gashes from bullets and shrapnel. But what was curious was the tree's sap; it was red, like blood. The trees were actually bleeding. The area scared me. It was at Sui Tre in March that nearly a thousand soldiers of the 272nd VC Regiment charged headlong into the artillery guns of the Third Battalion, Fourth Infantry, and Twenty-fifth Division. US soldiers on the edge of the small clearing were quickly over run and killed. In a desperate, wild act, the artillerymen leveled their guns horizontal and fired Beehive (steel darts) rounds into wave after wave of charging Vietnamese soldiers. My unit was on alert along with some one hundred or so armored vehicles and tanks from the Calvary units. We couldn't get to the artillerymen before dark, and a night travel and assault would have been a disaster. By morning the next day, some 423 enemy lay dead and mangled across the clearing at Sui Tre. My unit was never called. I was thankful again. Before March ended, over two thousand one hundred VC where killed in the area and sadly many GIs also.

Sabbath, March 4, was significant in that I had only three hundred days left in Vietnam. The sixth was significant because a mortar round landed fifty yards from me while on a patrol, and I wasn't killed. The eighth of March was the first time I dreamed of marrying someone. That really was a stolen moment in sleep because when awake, I never allowed myself to think or hope about such things again. The ninth saw tracks 22 and 24 (my old first track) blown up by landmines. Thankfully, all the soldiers got only minor wounds. I had been transferred to the headquarter medic track by then.

Of all the days of March, the tenth was the best! Returning form a search and destroy mission, I took the wounded soldiers to the battalion aid station; then as usual after returning from the field, I went to the small green chapel to pray and thank God. Walking across the powdery ground toward the chapel a sudden, deep sadness filled my heart as I thought of the deaths behind me and the ones to come in the months before me—even my own. It was late Friday afternoon, and the searing orange sun was setting. Dirt and sweat blew from my uniform as the evening wind made its usual pass before night settled in. Though everything under the rays of the sun still sizzled from the heat, the dusty concrete floor of the little green chapel was cold and hard. The stifling Vietnamese air hung still and humid inside the chapel. It was quiet. As I knelt and bowed my head, tears rimmed my eyes. "Lord, I'm not gonna make it. I'm not gonna make the whole year. Father, I . . . I need help." The rivulet of salted tears turned into a flood. Long sobbing moments passed before I had the strength to rise. Looking down, I left the chapel and headed back to the hooch. Slowly raising my eyes, they met other eyes—happy big round eyes. Surprised eyes. Eyes that was as tearful and overjoyed as mine. It was Albert Marks! "Oh my God!" he shouted, and we ran and embraced each other. "Thank you, Lord!" I cried. Marks was my brother in Christ; he was my instant prayer partner, he was God's answer to my loneliness, and the answer to my need for fellowship. Through the providence of God, Marks had just arrived in country and was assigned to the Fourth/Twenty-third aid station that day! God anticipated my need. He knew I was frightened, lonely, and missed fellowship with other Seventh-day Adventist. To this day, I thank Him for Brother Marks.

I met Albert Mark in San Antonio, Texas, just before leaving for Vietnam. His dark skin was highlighted by the biggest brightest smile I ever saw. He loved the Lord and spoke of Him as one who knew Him personally. Marks's second love was music. He played the organ and a little piano. His humming was a little off-key at times, but his powerful, heart-rending prayers made up for that. He was about five feet six or seven inches, a little chubby, and rich in experience and good humor. In San Antonio, we visited nursing homes, sang and prayed with the residents. We passed out literature and talked often of God blessings to us. Marks never went in to the field, but every time I left for missions, we got together for a season of prayer. Those precious times meant all the world to me and gave me the courage I needed to be faithful and hopeful.

The next day, March 11, Sabbath, was just as momentous. Friday night, I was surprised when the company commander, Captain Trammell, said yes when I asked permission to go to Saigon for church. I agreed to be back in time to go on the mission the following Sunday morning. Now the problem was finding a ride for Marks and me. The cool morning was dark as I roamed the camp looking and asking for a ride. I think the devil was trying to break my neck when I fell in to a trench and scraped my knee pretty bad, but I was determined not to let that stop me. Short while later, Marks joined me' and together for over an hour and a half, we looked for a ride. By 7:30 a.m., we hitched a ride to the assembly point for the truck convoy but no trucks. We wondered if we were late and missed the only way to Saigon. We prayed. At 7:50 a.m., we could barely make out the cloud of dust approaching us. It was a quarter-ton open bed truck noisily creeping to where we were standing. Minutes later, more trucks arrived; and by 9:00 a.m., more than fifty trucks lined up for the dangerous run to Saigon.

The ride was simply exhilarating! Though the air was cool, the sun was bright and not so harsh this morning. Something about the Sabbath, going to worship and fellowshipping with my brothers and sisters always, even to this day, feels me with joy and happiness. Helmets and flak jackets flapping wildly, Marks and I sang standing up in the back of the truck. "We're marching to Zion, beautiful, beautiful Zion." Nobody could hear us but the angels over the roar of the diesel engines, but we laughed and praised God the forty-some miles to Saigon.

We arrived at Tan Son Nhut Air Base on the outskirts of Saigon a little past ten in the morning; the air was getting warmer and the sun brighter. Now the problem was where and how to get to the Adventist Church. One of the convoy drivers told us to get one of the tiny yellow-and-blue taxis and tell them where we wanted to go. He told us to be careful and be back at the assembly point by 4:00 p.m. (1600), or we'd get left there. "Be careful" hung in my mind. Why did he have to say that, I thought. *Click*, I was back in jungle mode. Gazing cautiously in every direction as if on a combat mission, I looked for booby traps, ambushes, and places to duck into in case we received fire. But of course, "It was the Sabbath. And God had allowed us to come this far," I queried myself. "And besides, there ain't nothing going to happen, at least not today."

My fears calmed, and Marks and I squeezed into the tiny yellow-and-blue go-kart. Rush hour in New York City didn't have anything on Saigon at any hour. The streets were painted with a million people it seemed. Bicycles, rickshaws with stringy leathered men gripping poles and bouncing rhythmically through traffic, dodging other hurried vendors and motor vehicles. Sights, sounds, and smells overwhelmed the senses. What excitement! Finally and thankfully, we arrived at 273 Dailo Cach Mang Street. It was an old French compound with high plastered brick walls studded with multicolored broken glass along the top. Inside the compound were neat, well-kept bungalow-type homes of American and other nationals. The center of the compound where Marks and I stood was open and partly covered with faded green grass and powdery sand. Along one side was a small mission school with a red roof and a matching dormitory. Standing in the middle of the compound with dusty boots, helmets, and open flak jackets, we looked like characters form an old Western just rolling into town.

As funny as it may seem the lives of the missionaries and the day-to-day activities around the compound were pretty ordinary. The war that raged in the rice paddies and jungles only miles away was events experienced mostly on the radio and read in the newspaper. So Marks and I were an instant curiosity. Two young girls, Cherry and Ela, walked up to us, introduced themselves, and showed us around. The girl with long blond hair—set off by an equally bright smile—was Cherry, the daughter of the head missionary. Ela Gutierrez was a little shorter than Cherry. Her short silky black hair was crowned by a tan-colored barrette. That bubbly little Filipino girl with the pastel yellow sundress was simply beautiful! Her soft, smooth skin, innocent angelic voice, and girlish smile won my heart almost immediately. From long talks about everything, but the war, slicing pineapples and fruit for potluck, stolen glances at each other, listening to music and sitting on opposite sides of the tiny church praising God in fellowship, we became friends.

In the months to come, Marks and I would return to the compound, the small church, and the famous Saigon Adventist hospital many times. The Vietnamese name for the hospital was Benh-Vien Co-Doc. In 1952, the Adventist Vietnam mission received permission from the largely French Catholic government to open a medical facility. With the help of a $2,500 contribution from the Bangkok Adventist Hospital, the small Saigon hospital opened in May 1955. It soon expanded to a thirty-eight-bed hospital with an operating room and a small nursing school. Eventually, Marks and I would get helicopter rides from an Adventist captain named Equid who was an American army pilot. Perhaps the most memorable of times was the communion service, the washing of our Vietnamese brother's feet, eating at their homes, and listening to unbelievable mission stories of Vietcong prisoners accepting Jesus Christ. We ate sumptuous potluck dinners from a mile-long picnic table with other visiting soldiers, lounge at one of the missionary's home and listen to music, or sleep until time to get back to Cu Chi base camp. One army doctor I met I will never forget. His name was Joe Ryan.

Dr. Joe Ryan was a family practice doctor, I think. He was my Afro American brother and was full of life and humor. He laughed and joked as easily as I did. We were instant friends. Joe was a little older and a strong Adventist. He occasionally came to the mission compound for potlucks and always carried on lively conversations with everybody. He loved to sing. In fact, he and another friend who was a good friend of Joe Ryan was Dr. Leonard Johnson. I met Leonard while going through training at Fort Sam Houston Texas some six months before. We met at the Ephesus SDA Church on Hackberry Street. Joe and Leonard were members of a quartet during their college days and often reminisced about those great times. In the future, I would meet both friends again and have wonderful times. Dr. Ryan would set up practice at Riverside Hospital in Nashville, Tennessee, along the Cumberland River, while Dr. Johnson, would put on the wings of a full-bird colonel in the air force. Leonard would become a valued mentor and a sympathetic ear when I returned from Vietnam and my life turned upside down. He was the person who gave me the inspiration and hope to change and start fresh in the Lord. He reminded me how wonderfully God loves and forgives.

Both would die young—Joe of stomach cancer and Leonard in a plane crash. Both would be greatly missed.

Each visit to Saigon for me was to see Ela. She was like dessert—sweet, innocent, and refreshing as a glass of cold orange juice for which I constantly craved. In reality though, I never thought of her or anyone while I was in the bush on a mission. It seemed bad luck or at least a foolish thing to believe I would ever get out of there alive. But each time—by the goodness of God—I went to Saigon, we looked for each other. She was my sister in Christ, and even though she looked thirteen years old but was actually eighteen years old as she would proudly boost, I greatly respected her in every way. I think I loved her without really knowing it at the time because she represented hope and beauty. The war was pure ugly, pure fear, and absolute depression. She was life. She was what life could be. What real life felt like to one who seemed alone all his life. I miss her to this day and wonder where she is.

In April 1975, the Communist North Vietnamese and Vietcong were on the outskirts of Saigon. The city was in total chaos. Ela and most of the Adventist missionary families fled Vietnam. She wrote me from the Philippines and said how she missed me and wanted to see me again one day. A time came when the letters suddenly stopped coming. Years passed before I received a letter from a friend of Ela's who said she was in trouble and had gotten mixed up with the wrong crowd and was on drugs. No one knew where she was. Had I not been married by then, I would have gone to the Philippines to find my beloved sister whose smile was the light of my life in such a dark place, in such a dark time.

# CHAPTER TWELVE

*When the storms of life are raging, stand by me, stand by me*
*When my world is tossing me like a ship upon the sea*
*Thou who rulest wind and water, stand by me*

*In the midst of tribulation, stand by me, stand by me*
*When the host of hell assail and my strength begins to fail*
*Thou who never lost a battle, stand by me, stand by me.*
*—Charles A. Tindley*

Visits to Saigon were an aberration, a tease of normalcy, out of place, an unintended diversion from the nightmare to which I had to return. I tried not to think about my death too much because somehow I felt special. Not special in the sense that I couldn't die as easily as those around me, but special that I was protected. My fears and tension still hung on me as firmly as the sweat and dirt clung to my skin, but there was something strange and frightening protecting me. The months that followed were full of mundane details, the drudgery of which could only be appreciated by one in an infantry company. Fire fights, body bags, mosquitoes, letters to and from home, jungle heat, chow lines, KP, digging foxholes, bandaging wounds, cringing from artillery shells, ignoring the bullets that missed, rain, mud, laughing, crying, singing, moaning, praying, and even cursing at times. I gave many Bible studies, cheered the home sick, and dreamed with those who dreamed of something, anything, better than Nam. Flicking images, out of sequence, caught swirling end over end as I try to remember and am amazed that I was so protected. Here are some of those memories.

## The Monkey from Hell

I never knew that monkeys could be evil. I knew that monkeys loved fruit, candy, and, an occasional cold beer. I knew they were playful, but never pure evil. In fact, as a kid I begged my parents for a monkey after seeing them at the state fair. Now I know why they said no!

It was hard to tell who looked more like a monkey: the monkey itself or its owner—the maintenance sergeant. Of course, the sergeant was slightly taller, but still they resembled father and son when together. Both were gruff with sand-colored hair, slightly bowed-legs and bad tempers. No one could touch the monkey without a vicious bite from the thankless beast or a "keep you hands off'm" from the sergeant. The little devil would steal objects or snatch food, then run silently or screaming "monkey profanity" if caught. The two were inseparable in base camp and in the bush. When riding on a tank retrieval track or walking around, the sergeant kept it on a leach most of the time; occasionally, it would run loose around the camp, looking to get in to something.

One night while camped in the bush, the quiet was suddenly shattered by a scream and a "oh sh—t!" then that familiar high-pitched screech for help from the monkey. Cradled in the protective arms of the sergeant, the little devil seemed to close its ears to accusations that he had just hit a sleeping soldier across the nose with a beer bottle. I patched up the soldier's nose, and like the others, I was upset that the monkey was causing more trouble than the Vietcong.

As the saying goes, "God don't like ugly," our prayers—with some sadness and joy, it was hard to tell the difference at the time—were answered. The next morning after the beer-bottle attack, we got an urgent call to break camp and intercept a Vietcong battalion moving into our area. Tanks, APCs, and adrenaline-charged soldiers rushed to get ready. Engines growled to life; dust and exhaust fumes filled the air as tracks sped to from a long column. As the column started to rumble forward, above the deafening cacophony of mechanized sounds, one sound brought the whole column to stop cold—it was the sergeant screaming or the monkey; nobody was certain. Anyway, there in the design of a track pattern on the dusty road was the little devil—flat as a pancake and quiet for once. In the haste to leave, the sergeant forgot to untie his protégée from the track wheel. We actually felt sorry for the sergeant, his lost, but for the monkey, if that's what it really was, we were overjoyed.

## Revenge

The rumbling yellow Caterpillar bulldozers did their destructive job well. Most infantry and armor units hated pulling security for the combat engineers mostly because of the first part of their name—combat. Guarding the engineers was always a dangerous job. We rode along side them as they cleared jungle trees and brush, exposing enemy hiding places. At times, they were ordered to demolish whole villages and relocate the less-than-happy villagers to safer areas. Sometimes the engineers helped us uncover VC tunnels or clear mines and unexploded bombs. On one such operation, a Tunnel Rat (small soldiers with flash lights and .45-caliber pistols) crawled in a hole searching for enemy soldiers, supplies, or underground complexes. The tunnels of Cu Chi were famous for the hundreds of miles of interconnecting tunnels in which large numbers of enemy units could travel the countryside without detection or hide from the deadly air attacks from US forces. The Tunnel Rats were the only soldiers courageous enough to venture into those tiny often booby-trapped corridors. The Tunnel Rats themselves had their own set off fears. The worst was being covered by hundreds of large black spiders or running into venomous snakes. Vietnam had some 140 species of snakes, 30 of which were poisonous. The ones the Viet Cong, booby-trapped the tunnels with where large snakes like the 4 to 8 foot King or Asian cobras, the coral snakes or the smaller pencil width green Krait the GI's called "Two Step". The myth was that you took two steps before you died. Actually it was 15 to 30 agonizing minutes before death came.

One especially hot, overcast day our unit came across a tunnel entrance. After searching the tunnel for a while, one bare-chested Tunnel Rat was ordered to come out by Lt. Dewalt. Moments passed, and then everyone flinched as muffled gunshots echoed from the black hole. Tensed seconds passed slowly like time and mud and fear gelling into a wall of our worst nightmare. Everyone stared at the black hole as grayish dust colored smoke snaked its way to the outside; the Tunnel Rat didn't come out. "Hey, Ray! You okay?" His friends shouted, but nothing. The black hole stared back mutely. An hour or two passed before the engineers arrived to dig up the tunnel complex, unearthing the top as it twisted maze-like. It didn't take long to find Ray. Thick dark blood coated the walls and floor of the tunnel; he had been shot in the head, and a bamboo stake driven through the hole to prop him up to block the passageway. The enemy cut off his male organs and grotesquely stuffed his testicles in his mouth with the penis hanging out. Shock and outrage rose like the hot jungle air that day, setting the stage for the horror that followed a couple of weeks later.

Charlie Company circled the tracks in a small open field near a quiet neat village some eight miles from Cu Chi, our main base camp. Without incident, the evening ritual of setting up camp, unloading bedding, equipment, spraying for mosquitoes, and getting comfortable for the night went as usual. However, in the providence of God, as it happened so many times during the year, I was mysteriously ordered back to Cu Chi for a few days to work at the battalion aid station. I was told the day after leaving the field another unit's ambush patrol had killed a number of VC on a night operation. Remembering the mutilation to our soldier in the tunnel and the ghastly atrocities done to many other American soldiers, the American ambush patrol, lost it and cut off the ears of the dead VC. This brutal payback started after finding Ray's watch, family pictures, and other items on one of the VC. To add insult and a message of warning to other Vietcong in the area, the mutilated bodies were hung on the village gate. It was the same village Charlie Company made camp near. The second night, for some unknown reason, the new platoon leader, who just arrived to take charge of one of the platoons, failed to follow the practice of checking the perimeter defenses just after dark. The old timers and seasoned guys knew better but felt secure so near the big guns and air support from Cu Chi only miles away. Having just been with them, they were also simply too tired to do what they always did—check their positions, put out flares, set booby traps, and send out listening post. Stranger still, it was the first time the company commander, Captain Trammell, busy on the radio with HQ operations did not check the perimeter himself. Usually our commander was the last person seen walking around before it got too dark.

About one o'clock in the morning a group of villagers, friends, or relatives of the dead VCs walked straight into the center of the camp. Guards were sleeping, the sound of snoring crackled here and there around the dark circle. No alarm was sounded. Revenge shattered the stillness with horrific cascades of fire and steel—exploding machine guns, AK47 rifles, hand grenades, and RPG rockets swept the camp. Too paralyzed to fire back across perimeter at the VC standing in the middle of the camp, many took cover, crawled into the darkness, or played dead. One shaking black sergeant from Chicago told me as I bandaged his wounds at the aid station, the carnage lasted less than two minutes. The glow from the red hot barrels of the avengers faded into the dark and except for crackling fires of burning tracks and bodies, a rude, irreverent silence fell over the slaughtered, over the night. The shadowy group from the village slowly walked out as casually as they had walked into the camp.

As a woman starting labor pains, the stillness of the night summoned the cries of the wounded. The dead said nothing. The surprise was complete. Ten to twelve was killed outright, including the new platoon leader who was torn to shreds in the first seconds. Fifteen or so others were wounded, some seriously, others slightly; but all will forever bear the scars and memory of revenge from that night. I too will bear a memory—a memory of how again my God had protected me.

## The Voice

As I said, no one liked working with the engineers. They fought as hard as infantry or cavalry units and at times were magnets of trouble drawing every conceivable bad thing. In fact, it's hard to remember a time guarding the engineers when something didn't happen.

Near the poor, smelly, thatched-roof village of Phu Hua Dong, some five miles northeast of our base camp at Cu Chi, Charlie Company sat sweating and lounging as the engineers were rearranging the landscape. They were clearing a large swath of trees and vegetation to give artillery and spotter aircraft better views of the surrounding area in case enemy forces mounted large-scale attacks against the base.

I was busy playing with about fifteen happy, silly, lovable village kids, tossing candy, laughing and trying to practice Vietnamese phases. They giggled and waved their arms at my efforts, I laughed too. Overhead, a helicopter circled the work area and slowly descended to land. Our track radio announced a top engineer officer was coming to make a quick unscheduled work inspection. Across the field, an uncovered jeep bounced along the uneven ground hurrying to meet the helicopter. As the helicopter settled down amid a whirlwind of dust and grass, the jeep came to a rolling stop a few yards from the aircraft. A lieutenant colonel from the Twenty-fifth Engineer Battalion with a shiny silver oak leaf insignia centered on his freshly starched cap stepped out; at that moment, the excited engineer captain eager to meet his boss stood up in the jeep to render a crisp salute. Why he saluted in the field was probably due to his inexperience and being fresh from the states. The ol' timers knew better then to salute in the field, it was unspoken common sense; but even common sense can fall prey to virgin innocence and useless gestures of respect in the field. The ol' timers like me knew the price of a thoughtless moment. The air flashed crimson for a brief second as a faint popping sound mingled awkwardly with the rhythmic swish of the spinning helicopter blade. In an instant, the captain's head and right hand were gone. His body hung for a second, then toppled over. I did not rush to the scene. From where I was, I knew there was nothing I could do. I turned from the children and sat down in side the track. The happy moment was just that—a moment—and the creeping sense of depression that was the usual situation *de jour* returned to things familiar. In my sadness, I closed my eyes and whispered a prayer for his family.

About the "Voice," well, it came on another such oppressively hot afternoon some months earlier as we watched over the engineers clearing a dense jungle area. This was the heart of VC country. In fact the whole darn country was Charlie's, and we were definitely unwelcome guest. As usual around noon, the engineers broke for lunch and rest. Eight armored tracks and a M48 medium battle tank formed a wagon train circle around the engineers and their equipment. Several of the beat-up yellow Caterpillars were grouped in the center of the hundred-yard clearing. All around us was thick, steamy jungle, buzzing insects, and suffocating humidity.

It was noon, and I prepared to have devotion as was my habit, my moment of peace, God's time with me. Nothing in all of Vietnam was as important to me as those moments of noon worship. No matter what was happening around me—whether riding, walking, crouching and shivering in a gun battle, or sitting quietly on my bunk at base camp—I stopped for prayer or a Bible verse from Psalms.

"Hey, Doc!" the track's driver called down to me. He was sitting behind the .50-caliber machine gun on guard duty. The sun, as usual, was merciless and unforgiving. "Hey, Doc, can you give me some Z time. Was on patrol last night, I jus' gotta get some sleep. Nobody else is around to ask." With some reluctance, I said, "Okay." My reluctance was because he was right, "No one else was around" and sitting behind the machine gun meant I was not a medic now but a combatant. Also, I didn't want others seeing me there, start to demand I carry a weapon, or pull regular guard duty and go out on more ambush patrols. But for that moment, my friend was tired and needed a break; he awkwardly stretched his tired legs across the inside seat and instantly fell asleep.

I squeezed snuggly behind the large heavy gun, looked down its long gray barrel, and prayed silently nothing will happen with me sitting here. I returned to reading the small pocket Bible. Behind me, about twenty-five yards, a group of young engineers sat laughing, joking and smoking cigarettes. Almost imperceptibly, a sense of dread moved over me. I thought how quiet the jungle was. I lowered my Bible and stared casually at the green wall of barely moving palm leaves and thorn bushes, then more intently as things just didn't seem right. I resumed reading. A few moments passed, and again my eyes drifted back to the quiet stillness in front of me. "Robert." I turned to the voice behind me, thinking it was my friend, looked down at the sleeping soldier, and felt puzzled at the clarity of the voice. I turned back forward, feeling uneasier. I raised the book to read again. "Robert," the voice spoke more firmly. I whirled around again—no one. Turning back, feeling fear replace curiosity, I heard, "Robert! Get down now!" Without hesitating, I brought my arms and hands together quickly, like praying and dropped straight down behind the machine gun in to the inside of the track. At that instant, a loud swish passed overhead followed by a deafening, bone-rattling explosion. From that adrenaline moment, time accelerated to hyperspace. The sleeping gunner jolted up to his weapon, and in seconds, the ear splitting crack of the heavy .50 caliber joined the madness of every weapon in the jungle clearing, firing at once. Other crewmembers of my track came from nowhere slammed their weapons in place and fired wildly into the jungle. The inside track filled with smoke and cascading 50, 30 and 7.62 M16 brass casings as I struggled to put my flak jacket on. "Medic! "Medic!" Cries rose up over the terrifying noise of the main battle tank's canon. As my track spun into a fighting position, I flung open the back door and dove out into the powdery dirt and sand. The blast from the nearby battle tank almost knocked me off my feet as I tried to stand. Crouching with medic bag tucked to my stomach, I looked up, and my heart sank. The engineer's Caterpillar just behind where I was sitting earlier was in flames. Smoke and fire poured from the seating area. I quickly crawled to the vehicle. Along the bottom track of the Caterpillar was a dazed bleeding engineer with his hand blown off. Bullets and flaring tracers crisscrossed the clearing. I don't remember if I was afraid or not; I just said over and over, "Jesus have mercy, Jesus have mercy." I took a deep breath then reached for the railing and ladder steps. Any second I knew a bullet would tear into me. Keeping low, I reached the top, and again my heart stopped with overwhelming sadness. Two men were wounded—one engineer had serious wounds and would live; the other, a brown-haired, happy, boyish engineer, sat frozen in mid-sentence where he died. His stomach and chest was a hollow black smoking hole; only his untouched spine kept him sitting erect. He looked as if he was still talking and joking with his friends. As suddenly as the chaos started, it ended. I knelt bandaging the wounded at the bottom of the Caterpillar. There was no further contact with the enemy that day. In the distant, I could hear the Dustoff medic helicopter thudding through the air. I started to tremble as soldier often did after the battle. Inside, I cried—cried for the lost and cried with thanksgiving for the Voice.

## A Bullet and Bomb for Me

The underlying tension of the expected unexpected became as natural as breathing. The hot breeze leisurely crossing the dried rice paddy was better than the stagnant, airless heat of the jungle. We had spent days crashing through tangled thorny palms and bamboo thickets on a search and destroy mission. It felt so good now to be in the open field making camp.

A Vietnamese village sat atop a small bank about two hundred yards from the far side of our usual wagon train circle of defense. During the monsoon season, the rice paddy in which we were setting up night camp was a lake. Just after arriving, the mortar team, for the second time in my tour, fired testing rounds in case of a night attack. Most of the guys ignored the mortar team; others matter-of-factly watched them fire their first round. *Thump!* The round invisibly left the tube, but instead of arcing off away from the camp, the faulty propellant made the shell start to fall back down toward the mortar team. This was not the first or only time. Everybody shaded his eyes to see if it would hit inside the camp. Somebody yelled, "It's comin' straight down!" The mortar team scattered and took cover. I didn't have time to run, only crouch. I too watched the deadly shell heading straight back at us, but as if gently caught by the wind, it was carried about one hundred yards outside the camp where it exploded in a fiery plumb of brilliant white phosphorus. Most of the guys laughed and made a joke about the mortar team.

Afterwards, everyone went about doing his thing in preparation for the night. Moments after the mortar incident, I was standing shirtless atop my APC when *pop! pop! pop!* sounded from the village. I looked up to see brazing tracer bullets coming straight at me. The first bullet went over my head three or four feet. Even as the first bullet sizzled passed, I was already leaping in the air the ten feet to the ground as the tracer rounds corrected to were I was standing. I hit the ground hard and spun to get inside the APC. Rounding the corner of the track I felt the excruciating pain of hitting my knee on the half-open ramp door. The pain could not have hurt any worst if I had been actually shot. I lay on the ground a few minutes, holding my knee. I thought surely something was broken. Thankfully, it was just bruised and started to swell right away. I don't know if the tears in my eyes were from the knee pain or that I was so thankful the sniper wasn't a good shot, used a carbine which is inaccurate at those distances, or that our guys didn't bomb that village to ashes in retaliation.

The Cambodian border on the western side of Vietnam harbored thousands of North Vietnamese soldiers and Vietcong. It paralleled the famous Ho Chi Ming Trail, the long jungle pathway through which the enemy infiltrated into the south and launched hit-and-run attacks. Aside from tall thick jungles, the mighty, snakelike Mekong River that twisted the length of both countries separated the two countries. The Fourth/Twenty-third Mechcanized (my unit), along with armored cavalry, M48 tanks, and artillery units were dispatched to intercept a large North Vietnamese force moving south along the Ho Chi Ming Trail. Although American units were forbidden from crossing the Mekong River, we could fire across it if fired upon. The long column of armored vehicles fanned out among the trees to set up defensive position. Just as the lead track from the Calvary unit entered a clearing the track commander was shot through the chest by a .50 cal. bullet. Some feared the weapon was from one of our tracks that was ambushed, all the crew killed and the weapons taken just a few miles down the road.

It was sundown Friday evening, despite the humidity, the warm breeze felt good after such a long ride. Everyone had settled into their night sleeping or fighting positions. My medic track was not on the perimeter defense line but nestled near the center of the camp. As usual I sat off by myself a few feet from the track to read a verse of the Bible and have silent prayer to open the Sabbath. As I sat reading, I heard the familiar distant "thump" of a 105 mm, American artillery round cutting through the air. These 'marking rounds' were actually white phosphorus shells that exploded in the air near an encampment in order to help ground troops adjust the high explosive (HE) rounds targeting enemy troops if they attacked. The first round came in like a freight train and exploded above the trees outside the camp. I thought, "Man! That was close." I continued reading. "Thump!" Sheeee, the second round was coming. The familiar Voice spoke, "Robert, take cover!" I'd learn never to hesitate when the Voice spoke. Immediately I half stood and crouched racing from were I was sitting and dove under the track. A bright flash shot through my body as I again hit the ramp door with the same knee I hurt in the rice paddy. *Kaboom!* the 105 mm marking round exploded in the center of the camp just above the treetops. Hot jagged shrapnel rained down from above in every direction. Had it been HE (high explosive) instead of a marking shell we would have all died. A whirling *sheee, sheeee, sheee* . . . *crash!* sounded as a large piece of shrapnel cut through the thick branches and limbs and shot deep into the ground exactly where I was sitting moments before. It would have killed me instantly if I had remained there another second. Though in severe pain from the knee injury, I was filled with surprise and gratitude that again the angel of the Lord protected me.

## Crippled, Busted, but Alive

It was late summer, and the drenching cool monsoon rains were just weeks away. The sky seemed covered by a seamless and dingy white sheet that the sun shone through like a light bulb. Most of the day the sun was more a heat lamp drawing moisture from body and land. The Fourth/Twenty-third Infantry scoured the countryside near Phu Hoa Dong. It was the same area the young engineer died saluting. Again, we were pulled away from the main battalion to guard the engineers; and as always, the omens of bad things prodded our fears. Two or three Caterpillars were flattening the homes of villagers and clearing trees in different sections of the small village; everything otherwise was usual. I was standing up inside our track, talking with some of the guys when the rumbling Caterpillar engines were joined by a piercing high-pitched scream. A Caterpillar violently dropped into a hole or tunnel beneath one of the houses, throwing the driver up and out of the cab on to the churning Caterpillar track blades. Wedged between the tracks and the building, his screams were continuous and desperate. I bolted up from the track opening and immediately felt a sharp, stinging pain just below my left knee. My pant leg caught a sharp metal edge and ripped. I continued my run to the Cat driver. Another engineer reached him first and turned the machine off. Thankfully, the frightened driver was only bruised from head to toe but alive. As the adrenaline rush subsided, the sting in my leg returned. I looked down to see blood pouring over the top of my boots. The dirty wound was long and jagged; it needed fifteen to twenty stitches, which would not happen in the field. We were too short of medics for me to leave, so the best I could do was clean it with soap and put a thick bandage on it.

In the following days, the wound grew red, hot, and painful. I was feverish and the infection caused me to limp, and rest often. I didn't want to leave to get treatment, we were too short of medics. After leaving the engineers we rejoined the battalion on a search and destroy operation around Phu Hua Dong. We swept the jungles on foot, blowing up tunnels and managing a few brief gun battles with two GIs getting wounded. Running, ducking, crawling was getting more and more difficult. Within days, on top of the leg problem, I got badly sunburned and developed a large dark fungal rash spreading over my right face and ear. Like everyone else, I was filthy and smelled like something dead. I was glad when we finally stopped to make camp in a wooded area. Almost immediately, everybody started digging foxholes in the hard dirt and thick tree roots. We knew a large VC force was in the area and expected a counterattack. My foxhole was shallow and body length. I was in too much pain to dig deeper. Night shadows drifted in like phantoms, and with them, the night crew mosquitoes that were truly vampires replaced the daytime mosquitoes. I smeared enough toxic bug juice on me to kill every insect within two feet of me, and besides, I smelled so bad they probably questioned if I was worth dining on anyway.

Just after dark, the rain came lightly at first; then it poured for about a half hour. My shallow foxhole quickly filled up with water. With the sun gone the jungle air cools quickly at night; before long I was shivering from the cold wetness. I slide deeper into the warm water of my foxhole. For a few brief seconds or maybe minutes, I felt safe. In an instant, it was Saturday night, and the bathtub was filled with bubbles and makeshift toys. Combs and brushes were submarines and slippery soap sea monsters. Billy, my older brother, splashed and dared me to hold my breath underwater longer than him. Colored lights dancing off soap bubbles, squinting suds-filled eyes, thick dirt rings around the bathtub, silly snorting laughter, and the rumble, rumble of—what was that? "Wake up, Robert!" The Voice returned. The ground vibrated from the M48 battle tank easing through the encampment in the dark. "You better move." The water felt so good, and the air was so cold, I thought. "Robert, move now!" the Voice demanded. At that moment, I whorled or was yanked sideways out of the foxhole. I don't remember; it happened so fast. The tank's two-ton treads crashed into my watery bed; water and mud covered me as my heart nearly burst from fear of how close I was to being quashed. "Lord, thank you," I whispered as the lumbering metal giant passed into the darkness.

The roll out of the foxhole was not without cost. I ripped a long gash across the back of my neck. It immediately stung mostly from the insect repellant. It did not bleed much, but in the dark, I felt how deep it was. Like my leg, it too was infected by the next day. Pain pills no longer helped. My fever got worst, and I was getting sicker. Finally, the company commander saw me, "Doc, you better get that taken care of. You're no good to us if you can't function." I called the Battalion Medic station on the radio to ask the deputy aid station officer, who was temporary acting commander if I could come in for treatment and supplies. I knew we were close enough so that I could catch a ride on the re-supply run and be back before evening. "No! Stay out there," he said over the radio static. "You're the only experienced medic out there. Don't come in!" "But, sir—" "You heard me!" The conversation ended, and the pain returned to taunt and remind me how cruel human nature could be.

It rained harder that night, all night. My new waist-deep foxhole also was filled will water but colder. I ached and shivered all night. The fever came and went in waves. The bushes seem to sway and turn into VC soldiers, while clicking branches became grenade pins popping. At night the demons of war's imagination came to life. "Oh, Heavenly Father," I prayed, "I'm afraid, but I thank you for your goodness and mercy. I thank you for the rain, and I thank you for the morning that will come." The rained stopped. The clouds parted, and I saw the stars come to comfort me one by one. In the east, the faint orange of a gentle sunrise brought renewed hope, and I knew God heard me.

By noon that day, it was clear I had to go in. The battalion was preparing another assault through the woodlands, and I was too sick to keep up. I told the commander I was leaving and would be back on the return supply run.

I got a ride on an APC (armored personnel carrier). The five-mile road was clear of any jungle on all sides. The road dipped and splashed mud and rocks as we raced toward Cu Chi; the air breezed warm but felt cool riding along at twenty-five meters per hour. Even the thick diesel smoke that coughed from the side pipes didn't bother me; I was just happy to be headed back to base camp. This same stretch of openness was where God some weeks before spared my life when base 105 mm artillery rounds crashed within yards of my APC. Not one piece of deadly shrapnel hit us. What a blessing! Other memories flashed into view as we roared past Ann Margaret, the outermost bunker and perimeter defense line. It was named after the actress Ann Margaret who visited Cu Chi some months before. It was there that one night I was awakened in my bunk by the glare of a flashlight from one of the other medics. "Gardner," he said softly, "we gotta go down to Ann Margaret to get Roy." "What's wrong with Roy?" I said half awake. "I don't know," he said, "come on." We got in a jeep and slowly crept down the dark road without lights. Crickets and my heart beating were the only sounds. The air was dense, damp and foul; it reeked of that sickly smell that steamed from ancient mossy swamps in Louisiana. A lone soldier appeared ghostlike out of the dark and gestured for us to follow him. We went inside the bunker. Half-eaten pizza, soda cans, and crumpled paper littered the sparse sandbagged fortress. "He's over there." The soldier pointed down the front slop into the tall elephant grass and reeds near the base of the bunker. My body quivered for the danger of being on the front perimeter at night and partly because of the night chill that was so penetrating. The other medic and I slide down the loose dirt outside the bunker and walked a short distance before seeing the faint outline of a crumpled body. It was Roy, and he was dead—blown in half when he tried to hurriedly put out Claymore mines after dark. We never found one of his legs, an arm, and a missing hand.

The last time I saw Roy was a couple of weeks before. We were at the dentist; he was getting complete bridgework done. And the next time was at the battalion aid station after he returned from R&R (rest and recuperation) in Bangkok with a case of gonorrhea. We talked, and he grimaced as I gave him a penicillin shot in the butt. We laughed and joked about a few things. He told me he had extended his tour in Nam so his younger brother didn't have to come. As he left the station, I wondered how I could talk to him about God. I never got the chance.

I arrived at the Battalion Medic station. The other medics responded quickly when they saw how sick I was and still in the field. They started an IV, dressed my wounds, and gave me antibiotics. I started to feel better right away. They told me to go get some rest. And rest I did; I slept for hours even well pass the return trip to the field. That evening, I strolled back to the aid station to see what was going on. I found out that eight new medics had arrived weeks ago and were just doing details around camp. I was outraged! We were so short of medics in the field, many having been killed, and to have medics doing camp cleanup and filling sandbags was ridiculous! My blood boiled further knowing that I was deliberately kept in the field two extra months beyond the usual six, waiting for replacements. After six months, the rule was to pull the field medic back to the aid station, if they lived that long. After resting I went back to the aid station to start re-supplying myself with bandages, medicines and other things to go back into the field. About that time, the white MSC (Medical Service Corp) officer I talked to on the radio came in; he had been drinking and partying with his buddies—a usual activity for some officers who were too scared to go in the field. "What the hell are you doing back?" he shouted. I told him firmly the field commander ordered me to get fixed up, "I told you to stay out there. You're busted!" His tirade continued. "You made sergeant, but that's gone now! You get your a—back out into the field in the morning." A heat rose from my stomach to my head like a dragon on crack. I felt like leaping forward, grabbing his throat and squeezing with all the fury that two hundred years of slavery could muster, but I didn't.

The next morning, the battalion elements that were in the field returned to Cu Chi at daybreak; the search and destroy operations had been suspended. I was still so angry I just wanted to get the heck away from that officer. Despite my anger, I was impressed it was indeed time to transfer out. I could sense bad things coming. I bypassed the Battalion Medic station chain of command and went directly to the battalion commander. Sitting in his tent, the balding commander was medium height, muscular and worried-looking. I told him calmly I had been in the field nearly eight months, and wanted a transfer. His surprise was not so much that I wanted a transfer, but that I was still alive after eight months; the Twenty-fifth had lost so many medics. The idea of losing an experienced field medic by transfer didn't sit well with him. "We're short of medics, don't think I can let you go." But I persisted, looking him straight in the eyes while praying silently. "Dammit" he said angrily, "Just get the hell out of here!" And with that, my transfer was set in motion. The other thing I was also impressed to do before leaving was to talk to all the new replacement medics. I pulled each aside and told them how to be field medics—not heroic medics, just good medics. I comforted them not to be ashamed to pray with the guys or be ashamed to let go and cry. I told them God loves them. They were so young and hopeful, but their nervous smiles and searching eyes tried to be brave but failed to hide the fears I saw in their uncertain futures. Moisture crept into my eyes, my heart ached, and my arms wished to reach out and hold them like a father holds a son. With my talk ended each thanked me for talking with them. After I left Cu Chi for Dau Tieng, my new assignment, the news came that all the new replacement medics had been killed over the course of a few months. I had no doubt they were good medics.

It felt good to speak up for the Lord when ever possible even though admittedly it was awkward on occasion. There were times when as the prophet Jeremiah exclaimed, "His word was in mine heart as a burning fire shut up in my bones (Jeremiah 20:9)." Those times I couldn't keep quiet about the Lord even if I tried. Then there were times that panged my soul for the things I wished I had said but didn't. Such was the morning of 27 August, the day before I left for Dau Tieng. I sat across the table from Corporal Leggett in the nearly empty mess tent; it seemed that only he and I wanted breakfast that humid morning. The air was still and lifeless as we exchanged short "what's goin' on" greetings. Leggett was a thin brown-skin brother with black short-cropped hair; he worked in the mess hall. I liked him and enjoyed being around the brothers like him. I saw Leggett numerous times doing his mess hall duties; now he sat across from me buried deep in his thoughts. He ate slowly, looking down at his food while I sat staring at him. The lifeless air stirred chillingly, and a fear came over me. Something was not right. I knew fear well; I'd seen it in the eyes and faces of many soldiers during the year. It frightened me because what I felt was death. For that very reason, I tried never to stare at soldiers because I didn't want to see or sense the aura of bad things. My friend, Leggett, had worked as a mess specialist (cook) and all-around slave to the mess sergeant. The mess sergeant enjoyed making everybody's life miserable, even mine when I got assigned to KP (kitchen police). I don't know what the straw was that broke the spirit of Leggett, but he transferred from the relative safety of kitchen duty to the most dangerous job in the Twenty-third Mechanized Infantry—recon. Recon, or reconnaissance platoon, was comprised of two or three heavily armed APCs. Their job was to gather information about Vietcong activity and try to avoid contact with them. But many times, because of the noisy vehicles they rode in, most encounters with the VC ended up in a firefight with recon casualties. The VC knew the routine and procedures of the recon platoon more than anyone realized. "Say something to him, Robert," the Voice urged. I searched for words, but none came powerful enough for the moment. "Say something, Robert," the Voice desperately pleaded. I don't remember if I said God loves you or just opened my mouth to speak. He got up and left. A sorrow I could not describe came over me; I consoled myself into thinking I would really speak with him the next time. There would be no next time; Leggett's hourglass had run out of sand. The one APC patrol rumbled pass the perimeter gate as it had done numerous times before. About two hundred yards down the dusty road, several APG (rocket propelled grenades) slammed into Leggett's track at once; all four soldiers inside died immediately from the exploding VC rockets. Thousands of flaming steel shards, exploding ammunition, claymore mines, and hand grenades turned the inside of the track into a crematorium. One soldier riding up top was blown free from the inferno and lived. Later that evening, the track was towed in. The ashes of lost futures lay quietly in the twisted hulk. "God," I promised, "help me never to keep silent."

# CHAPTER THIRTEEN

*There are no heroes. There are only ordinary people who train and strive to be the best at what they do, here and now. They don't expect to live forever.*
—Robert Gardner

Forty miles northwest of Saigon and twenty miles northeast of Cu Chi was the Third Brigade of the Twenty-fifth Infantry. This small fire support base with a C-130 airstrip was in the heart of the Michelin rubber plantation next to the villa of Dau Tieng. The Third Brigade occupied an old 1940s or 50s French compound. Remarkably, despite the age and being surrounded by war, the buildings were immaculate and very well kept. The buildings were freshly painted cream-colored stucco with red slate roofs; some were two stories, but most were single level. I was amazed to find a well-stocked library of hundreds of books, magazines, audiotapes, and records. The two Vietnamese girls that ran the library were of French-Vietnamese parentage and were simply drop-dead gorgeous. They had small angelic faces; gentle, graceful smiles; and long silky black hair that hug to their waist. They didn't speak English too well, but they managed to understand me more then I understood their Vietnamese. One of them, I learned later, liked me because I was "not like the other soldiers." I was "quiet and respectful." I had to admit a tingle of hope flared briefly but brightly in my heart for the possibilities that could have been under different circumstances. But a lingering uneasiness always dampened my feeling toward the Vietnamese, a weariness born of experience of seeing too many GIs die for being careless and thinking such thoughts.

Another place caught my eye and excited my fancy when I discovered a sparkling, crystal-clear, twenty-feet-long elevated swimming pool atop one of the buildings. This was where I met Mike Handley whom I will mention later.

Dau Tieng itself was like most Vietnamese villages—busy with noisy trading, crafty vendors, and docile farmers—but here the economy was largely from the latex gatherers who worked the neat even rows of rubber trees. Ironically, the GIs were ordered not to fire their weapons unless absolutely necessary to prevent damage to the lucrative rubber trees. It was rumored the VC were paid not to bother the workers, and some said the wealthy Michelin Tire family also had deals with the US government to limit dropping bombs or firing artillery into the plantation. Of course, those dealings did nothing to stop the VC from killing American soldiers or setting booby traps for them. Americans and Vietnamese forces had been battling in the area for years with no clear winners. The one unquestionably clear fact was that the village of Dau Tieng and surrounding countryside belonged to the VC, and only a simple barbed wire fence separated their world from the base.

The medical unit was spread out under the ragged canopy of thinned-out rubber trees. Each tree was as round and tall as a telephone pole and had the familiar spiral cut that once milked the latex sap from its weathered bark. There was no grass, just hard-packed grayish Vietnamese dirt. The sleeping areas were wooden fames with large screen windows all around, corrugated tin roofs and a double row of sandbags surrounding each of eight to ten hooches. These buildings four or five on each side were separated down the middle by a sandbag walkway. The sandbag walls were high enough, so if a mortar shell exploded nearby, the shrapnel wouldn't injure soldiers sleeping on their cots. The sandbag walkway in one direction lead to the wood-framed oblong olive-colored building that was the main clinic. Oddly, I don't remember it having sandbags around it. At one end of the clinic was another long wooden building, the newly built medical surgical ward. Patients never stayed there long; most were air evacuated to Cu Chi or Saigon. The clinic itself had concrete floors and was divided down the middle by a wooden wall. The laboratory, where Gary Wicklund, a mustached slender, six-foot-tall Adventist medical technologist from Oregon worked and where I eventually got a chance to work, was next to storage areas and treatment rooms on one side of the center wall. The other side of the wall was toward the main village; the gate that separated the base from the main street to the village was only seventy-five to one hundred yards away. That bothered me because sniper or rocket fire from the village could easily rip through the wooden siding. The other thing that scared me was if the VC charged the gate, we'd be the first place destroyed. The village side of the clinic contained the large mass casualty bay with a small portable x-ray unit at one end. This casualty bay contained ten to twelve stretchers on inverted V-shaped stands, IV poles, Ringer's lactate IV solution, scissors, and emergency supplies hung close by.

The other direction along the sandbag walkway lead into a open area that was in front of a makeshift movie theater replete with gray-painted-white pine planks forming bleachers six to seven rows high. Farther along, the path lead to the small PX (post exchange) store, post office, and on to a small plaza with thatched roofs, bamboo walls, and beautiful ceramic title flooring, where pizza, soda, beer, and after-hours parties and hanging out was a much-awaited event. This was the closest thing to being back in the States most of the guy had and enjoyed.

As always, the first thing I looked for was other Seventh-day Adventist and the local chapel. To my surprise, I was placed in the same hooch as another Adventist I met during basic training in Texas; it was Pvt. Downs. He was likable but sort of nervous and awkward when walking due to some birth defect problem. We were glad to see each other. I quickly ask about other SDAs we knew from training and if some were there. He suddenly looked panged and hesitantly said some were there, but they didn't hang out much together. I asked if they got together on Sabbath. He said no, most of them had to work. Later, I discovered some of them ran the bar on Friday and Saturday nights; the job kept some of them from going into the field. Some drank alcohol, smoked cigarettes, did marijuana, had sex with the local Vietnamese worker girls, and partied as hard as the other GIs. I suspected when the topic of religion came up or if asked what religion they were, their silence spoke volumes. Some of them when they saw me became instantly uncomfortable. They remembered me from basic training, first as the top cadet officer (sergeant) in charge of training and second as the devout Seventh-day Adventist who loved God more than anything else. They remembered me sticking up for them as SDAs but showing them no favoritism over other Christian and non-Christian conscientious objectors. I was hard but fair.

Drifting back to my basic training months at Fort Sam Houston, I remembered how even those Adventist who weren't too happy with my leadership style united in sympathy along with the drill sergeant staff and other enlisted training staff when I got cheated out of the much-coveted Top Training Officer award.

The training company of some ninety-plus soldiers had won top honors nearly every week of basic training. We marched, ran, sang, crawled, sweated, and triumphed as a group during those hot July-August days of 1966. My ROTC training paid off, and I was responsible for, it seemed, everything including discipline. The eight weeks ended and the senior drill sergeants congratulated me for an outstanding job and proudly informed me that I was the sole nominee for the Top Training Officer award. The award included standing in the grandstand during graduation to review the troops, my parents were to be invited to come for the ceremony at the expense of the government, I was to receive a large trophy, get my private first class stripe, and have the choice of duty station anywhere in the world after advance medic training. The week before the big day, on a Friday, a new army officer fresh out of school showed up to take charge of the training program. He was a very thin young white officer from one of the Southern states. Bringing the new officer up to speed on what was going on with the class that was finishing basic training, the senior drill sergeant told him everything including the planned ceremony and the award candidate. All was well until he discovered I was black. I was to be the first Afro American to get that award I learned later. Despite protest from the senior drill sergeant, the new officer insisted that there be a competition for the award not just the unanimous recommendation of the whole training staff. He ordered a board of review. The drill sergeant told him, "There was no one to compare or compete with Sergeant Gardner. He excelled as a training leader and successfully got nearly everyone through the program." The new officer was irritated and immediately called for the trainees to line up in formation. He slowly walked down the rolls of rigid soldiers and at the back of the formation picked out a wiry-looking, surprised white troop from a Southern state. "You and Sergeant Gardner will appear in class A (khaki dress) uniforms on Sunday for a board of review."

Nervously, the other soldier sat in a chair across from me. It was Sunday morning, quiet and hot as usual. I was the first called in to a small room on the second floor of the barracks. "Sit down," the officer said curtly. Another Sergeant I never saw before sat next to him behind a desk. "You like the army," he said. "Yes, sir," I answered crisply. After a few moments of small talk, he said, "Let's get down to why you're here. Who was the second baseman for the last World Series?" Caught off guard by the question, I answered, "Sir, I don't know. I don't have much time to watch TV with my duties." "Thank you. You're dismissed," he said flatly. I stood, saluted, about-faced, and left. Later that afternoon, the senior drill sergeant called me to his office. The wrinkled forehead, squinting eyes and flushed face told me every thing before he spoke a word. The words crossed his dry lips slowly, "I'm sorry, they chose, Private H." "What!" I said angrily before I could gab the words. "I'm sorry," the consoling drill sergeant said again, looking more dejected than I ever could have. Seeing my disbelief, the drill sergeant leaned forward, looked me squarely in the eye more like a friend than a superior, and said, "Everything's gonna be all right, just hold it together, Gardner. You've done a damn good job, and I just don't know what else to say." I left stunned, and like being stabbed by a bayonet twice, the white officer passed by smiling. At that moment, welding up in me was a fire and rage hotter than any Texas afternoon. I didn't pray, I couldn't, but I'm sure the Holy Spirit was near. Private H ran to me breathlessly. "Sergeant Gardner, I had nothing to do with it! I'm sorry. I didn't do nothin' to get this! I'm sorry." I said, "Don't worry about it. It's not your fault." My disappointment was obvious to all. The other Adventist, in fact, the whole basic training camp knew it was wrong. Everyone kept looking at me to see what I would do. An award never crossed my mind; I didn't know the army even gave awards for leadership. I was simply glad to be a soldier and even more honored that as a Seventh-day Adventist Christian, they trusted me to work hard, be fair, and demand excellence, and I didn't let them down.

It was hard marching around the parade field that next week. The smiles on Private H's parents' faces could glean no pleasure from me. The trophy was ceremoniously handed over by the new officer, and it was proudly announced that Private H chose to go to beautiful war-free Alaska. I, of course, ended up in Vietnam, like most of my classmates. At the time, I vowed I'd never volunteer for leadership again. I didn't know the stolen prize would not compare to the experiences I would gain from Vietnam nor bring me so much closer to heaven's treasures—a treasure for which I so desperately longed for more than any earthly prize.

Back from the daze of one memory, I drifted into another. On a number of occasions, I tried to get the Adventist of Dau Tieng to have midweek Bible studies in the mess hall, Friday night vespers, or Sabbath worship with me in the chapel; but despite a reluctant okay, I usually found myself alone. The next time I saw them, I didn't pressure them for why they didn't show up but continued to be friendly. I prayed for them often. It saddened me, but I knew that not everyone had the same strength of character or experience with the Lord that could help them to endure hardship or personal trials. At times, I too felt as fragile and fearful of failing. Once during a gun battle while I was with Charlie Company, the constant grinding tension and gnawing uncertainty gave way to surrendered hope and inner futility, I closed my eyes and stood straight up, waiting for the bullets to end my life, end it all. Moments passed like eternity, then amid the ricochet of bullets and deafening explosions, the Voice that had been my constant companion spoke, "What are you doing! Get down!" I hesitated a moment or two. I was in full view of anyone who wanted to kill me, but no one shot me. "Fool," I said angrily to myself, vowing never to do that again. As I thought of my Adventist brothers, I remembered how gracious God had been to me in my times of wandering, my times of bad choices, and how patient, how forgiving, and how wonderfully longsuffering He was. In Dau Tieng I met many wonderful people I appreciated and highly regarded among the Pentecostals, Baptist, Catholics, Christ of God, Mormons, and even Ba' Hai. But it was my Adventist brothers whom I truly loved the most. They had the greatest privilege to serve the Almighty, to be His witnesses in that terrible place, to be the link between heaven and earth, but they were weak in Texas, they were weak in America, and they were weak there. The courage that God develops in the daily small crises of our lives prepares us for the grand, awful trials that will test our faith. It is the small victories, hard fought and barely won, that will bind us to our Savior.

Alone, in the quiet of the base chapel, I praised God for the sweet fragrances of life as well as its bitter essences. I thanked Him for every day of my life because it was "extra" and undeserved. I thanked Him above all for the love and courage He gave me to point others to the Rock in a weary land, to the Shelter in a time of storm.

*Though we live with all diligence to be successful . . .*
*it is far more important to God that we be faithful,*
*even if by this world's standards we seem to fail.*
—Robert Gardner

# CHAPTER FOURTEEN

*Whosoever shall call on the name of the Lord shall be saved.*
—Acts 2:21

My whole family could swim. Dad had been in the navy and was a great swimmer and teacher. Riding on his shoulders was always the best ride of the day. We always looked forward to that unguarded moment when Dad would snatch Mom from the sandy beach of Belle Isle and run with her into water. "Bill, stop! Bill, don't you drop me!" We would jumped up and down, clap our hands excitedly, knowing that the drop was coming no matter how loud or defiantly she pleaded. Mom had good reason to avoid a dump in the cold, muddy Detroit River. Often seaweed the color of spoiled lettuce bobbed up and down accompanied by an occasional dead fish or a brown human log. The latter always caused shrieks of "uhhh" from everybody and the dash to exit far from the unwanted flotsam was immediate. But even that bit of ugliness didn't deter the Gardner family's fun on those hot summer days.

Like my father, my older brother Billy was half fish. Swimming was as natural as breathing or walking. By the time he entered Miller Junior High School, he was the prince of aquatics, the master of chlorinated swimming pools. Built like an Olympian with his gray eyes, broad chest, corrugated stomach muscles, and chiseled tanned legs, Billy poised confidently at the base of the diving board almost every day of the year, except Sunday. With quick short steps and a powerful bounce, he was airborne and graceful as any creature of flight could be. With perfect form his swoosh into the deep blue water caused barely a ripple. The crowd would explode with whistles, cheers, and thunderous applause; I cheered the loudest!

As if destined for similar greatness, my fourth brother Timothy shared the pool, the air, and the greatness with Billy. Tim, or Timothy Paul, we would call him jokingly, was small but solid. His hair was short and—seemed by fate—forever sandy brown, beady, and dusty. At three feet nine inches, a fierce scowl furrowed his brow always; sparkling brown eyes were focused and flashed determination. In the pool Tim was confident, but away from the pool confidence was as slippery as the soap he showered with. Tim stuttered. My uncle Floyd, my father's brother, delivered coal and fuel oil in the community; and early in the mornings after making his deliveries, he would come by our home on Joseph Campau Street; we lived with my grandmother. The first thing he did was rush into the backyard, then house, rise his arms like a grizzly bear, growl, and grab terrified Tim. Only two or three years old and light as a newspaper, Uncle Floyd would lift him high above his head then lower Tim to eye level. Like two large white owl eyes buried in a black tree hole, the coal-dusted face of my devilish uncle became Tim's childhood nightmare. He developed such a fear of my uncle that at the mention of his name Tim would shake uncontrollably, cry, and stutter as if freezing to death. Despite my mother's protesting, my uncle continued his joking for years. Only in later years did Tim get control over his nightmare. Swimming was the wonderful key that unlocked the paralyzing grip of fear that made him reclusive, self-conscious, and embarrassed by his speech defect. Like a tadpole and not much bigger, I would hold Tim just above the water with my outstretched arms, shouting, "That's it, Tim, kick your legs and move your arms!" Then slowly, I would lower my arms; and like a tiny motorboat, Tim began to swim—and did not stop swimming until he became Tuskegee University's star swimmer and Alabama State Diving champion. Tim's greatest attribute was not in the pool but in life. Like me, he gave his heart to God and to this day is much admired and loved for his faithfulness and staunched dedication to the service of the Lord. Swimming and diving carved into his soul the courage to overcome the impossible and master the unimaginable. Whatever life threw at him, Tim's determination never failed him. Quiet, confident, and focused, he was destined for greatness in this life and the life to come.

It was at the recreation building in Dau Tieng that I first met Mike Hanley. Mike's eyes seemed as blue as the water in the old French swimming pool. I watched in amazement as he splashed, choked, and flailed his arm like a chicken being chased around the barnyard. "Want to learn how to swim?" I asked. "I'm Doc Gardner, the new medic." We shook hands. "Sure! That'll be great!" he said, smiling broadly. I spent the next hour or so showing him basic stuff, like holding his breath, leg kicking, arm strokes, and gliding without kicking or stroking and the dog paddle. Before long, Mike was torturously zigzaging across the pool. He was elated. "I can swim!" Mike and I became friends. I would see him every now and then at the military shoppette, buying stuff or at the post office. We would stop by each other's hooch and talk a while. Of course, before long, the conversation turned to God. Even the hardest troops could not resist bringing the topic up when it seemed God was nowhere to be found in Vietnam. Soon, Mike joined me in prayer and listened to me talk about how wonderful and real my Savior was to me. Mike told me about his mother, Norma, how religious she was and how she was always trying to get him to turn to the Lord. He remarked that God must have heard her prayers and sent me there to become his friend.

It was October 28, and I had not seen Mike for some days. I went by his unit, the 188th, and found him in the enlisted men's club. We went to his tent, and he showed me a beautiful love letter from his mother. "Liar! She's a liar!" he screamed, then torn up the letter. Later that evening just before sunset, I was standing in front of a mirror, cutting my hair with electric clippers. The screen door of the hooch opened suddenly. "Doc." It was Mike. The usual ready smiles I had for my friend quickly vanished when I turned to look into wild blood-red demon eyes. Mike had his flak jacket on and carried his M16 rifle. "What's wrong?" I said. "Wanna talk with you," he said desperately. He was drunk, sweating profusely, and marijuana smoke hung heavily in the air around him. I put the clippers down and said, "Okay, let's go down by the theater." We walked silently the fifty yards over the sandbagged walkway to the open-air theater. The sun was setting, and the last glimmer of light was filtering through the trees. We stopped in front of the bleachers. Angrily, he said, "I was looking for you last night to beat the sh—out of you!" "Why!" I said surprised and stunned. "Somebody said you were talking behind my back!" "You know me, Mike. You know I wouldn't do that." "Anyway," he said dismissively and continued, "I just came by to say good-bye." "Where're you going?" I said. Looking down, Mike blurted, "Doc, I just can't take it no more, just can't take it no more!" "What's wrong, Mike!" I pleaded. "I paid this buddy of mine $15, we're on guard duty tonight at the bunker line. I paid him to shoot me with his 60 [machine gun] when I go back." Mike paused a moment, looked at me, his eyes aflame. "I just came by to say good-bye." I was speechless. I didn't know what to say. "Mike, you don't have to do that—" He cut me off. "You can't stop me! Don't try to stop me, you're gonna try to stop me, huh?" Anger suddenly turned to rage like a tormented animal. The night air seemed like a vacuum. It smothered and darkened like covered with a blanket. I could feel the dense evil all around me. He raised his M16 to my stomach; he was only inches away. "Doc, I got to kill you, got to kill you, right now, can't let you stop me!" My heart accelerated; my head whirled in disbelief. His finger tightened on the trigger. "Mike, wait!" I said desperately, "wait, wait a minute, give me a minute!" I gently pushed the rifle barrel from my stomach and stepped back a few feet to the other side of the platform. I bowed my head and prayed. "Father, I need you now. Not for me but for my friend Mike. The devil has taken his heart, and, Father, only you can save him. Father, have mercy on my friend." I started to cry silently. Time stopped, I don't known how long, but it was long enough for God to work a miracle. As the rifle fell to the wooden floor, Mike rushed over and grabbed me as tight as a python. "I'm sorry, Doc! I'm sorry, Doc!" We both held on to each other and cried as the gentle night air returned free of demons, filled with angels. "Doc, I gotta go!" Mike said abruptly as he torn away from me. "Where?" I said. "Gotta go back and get my $15!" With that, he disappeared into the rubber trees and darkness. I don't remember if there were stars out that night. But looking up I gazed past the trees, past the stars, past the millions of galaxies and past the majestic corridors of Orion into the courts of heaven that night. I saw in my mind's eye my forever friend Jesus, and I thanked him for hearing me.

I never saw Mike again. Some weeks later, as a door gunner on a helicopter gunship, he was shot and wounded during an air assault. In December 1968, nearly a year after I returned home, I received a letter from Mrs. Norma Hanley.

Dear Bob,

How nice to hear from you. I wish I could write something good about Mike. He arrived home safely in June by God's mercy. He has been acting strangely ever since. I feel he may be on dope. He has gotten in debt over buying a car, written a lot of bad checks, and is listed as a deserter from Fort Ord Army Post. He was to get out in November, but he went AWOL. He is running from God and is miserable. Remember him in prayer; only Jesus can help him.

Sincerely,
Norma Hanley.

My year in Vietnam was nearly over. Each day was filled with dread and excitement about going home and fear that at the last moment something would happen. My anxiety was not unfounded. There were many stories of guys with one week or one day left getting blown away. There was one story about a sergeant going home, getting on the Freedom Bird plane at Tan Son Nhut airbase near Saigon, and was killed by a mortar attack. There were rumors that I would be sent back into the field again because there was a shortage of field medics, casualties were high, and ten to fifteen killed each week. Bad things were coming, and everyone could sense it. The number of Vietcong and North Vietnamese regular attacks was increasing all along the length and breadth of Vietnam. At the time, we didn't know it was the opening salvo of the great Tet Offensive—the devastating attack that was to reach its deadly climax in February 1968. The Tet Offensive was the decisive turning point in the war that ended with the defeat of American forces and the humiliating helicopter evacuation from the rooftops in Saigon in 1975.

Dau Tieng was a small but important American and Vietnamese base and staging area. It was vital for the base to be taken, and the Vietcong felt no hesitation in making known their intentions. As a rule, I never took my pants off to sleep. Before lying down, I positioned my boots, flak jacket, helmet, and medic bag in quick reach. One particular night, I broke my rule and took off my pants. I quickly fell asleep. *Boom! Boom!* "Mortars!" After the first boom, I was already in motion. The thunderous explosions among the rubber trees were terrifying. I scooped up everything in my arms, including my pants and burst through the screen door, racing barefoot and half naked toward a sandbag bunker. "Oh my God!" *Boom!* They're walking the mortar rounds in. The Vietcong were targeting the medical area, command area, and nearby airfield. *Boom! Boom! Boom!* The explosions grew louder and closer together. They were coming straight at us! The above ground bunker I darted into was pitch-black. I was alone. Tiny jagged rocks covered the ground and dug deeply into my bare feet. *Boom! Boom!* The shell explosions grew louder still and were only a few hundred meters away. The deadly missiles were coming directly at my bunker. I knew if the mortar got a direct hit or even a near miss, I would be killed by the explosion or concussion. *Boom! Boom! Boom!* Only a hundred yards away. "Oh Jesus! Oh Jesus!" *Boom! Boom!* The ground and bunker were shaking violently from the approaching bombs. "Oh Jesus, have mercy!" on my knee in the darkness, I pleaded. *Kaboom!* Explosions in the trees near the bunker! I knew by experience the spacing of the mortars would put the next rounds directly on to the bunker. Awaiting the impact, I stiffened into a ball. "Oh Jesus!" I called once again. Silence, a long space then the next deafening explosive; it landed fifty yards directly across the road from the bunker. The shell meant for the bunker didn't hit! "Thank you, Lord!" I screamed. "Thank you, Jesus!" I said over and over again. There were two or three more explosions farther away from the bunker. Finally our own artillery gunners began to return fire back into the jungle, quieting the enemy mortars. The airfield had been hit and a couple of helicopters left burning. The smell of cordite (gunpowder) filled the air inside the bunker. I was sitting awkwardly and still on the floor. Suddenly, even with my ears still ringing, I heard a rattle. *Oh God, there's a snake in here!* My mind flashed, recalling the poisonous snakes I've seen around the base. The rattling got louder. My impulse was to run as fast as I could. But as I slowly stood up on wobbly legs, the rattling stopped. I put my hands on my trembling legs and let out a laugh. I couldn't stop and half crying; it was my knees knocking together.

There were many things that happened after that—both happy and sad things. The sad things were truly sad. November was a month of mass casualties filling the trauma room. Both American and Vietnamese soldiers with torn, mangled, and burned bodies were rushed into a bee-hive of scurrying medics with scissors to cut off their uniforms, hang IV fluids, and desperately grab pumping arteries spewing blood everywhere. Often there were so many the doctors just turned away from horribly wounded soldiers pleading and crying for help to those more likely to live. One soldier carried in a wounded friend. The soldier himself was also wounded from an explosion but otherwise looked well and healthy. The medics took the friend and began the drill of trying to save his life. The other soldier and I talked as I took him aside to check him out. He complained of a small wound on his chest and said he had trouble breathing. He leaned against the wall as I took off his blood-soaked shirt. I looked at the tiny wound in the chest similar to the one I had years ago in Detroit. He said, "I can't breath". I rushed to one of the surgeons working frantically on the other wounded soldier; he looked up across the room at the soldier now slummed on the floor, "I can't save them all". With that I knew there was nothing more I could do. I wished I'd learn more about medicine or knew what to do. I went back to the soldier and sat next to him; he leaned against me. "Doc, I'm not gonna die am I? He looked at me and I stared at him with tears in my eyes. "You're gonna be alright." He smiled and began to breath slower and slower. I put my arms around him and my mouth close to his ear and whispered, God loves you; then he died.

The next four to fives weeks saw the tempo of battle injuries, mortar attacks, shot-down Medevac helicopters, frantic mass casualty drama increase. Something was wrong. Later we learned the Vietcong and North Vietnamese were working their way south one village district at a time for their eventual surprise attack against the capital in Saigon. The 1968, February Tet Offensive was starting. Probably the worst event was the armored attack up the slops of the Black Virgin Mountain, Nui Ba Den, just before Christmas. Some general somewhere wanted to end the year, 1967, with a large body count for enemy soldiers so the young troops of Dau Tieng and other units went up the mountain and died. Many of them I saw days earlier at the store buying Christmas cards and gifts to send home. Others were putting up decorations and getting ready to party and relax; then the order came to attack. I cried as the bodies started arriving and I stacked then high on top of each other in a small tool shade behind the hospital. All I could do was cry.

There were also happy things during those weeks. I gave more Bible studies in the mess hall with my little fan-less filmstrip projector. As many as 7 to 10 guys would show up and afterwards ask questions. My Pentecostal friends like Roby, the Mormon doctor and others of different persuasions were most impressed and showed conviction of the truth. Few accepted fully the things they heard, but they knew at some point in their lives they would have to search the Bible again to make sure the truth was really the truth. The Holy Spirit was speaking to their hearts and they knew it.

Finally, of good things, the news came that I was going home! That day came too fast and yet too slow—when it came I sat on my empty cot, duffle bag packed and my heart heavy with memories. A C-130 plane sputtered on the runway waiting for me. Inside I was torn between opposing emotions. Someone came to the hooch door. "Doc, they're waiting for you!" Before I could think, I said, "I can't go. I don't want to leave." "Doc, if I was you, I'd get out of here." I sat there motionless a moment longer. A fierce struggle raged in my heart. I was afraid to stay and afraid to go. Vietnam was my home. War, pain, death, and fear were my life. These young soldiers were my friends; guys who needed to know there was hope. They needed to know God loved them more than they could ever realized.

"Robert," the Voice whispered, "go home." With that, I grabbed all I could and ran to the airstrip. I threw my bags onboard, and the ramp door closed; I was finally going home. The dense green jungle passed swiftness beneath the plane as it lifted noisily into a steamy blue sky and fleecy clouds. As if in a dream, my soul felt a deep uneasiness; I was caught between two worlds, two times, two lives. Things were already changing in my life. The clouds outside the window grew dim as my eyes slowly closed. Inside, other clouds were gathering; another storm was coming.

Back Row: Dr. Robert Gardner and Dr. Leo K. Edwards Jr.
Front Row: Michelle Edwards Griffin (Nurse) and
Virginia Alvarado (Accountant)

# Dr. Leonard Johnson dies in plane crash

ol. Leonard Johnson was
command surgeon at
elly AFB.

A Kelly AFB Colonel died in a fiery airplane crash over the weekend while on his way to a high school reunion in Indiana.

Col. Leonard W. Johnson, 55, Command Surgeon for the Electronic Security Command at Kelly AFB, was alone in the Comanche Piper Cub when it nose dived in the midst of a thunderstorm and crashed into a soybean field near Kokomo, Ind. investigators said.

He was en route from

Col. Leonard W. Johnson, friend and mentor of Robert Gardner

Break for lunch during mercenary training

Robert firing the Mac-10 sub-machine gun

Albert Marks and Gardner pausing at noon to have devotion in the 12th Evacuation Hospital Chapel, Cu Chi Viet Nam

Col. Tom Slyter presents awards to Col. Robert Gardner at his AF retirement in Oct 2005. Robert served 19 years

William and Roberta Gardner, parents

Siblings:William, Michael, Tim, Darrell, Lester, Beverly and Robert (Center)

# PART II

## MOTOR CITY

# INTRODUCTION

Every year, in October and November, huge cold air masses race from Canada's frigid north, spreading icy temperatures eastward through the Midwest toward the Atlantic States with feared regularity. Unlike the cold Antarctic currents that rise along the Pacific coastline, the currents of the eastern seaboard are warm and subtropical, straight out of the Caribbean. In late October 1991, the last hurricane of the season, Hurricane Grace, which had formed on October 27, was slowly moving up over the warm waters of the Carolina coastline, heading north. The high pressure in the upper atmosphere and lower pressures near the surface were locking in the forces of nature for a confrontation of unbelievable power. There it was, two gigantic air masses—one cold over the land, the other over the warm sea converging into what was to be called the Halloween Storm, the Perfect Storm, and the Storm of the Century! The cold Canadian air mass punched into Hurricane Grace like a rampaging bull, tearing all its energy away and leaving it scattered within the larger coastline storm called the nor'easter that stretched from Nova Scotia to the Georgia coast. Sustained gale force winds extending over three hundred miles from land out to sea screeched at over seventy-five miles per hour and waves topped fifty feet. Coastal tides crested at over nine feet and inland flooding caused beaches to disappear from erosion and hundreds of boats, homes, and building to be destroyed; damage was in the hundreds of millions of dollars. Then it happened. One day later, November 1, from the southern end of the terrible Halloween Storm, the warm eighty-degree temperatures of the Gulf currents gave birth to another tropic hurricane! It was so unusual it was simply called the Unnamed Hurricane.

Perhaps this too describes the Perfect Storm that began in my life during the early 1970s when forces from every direction were converging. The fresh warm currents of Vietnam's nightmare meeting the cold pressures of family, work, and school setting the stage. Then, the unexpected turbulence whirling from within in the church I loved tore my heart into frozen shards of confusions and neutrality. Here is how the "storm" raged.

# CHAPTER FIFTEEN

*Oh that I had wings like a dove! For then would I fly*
*away, and be at rest.*
*Lo, then would I wander far off, and remain in the*
*wilderness.*
*I would hasten my escape from the windy storm*
*and tempest.*

—*Psalms 55:6-8*

The flight back to San Francisco was as much a dream as leaving a year ago. My feelings were vaporous and dense like the clouds that engulfed the bay and the fog that rolled leisurely on to blue California shorelines. What was I feeling? Was it numbness, fear, or depression? Maybe it was all three. It was like waiting for an exam score to be posted from a test. Did I pass? Did I fail? Was this a sick joke, a mind trick to raise my hope? Was this a terrible dream or a terrible reality? Was I actually coming home? Then an overwhelming, nameless dread seized me; I wanted to go back to Vietnam. There I was safe, safe in the routine of war. Home, what did that mean? I was afraid to go home, afraid of the unknown, afraid of how much I had changed. If I could just see Mom and Dad for five minutes, five minutes to hug them, five minutes to tell them with my eyes how much I loved them, then in five minutes I would have been gone, back to the night, back to the pain and back to the death. Vietnam was my home. America was the place where nightmares ended and nightmares started. I was lost in America, a 21 year old stranger.

"Thanks." I handed the cab driver two twenties as he drove off. I stood for a moment in the cold, crisp January night, looking up at the billions of stars in the cloudless sky. I had forgotten how cold January was in Michigan. Now it seemed even more intense after spending a year in the tropics. How strange yet how familiar those stars; the same stars over Vietnam hung over Detroit. How strange, two different worlds on the same planet. A wisp of coldness brushed my face, signaling a need to get inside. The crunch of ice and snow seemed amplified as I climbed the brick steps to my parents' home. I sat my bags down and stood quietly, listening to my muffled heartbeat and the wind sliding through the tree

---

branches. Was I dreaming still? Was I really home? Am I going to wake up again drenched in cold sweat looking up at palm trees? The wind blew harder. "Yes, Robert, you're home," the Voice spoke. Tears weld up uncontrollably. *Yes, I'm home!* I fell to my knees and wept. "Thank you, Jesus, thank you, Father!"

My short stay in Detroit was wonderful. Everybody was glad to see me, especially when I donned my uniform. I wore a red beret proudly slanted to one side; medics were allowed to wear them at that time. Draped smartly across my shoulders were twisted bright white-and-red unit ropes with gold tips. My left chest garnered multicolored service ribbons and the medal I cherished the most—the Combat Medical Badge (CMB). The CMB was a silver-colored cross, a stretcher, and two coiled snakes surrounded by a wreath. "The wreath meant grief," I would always say when asked.

I stayed a few days with my parents but eventually went back to stay with my other family—David and Hattie Fulton. I first stayed with them after I joined the Adventist church at seventeen years old. They were my spiritual parents in Israel. I loved them so much and felt more at home with them then at my real home. I loved my family, but it was hard to keep the Sabbath and find quiet time to read or study in a house full of people. Before the war and before Andrews University, I would gather my younger brothers—Darrell, Timothy, Michael, and Lester (if he wasn't with my grandmother)—and my cousin, Joann, to open the Sabbath every Friday night. I would first feed them beans drowning in butter and sprinkled with sugar or canned spaghetti floating in watery tomato sauce along with jellied toast. Then off to worship we would go. Like a herd of buffalo, we'd raced up the stairs to my cramped bedroom. I would have them kneel while one of them prayed. Afterward, they would spring up, sit in a row at attention, waiting for my dramatized Bible stories filled with hilarious sound effects or totally original facial contortions; they loved it. Best of all, though, was the singing. At the top of our voices, we'd sing, "We're marching to Zion, beautiful, beautiful Zion" or "Deep and wide, deep and wide, there's a fountain flowing deep and wide." After about an hour, I would put them to bed, then pray in my heart that God would save each one of them.

The Fultons were easy to talk to; I always received straight answers whether I agreed or disagreed with them. They would always say, "Let's ask the Lord." Mrs. Hattie Fulton was the Lake Region Conference Bible worker. She was one of their most successful soul winners. Ministers from all over North America wanted her for their evangelistic meetings because she got results. When it came to one-on-one soul winning, she was deeply spiritual, intensely focused, and well armed with Bible truths honed in the furnace of her own life experience and love for Jesus. She mastered the art of decision-making and led hundreds of souls to know and accept Jesus as their personal Savior. Hattie Fulton was herself only a teenager when she accepted the Lord. Though a shapely, smiling beauty in her youth, the battle with appetite was her lifelong nemesis. In later years, her short, rather full figure, gunfighter walk, and piecing call "David! Come here, honey" even now makes me laugh. Brother Fulton himself—a stately, slightly balding man with a quiet, submissive look—would quickly gaze at the ceiling for grace and patience before tenderly saying, "Yes, honey bun. What do you want, little girl?" Mrs. Fulton would flash a girlish wink, raise her eyebrow, and say seductively, "Take out the garbage, dear" or "David, be a honey bun yourself and wash my car."

We had lots of fun talking, studying, going places, or just sitting around doing nothing. As I mentioned earlier, David Fulton made the greatest impression in my life one troubled day; before I left to go to Andrews University. I was confused and didn't know what I wanted to do in life like most teenagers, so I told him my problem. I told him I couldn't decide if I wanted to be a minister or work in the medical field. His advice was priceless.

Mrs. Fulton eventually retired, and she and David moved to San Diego, California. David had diabetes that took his life one day. It was that very day Mrs. Fulton began to die from a broken heart. She comforted so many in their hour of heartache, but her own grief was so intense, her loneliness so complete she found little comfort by others. Many nights in quietness she cried, rocked, and prayed to see Jesus. She asked if I could come and live with her when she moved to Monticello, Alabama, to be near her daughter Mildred. We were bonded spiritually; she was my mother in Israel. I would have stayed with her had I not been in the military at the time. I visited her twice in 1986 while stationed in Florida. I saw her melt away in grief like wax before a flame for the love of her life, David. The last time I saw her, I held her as I fought the tears that came anyway. Weeks after her death, I was told of her passing. My grief too was almost overwhelming but not complete. I know that God can fix anything, even broken hearts. I so look forward to seeing both of them again in the resurrection when God shall wipe away tears forever; this I believe with all my heart.

What is a life or a story without love? Genora Daniels became the love of my life. I met her through my friend John Tolson. John loved Travis, Genora's sister; and while we were stationed in Texas before going to Vietnam, he asked me to deliver a letter to Travis. While on leave, I visited the City Temple church where the Daniels family worshipped. After the service, I looked for Travis whom I'd never seen and was told by someone, pointing across the hallway, "That's her sister." Genora was hurrying down the stairs. She was simply beautiful. Her brown skin glowed with the light of youth and a smile that stopped by heart. Her short sassy black hair, entrancing large eyes, curvy legs, and sculptured body took my breath. She was the fantasy of every teenage boy, the dream made for special moments like that. Gaining control of my emotions, I introduced myself and handed John's letter to her. The next time we met, my friend John too had come home for the Christmas holiday in 1966, and the four of us went out on a date—bowling, I think. I tried not to like Genora too much or stare too long into her beautiful dark eyes. The hesitation and wounds of my first Adventist girlfriend, Sharon Jowers, had not healed. Sharon was a member of the rival church on the eastside of Detroit, the Burns Avenue church. I loved Sharon more than words could say. So much so that one courageous, perhaps foolish, but certainly climatic day, I asked her father if I could marry her. I was young, only eighteen and didn't have a real job or a career or, for that matter, a clue about most things. Preston and Mable Jowers, her parents, were my second mom and dad in Christ. I have never had such fun or closeness with any family in the church as with the Jowers. Sharon and I attended Eastern High School, and on weekends and a few weekdays, we spent a lot of time together talking, walking hand in hand, and ever teasing one another. She was a songs tress *par excellence*. Her soprano voice was celestial and pure; she sang professionally at hundreds of engagements and always electrified and inspired her listeners, especially me. Mr. Jowers, her father, said, "No." Then with all the sympathy a father and friend could muster in such a sentinel moment as that, he said, "Rob, I think it would be better if you waited. You have to be able to provide for yourselves. You don't have a real job and haven't finished school. Sharon wants to go to college, and once kids come, that's the end of that. Wait, your time will come." I was disappointed but knew he was right. Eventually, I went off to college, Andrews University, and Sharon went to the University of Kentucky at Lexington. One day, a letter came from Mrs. Fulton, saying Sharon was dating someone else, a non-Adventist; by then, I had been drafted into the army and was stationed in San Antonio, Texas. Mrs. Fulton knew how much I loved Sharon, but as a mother, she didn't want me to get hurt. When she confronted Sharon about why she was dating someone else, Sharon told her cutely, "I'm not going to be sitting around waiting for Robert, and I got a life to live." A frost settled over me like a January morning; my emotions became encased in ice. I was devastated. But like an epiphany, like Paul's Damascus road experience, one warm, sunny, and cloudless Texas afternoon, a thought came, "You're free now, Robert. You're free!" A great weight lifted; a change occurred. I can't explain it, but it would affect the rest of my life. "You're free!" And with that, spring's thaw began and Sharon left the throne of my heart.

Genora's perfume, her sensuous walk, her magnificent voice, like Sharon's, was all that a young stud like myself could take at one time. She was gifted to sing. Her music rivaled the voice of an angel and silenced the mediocre; she captured my imagination and wrung chains of love around my heart. Her smile, her touch, her essence was electrifying. All during my time in Vietnam, I dared only to think about her in the briefest of moments, only special moments. Moments handled like fine, expensive crystal only to be admired with delicacy and care. I knew my growing affections for her could vanish as quickly as life itself in Vietnam, so I put her away until I was safe at home again. Now I was home, and there she was. The more time we spent together, the more passionate our feeling became until finally I knew I had to marry her or die.

In 1972, we got married. It was a huge church wedding at the City Temple church. We honeymooned in Washington and Philadelphia and happily spent the first two years of our lives snuggled in a one-bedroom apartment on Detroit's near Westside. Just before getting married, I worked at Harper Hospital as a lab technician. I was fired after three months when an old decrepit, set-in-her-way lab supervisor found an excuse to get me fired. I didn't know if it was because I was so young or so black. The incident that upset her and gave her ammunition occurred when another technician suddenly swung open a door, causing me to drop a whole morning's worth of blood tubes. Despite everyone coming to my defense, the cranky lab supervision saw the opportunity to get rid of the only black worker in the lab. She lied to the lab director who refused to hear my side of the event; I was fired. I didn't know this would be only the opening round of a series of trials that would test my faith.

Thankfully, I managed to get a similar job some months later but was again laid off when asked to work on the Sabbath, and I refused. After much prayer, I then found a job more to my liking, a medical technician at the Six Mile Clinic. There I put my army training to good use, and before long, I was doing x-rays, physical therapy, and minor surgery; putting on splints and cast; and manning the front desk. It seemed like a perfect job. Genora would come and bring me dinner the nights when I worked alone, and we would listen to music and cuddle. Eventually, the Sabbath question came up. The boss knew from the first day, as did everyone else that I was a Seventh-day Adventist. He was a young osteopathic doctor, arrogant and treacherous. He had little regard for people or their problems. He had a lifestyle he needed to maintain, and at that moment, it meant reducing the staff. I was the most expendable one since I had the Sabbath problem. So it was; I was out of a job again. I knew I had to do something quick, find more than just temporary work. I knew the real answer was to finish college and get a degree.

Not too long after that, Genora also was laid off from her job at the railroad office downtown; so the pressure was on. Somber about what I was going to do next, I happen to read a newspaper advertisement one day. "Wanted: Persons with medical experience, former military medics, and hospital personnel interested in newly formed Detroit Emergency Medical Service. Please apply." *What providence!* I thought but at the time didn't realize the change this job would have on my life. A summer wind blow in from the street. The newspaper fluttered restlessly. It came again, stronger, more determined to shake the paper from my hand. Looking up past the curtains, past the buildings, past daydreams into the gathering clouds, the wind seemed to know the future and the storm this job would cause.

Before going further, I want to thank my Heavenly Father for his continued protection in the days and weeks after my return home. Like a speeding train passing the station platform, bits and pieces of images, people, and things passed mostly unrecognized, but a few images linger in the memory. Such were memories of Fort Campbell, Kentucky, and the Riverside Hospital-Sanitarium in Nashville, Tennessee. Fort Campbell is remembered for the day I and two other soldiers were trapped in a blazing forest fire caused by artillery rounds, for the night convoy in which my jeep was inches away from flipping over into a ditch and crushing me, for other jeep accidents that nearly killed me and a soldier I was transporting on a stretcher when the rains washed out the road and the vehicle nose dived into the gapping hole but settled back down, leaving us bruised but alive, and finally, for the tension and uncertainty the day Martin Luther King Jr. was shot. Kentucky is also remembered for the warm hospitality of the white Adventist church in Hopkinsville. In those days, the racial climate of the south was uncomfortable when blacks and whites were together in any setting, even the church. Then the finest memory was the purchase of my first car—a two-door Chevy Impala. It was my freedom chariot, my ticket to anywhere in America. It took me back home to Detroit in July 1968 when the army discharged me. Nashville will also remain a treasure chest of memories. It was there that I met such wonderful Christians like the mother of Elder E. E. Cleveland, world evangelist; and Lane Todd, champion lay activities leader; Ted Brown, draftsman and artist; and, most memorable, Betty Mae, the lovely nursing student who competed for my heart. Of all the reasons not to return to Detroit, she was the most important. I think if I had stayed in Nashville, I would have married her and certainly had a different future. Betty was from Meridian Mississippi and was at the Riverside Hospital in training as a nurse. She was of shoulder height, wore neat dark brown hair, and flashed a smile as pleasing as a rainbow after a storm, as sweet as freshly picked roses, or as quiet and beautiful as the majesty of a beautiful sunset; she was a treasure both outside and inside. Her shyness and hesitant speech only delighted me more each time our hands found each other as we walked around the hospital campus. Holding her hand was the highlight of every visit and the desire of every moment I was away from her. My heart always raced, and my face blushed embarrassingly, neither of which escaped Betty who only laughed, brightened her smile, and squeezed my hand tighter. Betty knew me long before we met in person. During my first visit to Riverside as I sat eating lunch in the cafeteria, I watched a group of giggling nursing student across at another table. There was one, a short daring brown-skinned student with glasses and an embarrassed expression on her face being egged on to introduce herself to me. Awkwardly, she walked over to my table and said, "I'm . . . I'm Betty . . . Betty Mae . . . can I have your autograph?" "What?" I said surprised. "Your autograph for my book." "Why?" I asked with growing curiosity. "Aren't you Robert Gardner, the medic in the book?" The book was *No Guns on Their Shoulders*. In October of 1967, while I was in Vietnam, an army photographer flew up to Dau Tieng to take a picture of me. Earlier in the year, Herbert Ford—the author—wrote me, asking about my experience as a conscious objector Seventh-day Adventist in combat without a gun. There wasn't much to talk about so early in my tour, but I wrote a short letter he later titled in his book "Some Will Die." Seeing Betty with the book left me totally speechless; I had completely forgotten about Mr. Ford and the army photographer. Betty again mentioned a letter that caused me without thinking to grab and hug her tightly. All eyes were on us in the middle of the cafeteria. Although this was my first time seeing Betty, I felt I already knew the spiritual person she was. Jacinta Wilson, a friend from Detroit and a former nursing student, asked other students to write to the soldiers in Vietnam; hers was one I received at just the right moment when I needed encouragement the most. After the long embrace, and stunned astonishment of her huddled friends, I signed her book and sealed our friendship.

It was on one of those weekend passes to Nashville that the Lord's mercy and grace again found me. "The angel of the Lord encampeth round about them that fear him, and delivereth them . . . Behold, he that keepeth Israel shall neither slumber nor sleep . . . the Lord shall preserve thee from all evil: he shall preserve thy soul . . . (Psalms 34:7, 121:4-8)." It was nearly midnight, and four of the five Adventist soldiers curled up inside my Impala were bone-tired and sleepy from the long day at Riverside. We had attended morning service, ate lunch, walked around campus, and talked with the nurses and other friends. The only one missing was Lester, the suave, perfumed, unnaturally neat, brilliantly white-teethed playboy who was feverishly petting his girlfriend at her home. She lived off campus, and Lester asked me to pick him up around ten o'clock, but now it was almost twelve. Finally, with clothes in disarray, Lester sprinted to the car; I was mad to say the least. He laughed off the groans and evil stares from the other guys as well as my complaints. Ten seconds of unapologetically squeezing between three other guys in the backseat, he was asleep and beyond further censored tirades. The night was star filled and dark. The gentle long hills of Tennessee's countryside undulated up and down in the beam of my headlights. The engine sound seemed in sync with the symphonic snoring that came from my exhausted friends and the player. Mile after mile seemed to pass like molasses, and my brain throbbed for rest. The hypnotizing alternating patterns of black-and-white road strips seemed to draw me to them. I shook my head over and over to force my eyelids to stay open, but somewhere between reality and dreams, the image of the road froze. My brain forced beyond its capacity and desperately crying for rest switched to autopilot, and I was dead asleep at sixty-five miles per hour. "Gardner!" one of the sleeping guys awoke and screamed. The frozen picture thawed in a flash. The road had changed to the tops of trees and black emptiness. I slammed on the brakes with all the force my panicking legs could push. The tires squealed, and the car twisted wildly before coming to a violent stop inches from a deep ravine that disappeared into darkness. Needless to say, everybody was wide eyed by then. My legs and arms were shaking badly, but I couldn't let go of the steering wheel or take my foot off the brakes. "Thank you, Jesus!" I said out loud. "Hey, Robert, you better let me drive," Lester offered. I scowled at him, thinking he was the cause we stayed so late in the first place. "Okay," I said. I moved to the passenger side, leaned my head against the window as Lester drove off, and quickly fell asleep. The other guys decided to all stay awake and watch Lester maybe because they didn't know if the angels were going to do the same for him because of his antics. Later, I asked the guy who woke and screamed why he woke up since everybody was fast asleep. He simply said something told him to wake up.

# CHAPTER SIXTEEN

*Life is a flash between two darknesses . . . birth and death*
*It is a light of imperfect glow, bearly visible,*
*bearly sensed before as a dying ember it darkens*
*to ash and is blown way by the winds of time.*
—Robert Gardner

It was the thirteenth day of the month in 1972. I was assigned to medic station 13, we had thirteen emergency runs, and my badge number was 13. I'm not superstitious; at best, I'm cautious. As 13 was a sign of bad things for many, to me it was as much a talisman of good, a sign that all was well. But in reality, I didn't trust 13 fully for as easy as 13 was a friend, it could be the worst number or worst day of my life.

The emergency medical service was attached to the Detroit Fire Department. Everything was brand new from the fresh, eager faces that went through the fire fighter's fitness training to the bright, shiny orange and white box-type modular ambulances. It was exciting to be back in uniform—crisp tan shirt, brown clip-on tie, dark green pants, and of course, a green garrison hat with a glazed black visor like army officers. The whole city was equally excited and anticipating this new emergency service. Long had been the outcries and terrible tragedies of victims of accidents, crimes and sickness being carelessly thrown into the backseat of a police car still bleeding or gasping for air. Hardened by the streets of the Motor City and oft seething with glaring racism from white officers the ride to the hospital—Detroit Receiving Hospital—was often without haste and at best leisurely if you happen to be black. Sadly, it didn't matter how desperately you pleaded or hopelessly you clung to life, apathy and distain was the rule. The demand for better service was obvious and much needed; the early 1970s was the era of drug wars, the rise of crack cocaine, the all-pervasive marijuana, ruthless gangs, and the violence that torn the life away from over seven hundred people each year in Detroit and surrounding communities. Although a few victims were white, most were black.

During the 1943 race riot, the thirty-four hundred nearly all-white Detroit police force won notoriety for its brutality toward the black community. US Army Brigader Gen. William Guther, who was in charge of troops sent to help quell the riot, said of the Detroit police they are "very harsh and brutal . . . they have treated the Negroes terribly. They have gone altogether too far (Detroit Free Press)." This unchallenged injustice continued into the 1950s when the Detroit policed organized four-man patrol squads known as the Big Four; they were detectives in plain clothes. In my neighborhood, one of the four was a six-foot, muscular, dark-skinned black detective named Ben Turbin. He was the token black who as in slavery days did all he could to please the white masters. Ben Turbin, shot, beat, and publicly humiliated every black he encountered. Ironically, he actually lived in the Black Bottom of Detroit, on Waterloo Street, a half block from my home on Joseph Campau Street. As popular as Ben was with the other white detectives, he was never good enough to live where they lived in Hamtramck, Southfield, Royal Oak, or Birmingham. On the east side of Detroit, the Grand Boulevard was the frontier beyond which blacks were only allowed to clean houses but never live in them. To think you could violate the white-line rule meant you faced harassment, police intimidation, beatings, cross burnings, or worst. My uncle Floyd, my father's brother ventured to be different from the rest of us blacks when it came to life-style; he brought a house across the line. One night, a large gasoline-soaked cross burned on his lawn; a night that acutely reminded him of who he was and that no matter how much money or prestige he tried to get, or thought he had he would always be black and unwelcome.

The black community desperately needed relief from the building pressure of ghetto poverty, crime, drugs, corrupt police, and hopelessness. Unfortunately, the riot of 1967 explosively released some of the pent-up frustration; and again, the police response was brutal and venomous toward the black neighborhoods. Military tanks blasted residential areas while armored personnel carriers rumbled down main streets like Linwood Avenue, Twelfth and Fourteenth Streets. Police and civilian snipers exchanged gunfire, and of course, those with nothing to do with the riot often lay among the victims. That was a particularly trying time for black soldiers in Vietnam. Watching a full military police and National Guard assault on our neighborhoods filled us with anger and outrage. Why were we in Vietnam fighting an enemy who only attacked us because we were invading their homeland? Tension was extremely high in various military units so much so that many black soldiers and whole units were put under guard and watched during the riots back in the States. Not until the mid to late 1960s did inner city heroes emerge. Men such as Malcom X, Bobby Seals, the Soledad brothers, Martin Luther King Jr., H. Rap Brown, Elijah Muhammad, Coleman Young, and Chokwe Lumumba raised the touch of black pride, self-esteem and power. Organizations like the Nation of Islam, Black Panthers, Republic of New Africa, NAACP, The Southern Christian Leadership Conference and a few others not controlled by the white power structure provided scaffolding to build the hopes and dreams of black aspiration. A flash point in the drama of the times was in

1971 when Detroit undercover decoys called STRESS squad (Stop the Robberies, Enjoy Safe Streets) ignited widespread protest after its members killed twenty people, seventeen of them black. The .357-magnum pistol was their trademark weapon and the spine or headshots their favorite aim target. Although I paused to give due attention to the Detroit police, their brothers—the Detroit Fire Department—was not sterile from racial bigotry and favoritism rampant during those times. Both, especially the Detroit police, set loose in me a rage that proved nearly fatal for all.

How can I put a nightmare on paper? How can I capture sight, sound, smell, touch, emotion, and tears with ink? How can I chase away in memory those festering years, the early flashes, and the distant rumblings of a gathering storm? Here are some of the flashes for which the enemy relished and crushed my spirit and for which my eternal Father sought to teach me ever so patiently His marvelous grace.

## The Greyhound Bus Station

She walked in to the Congress Street Greyhound bus station noticed, but too ordinary to look at a second time. The long faded tweed coat she wore bulged a little but brought no attention from the milling crowds of travelers waiting for buses. Outside, the sky was overcast with the sun breaking through now and then to heat the already-muggy summer air. Blue haze drifted from sputtering cars and grinding trucks, and people in business suits, homeless attire, print skirts, cutoffs, sandals, and shoeless waited for the traffic lights to signal go or stop. The cacophony of city noises for the young lady with the bowed head and ordinary face was but a whisper as she made her way to the ladies' restroom. Buried in her heart was hopelessness for some life issue that to her had no answer. The second hand on the large clock on the station wall never slowed, not a second, but time stopped in the ladies room as a loud explosive boom echoed out into the waiting area. Screams and hysteria raked the station. People ran for cover, others burst through the station doors, cars screeched to a halt as people darted between traffic. "Medic 13", the EMS dispatcher's tinny voice crackled through the radio. "Dispatch, Medic 13" I answered quickly. "Medic 13, respond to a shooting at the Greyhound bus station." Moments later we were there; I raced across the dirty speckled marble floor of the bus station and was nearly hit in the face by the swinging restroom door as a detective rushed out holding his mouth, trying to stop the vomit seeping through his pale fingers. I stood transfixed at the large mural of blood, bone and brain spattered on the stall wall and the headless body wrapped in a tweed coat lying crumpled on the floor. The pool of slowly spreading redness darkened as it gelled and clotted. There was nothing I could do but leave. I turned to walk out but paused to notice a piece of wrinkled paper or clothe on the floor. I stooped to look closer. Was it a note? Was it a piece of treasured memory she clutched tightly in her hand until death released it? Or perhaps it was just a piece of litter carelessly dropped on the floor? Looking closer, I cringed and turned away; it was her face torn apart by the shotgun blast, the young lady with blond hair, so ordinary yet so precious. I could not imagine how people could become so hopeless that destroying themselves seemed the only way to end the pain of life. I didn't know then, but in time, I would. I would sit motionless on my bed each day, holding a gun as that young lady did. I would listen to my heartbeat. I would sense time and eternity waiting like the clock on the bus station wall and wonder as the seconds ticked away, *is this the day?*

## So Beautiful, So Dead

It must have been a beautiful wedding. Candlelit, rose-strewn aisle graced the delicate feet of the radiant bride arm in arm with her beaming father. Adorning family, friends and well—wishers smiled, cheered, took pictures and waved handkerchiefs. Before her, her dream, the man who would fill her life with joy and love. She knew by his smile, his eyes, his hands she was safe; she could trust him with her heart, trust him with her life. Hand in hand, they said their thank-you and good-byes to the guest. Her father kissed and held her tightly. Her mother fought back the tears, dabbing her eyes with a napkin and remembering her bubbly little chocolate muffin now all grown up. The place where love would find its first fulfillment and ecstasy was the twenty-five-story Pontchartrain Hotel overlooking the river in downtown Detroit. The happy couple reached the door; he opened it, then swung around, lifting her gently and stepping into the bridal suite. They laughed, she kissed his ear, and he closed the door with his foot.

"Medic 13, Dispatch". "Dispatch, Medic 13, over." "Medic 13, got an unconscious female at the Pontchartrain Hotel." Two police officers rode the elevator up to the bridal suite with us; the hotel manager let us in. Lying face up across the bed in her laced white wedding gown, the beautiful young bride with short silky black hair was motionless and cold. On the floor at the foot of the bed, still dressed in his tuxedo pants and half buttoned shirt, the groom moaned in a drunken stupor, oblivious to our presence. Near the bride, the empty syringe of heroin sparkled in the dim light from the dresser lamp. The love of her life, the one she trusted, the one who would fulfill her dreams said, "Just try it, sweetheart, and we can make love all night." Somewhere in the city, a telephone would ring, and the joy of that day would turn to sorrow. Standing there, my own soul felt something slipping away, futility and depression were building into an avalanche of despair from which I could not escape. Looking out the Ponchartrain window, it was hard to tell if the drops of rain streaming down the glass was only water and not the tears I tried to hide. "Lord, have mercy on his child. Please, have mercy on her family who will call on you this terrible night."

In the weeks and months that followed, I saw the death and darkness of drugs over and over again, a hundred times. I saw brains spread across kitchen tables and dashboards of cars, slashed throats, families gunned down, glassy-eyed addicts tripping out, dilated and fixed pupils of drug overdoses, knives in the back, people thrown or jumped from windows and bridges, church members murdered, girls raped or sold for drugs, and blazing infernos caused by methamphetamine labs. Every emergency run, every trip to the hospital trauma room and morgue, every useless word to wailing families and friends chiseled away at my soul. "What's the use? When will all this craziness end? I can't keep doing this . . . I can't!"

## Bullet in the Back

Washington Avenue in downtown Detroit had the usual nighttime traffic just after rush hour. We were driving and within a half block from the busy intersection of Griswold Street when the call came, "Medic 13, dispatch! Dispatch, Medic 13! Medic 13, respond to a stabbing at the all night drugstore on Griswold Street!" *Blammm!* At that moment, a bright flash about seventy-five yards off to my left, and a person was falling! Sirens and lights snapped on, and in thirty seconds, we were there. Turning the corner, I saw two policemen—one black, the other white standing over a small black woman lying on the sidewalk. My partner got on the radio to talk with dispatch while I rushed around the ambulance to check the woman on the ground. One of the policemen was holding a hysterical younger black crying woman who had been handcuffed. "They didn't hav'f ta shoot her," the handcuffed lady wailed! The older lady on the sidewalk reached toward me and said, "Mista, please help me, they done shot me, please help me!" I bent down to help her, and the white police officer scolded, "Leave her the hell alone, there's a guy down the street who need you guys." "I'll just take a quick look at her," I said. The white cop warned more menacingly, "I said, leave her alone, she's all right, she ain't hurt!" I looked angrily at the cop, then at the pleading woman. "I'll be right back," I told her. Jumping into the ambulance, my partner and I raced the half block to the drugstore. Bright red blood and hurried footprints covered the entrance and trailed to a middle-aged white customer sitting on a box. Someone had given him towers to hold to his bleeding hands and arms. There was a ugly long laceration on his neck that had clotted and was not bleeding but could open up, easily killing him. As I approached him, he blurted, "Keep away from me, nigger! Don't put your g—dam hands on me!" I stared at him, then without saying a word, turned away as my white partner tended his wounds. "You stay here, I'm going up the street to check on the old lady." I ran to where a small crowd of other police had gathered. The old woman lay still on the ground with a dark pool of blood seeping from her back and chest. She was dead. I shouted at the cop, "Why didn't you let me help this lady!" "She pulled a knife on us," he said matter-of-factly. He held up a small pocketknife, and then pocketed it. The black cop looked away as I glared at him. Another cop stepped in, saying, "They tried to rob that guy in the drugstore, and they took his wallet, then cut him." Captain Bonavich, the medic commander, arrived. I told him what happened. He said, "Gardner, just let it go, don't get involve." "Two six-feet cops couldn't take a knife from a hundred-pound old lady, they had to shoot her!" I shouted so all could hear. "Gardner, let it go," he said again.

But I couldn't let it go. I couldn't silence the plead—"Mista, help me!" I couldn't stop the building anger I felt toward the police.

## Death Respects No One

Medic 13 weaved between cars stopped along I-94 expressway; it was 8 pm and traffic was heavy. Three or four cars were crumpled and smoking as water, transmission and brake fluid leaked out across the road. Someone had slammed on brakes causing a chain reaction and three cars collided into each other. The front car spun to the shoulder off the highway leaving the second and third cars locked in a tangled grip of twisted metal and broken glass. Both drivers had face and forehead cuts and were quickly attended to by other drivers using towels and shirts before we arrived. I jumped from the ambulance and went to the second car. The second car was an older beat-up car seamed with rust, gapping holes and dents from many Michigan winters. The thin black lady, in her late twenties or early thirties with short unruly hair wore cut off-shorts, dirty ragged t-shirt; she sat slumped sideway against the door. I spoke loudly, "Are you alright?" Eyes half open, she was still and not breathing. I gently turned her head that flopped like a toy doll; her neck was broken. She was dead. I slide across the seat of broken glass and rushed to the third car. The third car was bright, shiny black, and spotless like a limousine belonging to someone with money and power. The passenger door with tinted windows was locked so I crossed the seat from the driver's side. The middle-aged white lady with silver hair was beautiful in her sparkling black evening gown, diamond necklace with matching earrings. She sat dignified with her head resting on the back of the seat as if sleeping. Her blue-mascara eyes were closed. "Are you alright" I spoke and nudged her shoulder. She said nothing; her neck was also broken. She was dead. Another EMS ambulance came and transported the drivers of the cars. I placed another injured man on our only stretcher and stacked the two ladies one on top of the other tying them together with a strap on the long leather seat across from the stretcher. The driver started up the engine while I sat in the back of the darkened ambulance. I looked at the two ladies and thought, one very poor and one very rich. In life they would probably have never spoken to each other or had anything kind to say to each other. But here and now they were together, locked in destiny and death. My sadness deepened and I wished eternities best for both of them.

## Medics Still Die

During those months with the Emergency Medical Service, the other half of my life began to splinter from other pressures. I started taking a few undergraduate courses at Wayne State University (WSU) using the GI Bill student stipend program. It was hard working at night and struggling through a few classes during the day. I was aiming for a bachelor's degree in science or biology and wasn't sure if it was possible, but I needed to do something different to take my mind off the depressing job I loved and hated. Added pressure came when Genora announced she was pregnant and wanted to start nursing school almost at the same time. I knew the baby part was due to pressure from her cousin, church and work friends themselves wanting or having babies. "Can't you just wait till I finish school?" I pleaded. "I want a career too, I have a life," she responded flatly. "We just got to work things out." It was futile trying to persuade her to wait; her competitive spirit and uncompromising ambitious was set. Things at church had its ups and downs. The ups were truly wonderful. I was Lay Ministries assistant, then leader. I took the role as Sabbath School teacher and leader and mastered my fears of standing in front of people. My mind was alive with hundreds of ideas and plans for witnessing and hastening the kingdom of God. My love for Jesus and the desire that not one soul be lost because of me burned like a fire in my bones. With much prayer and fasting, a small group of Burns Avenue church members organized the one and only combined witnessing event ever involving all the other area SDA churches. Several hundred Adventist in automobile convoys ascended from different directions onto the city center and literally sweep through all of downtown Detroit with literature, street prayers, and music! It was a fantastic and glorious day! I also had the wonderful experience of being an Adventist youth leader and occasionally was talked into singing with the youth and adult choirs. It was a time when the church was missionary minded and more like a giant family than any other time I can remember. The young people were vibrant, exciting, and full of energy at church programs and social gatherings. My sense of humor was infectious as was my dedication to spiritual things. We never knew those were the best of times and would one day vanish into the blinding blizzard of time, forever lost, and forever missed.

The downs too came as an unwelcome guest. They came with changes in pastors at the Burns Ave Church. Thomas Marshal Kelly—baritone extraordinaire, pastor, friend, and mentor—represented the best of the best. Everyone loved him for his quiet demeanor, his compassionate counseling, his soul-inspiring music, and his deeply spiritual sermons. The antithesis was Pastor Little (not his real name) who was always immaculately dressed, short stature, defensive in the presence of others with equal credentials and autocratic in his leadership style.

It was Pastor Little who cut the heart out of the Burns church. From the low vantage point of a Napoleon mimic he blocked or voted down any activity that did not originate from him. He did not hide his dislike, disdain, or jealousy of anybody he felt threatened by. It was inevitable that a crisis or climax would come; such occurred one Wednesday night just after prayer meeting. Immediately after the "Amen", a brief business meeting was called. It was apparent from the start of the meeting that some long festering grudge was surfacing like an infected boil about to burst. Pastor Little and Brother Sam, from opposite sides of the room, squared off with escalating accusations and counter retorts. Before long, a tense shouting match erupted and reverberated like the clinker inside a large church bell. Clenched fist raised, and fighting postures flared like two kids on the playground. "You're disfellowshipped!" Pastor Little screamed. Brother Sam shouted back, "Who do you think you are, God or something?" The spirit of the prayer meeting that had just ended was gone and the Devil was fully in charge. I'm sure the angels veiled their ears and turned their backs on that terrible scene. Even while their voices clashed and others joined the fray, I quietly got up and slipped out the side door into the night. As I gazed past the streetlights into a faded star-filled sky, I sensed I was changing. My own personal depression and taunting demons were growing stronger every day, and in my heart, I vowed, "I'm not coming back here, ever."

It was about that time I learned that one of my EMS partners had shot himself in the head; another had severe brain injuries from a beating from a hammer-wielding patient, and still a machete-carrying gang member in the Jeffery Projects eviscerated another. The event that hurt the most perhaps was the death of a paramedic friend who was also a Vietnam medic like me. Medics had a bond, an understanding, and a kind of love for each other. We spent many hours in the fire station talking, joking, and shooting flies out the air with rubber bands. As always, I tried to spread a little hopefulness and the love of God into his otherwise-depressive life; occasionally, he'd listen, smile and say, "You're right". Shortly after leaving the EMS, I learned he hung himself in jail one night after being arrested for drunk driving.

# CHAPTER SEVENTEEN

*A merry heart doeth good like a medicine:*
*but a broken spirit drieth the bones.*
—Proverbs 17:22

I couldn't help but laugh as I lay on my bed, staring into the emptiness of the ceiling. It was one of those times when it felt good just doing nothing. Laughter and thinking of silly things or past moments always brought treasured release from the pressure of being me; it was and still is the best medicine for stress and for wounded hearts.

Genora, Robert Jr., and I had moved from the small one-bed room apartment on Seward Street to a rented flat on Martindale Street. The thoughts that made me smile were many, but the pet rooster I raised from an egg experiment during biology classes at Wayne State University (WSU) was the thought *de jour*. That burnish orange, red-and-black rooster about as big as Robert gave me as much joy seeing it as seeing little Robert when I came home; the two were inseparable. The rooster's favorite place to roost was on Robert's shoulder and sometimes perfectly balanced on Robert's head. Like a falcon, it guarded Robert and never considered itself a chicken. As far as it knew, it was human. It was hilarious to watch how content each was at dinner eating fried chicken; the rooster seemed oblivious to his ancestral meal. Then I thought about the thirty-pound rabbit from hell—big, white, and fluffy with penetrating pink eyes that stared at you uncomfortably like you were a meal, like everything was a meal. The rabbit was a "gift" someone in Philadelphia gave my mother during a visit there. We brought it back to Detroit and let it loose in the backyard with all the other animals my grandparents kept. There were three to six dogs always, sometimes as many as sixteen dogs. My grandfather had ducks, chickens, pigeons, rabbits, and at various times, turkeys and cats. My father kept a buried refrigerator on one side of the small backyard; it was filled with hundreds of fishing worms. It was like a farm in the middle of Detroit and like a farm my brother Billy and I had endless chores. Our chores began long before the rooster checked its watch. Mother, what we called my grandmother, would jump-start us in the morning with hot thick coffee loaded with milk and sugar, served with pan-fried toast dripping with real butter. Winter, spring, summer, or fall, we gathered eggs, dived into grocery store dumpsters for old lettuce and produce, changed animal water troughs and straw nest, suffered anemia from numerous bedbug bites, raked tons of dog and chicken pooh, cleaned cages, and emptied household trash and ashes from the basement furnace—all before school! Well, the rabbit from hell was let loose in the backyard; and immediately, all the animals knew the stranger was not of this earth. They scattered; even the dogs barked uncontrollably. The rabbit thumped heavily around the yard, ignoring the panic it caused and the menacing challenge of the dogs. Its pink eyes were searching, sizing up, calculating, and enjoying the yard of plenty.

Our first inkling that the new family pet was not just a pretty white ball of joy was when we heard it growl as we attempted to take some food away from it or when other animals approached it while eating. It bit me on the finger once, and from then on, I stayed clear of the beast and in my heart felt murderous thoughts. It was my grandfather who discovered the horror and carnage left by the "rabbit from hell." One morning, climbing up onto the chicken loft over the garage, my grandfather found nearly a dozen of his prized hens and roosters mangled and half eaten. Immediately, he suspected the large city rats that sometimes measured over two feet long that would kill small chickens. He thought perhaps it might have been one of the dozen stray cats that roamed the garbage-filled alley behind the garage. He was devastated by the slaughter. Some mornings later, I was up in the loft and heard a crunching noise, like wood being gnawed, and then I saw it with my own eyes—the rabbit was eating a chicken whole, both feathers and bones! The rabbit hardly glanced at me, growled a little, and continued its meal. I rushed and told mom and my grandparents. Right away, my grandfather caught the demon and caged it. The next Friday night, the decision was made to kill the beast. Like the Bible story of the demon-possessed man, the rabbit screamed like a crazed banshee, almost humanlike as my grandfather strung it up from its back legs. It snapped and clawed the air like a tiger, hissed and barked. With one swift motion, my grandfather slit its throat. Blood squirted everywhere as it thrashed about. It took nearly fifteen minutes before it died. Sunday afternoon, everyone sat quietly around the dinner table, staring at the rabbit from hell, roasted and splayed deliciously on a white platter at the center of the table. No one dared raise a fork or knife toward the platter for fear of possible reincarnation. It was my grandfather, however, who broke the silence and asked, "Is anybody gonna eat?"

Legendary tales are often born, recounted, or exaggerated at the family dinner table. A broad smile again spread across my face, and the ceiling became a movie screen. This was especially true when my family got together for holidays or visits. Never an occasion ended without the "ain't gonna do it" tale. The legendary, infamous, and unembellished saga of defiance, stubbornness, and strong-will always left me shaking my head and others laughing. It must have been a Sunday meal. Steam rose from the biscuits in wavy spirals as I watched in anticipation for the blessing to end. "Amen," and before other heads returned from prayer to normal position, my tiny hand had retracted a biscuit; and joyfully scanned the white table cloth for butter. My father glared at me but said nothing. "Bobby," Mother (my grandmother) asked, "can you pass me the biscuits." I stared at her as if to say, "I know she's not talking to me!" I continued my search for the butter. "Bobby, pass your grandmother the biscuits," Mom said. Without looking up and for no apparent known reason in the universe, especially being within arms reach of my father, I said, "I ain't gonna do it!" Beverly—my little sister, who wore thick, wire-rimmed glasses—smiled gleefully, exposing gaped teeth. She knew trouble was coming, and for her, it was entertainment. Billy, seated next to me, scooted his chair away from the crime scene. Mom said more firmly, "Bobby, I said pass Mother the biscuits!" *Blamm!* Everyone's head snapped toward the end of the table. Dad slammed his hand down on the table. "Dammit, boy! Give your grandmother the biscuits!" Without expression, I looked my dad right in the eyes and said evenly, "I ain't gonna do it." "Bill!" Mom screamed and stood up to intercept my father, knowing judgment was going to be swift and possibly fatal for me. "Bobby, go sit on the stairs until you say sorry to your grandmother! Now say I'm sorry," Mom pleaded. My face frowned and grew hot with anger maybe because the biscuit was cold, unbuttered, and uneaten or maybe for no known reason in the universe. I said with defiance, "I ain't gonna do it!" The dishes had been washed hours ago, and darkness was filling the kitchen and stairwell where I sat. I was in a trance of anger, locked in the recorded message played over and over in my brain—"I ain't gonna do it. I ain't gonna do it!" The hours passed slowly until all that was left was darkness, mental images of unbuttered biscuits, and the taunting noise of my parents watching TV upstairs.

I must have dozed a little because I didn't hear my mother come down the stairs behind me. She touched me gently and said, "Sonny, go to bed."

I never apologized to my grandmother, and to this day, I don't know why I said what I said. But what I learned that day and everyone knew even to this day was that, when I made up my mind to do something and said I would or would not do it, I would do it—even if it killed me. So when I accepted the Lord in to my life, I meant it; and when I began to slip away from the Lord, I meant it—sort of. What happened was I simply went into neutral, the worst place to be. I stopped fighting, stop resisting, stop making the best choices, stopped caring; and so the battle was on. My neutrality aligned with the devil; my conscience turned off to the will of God. A Christian writer once wrote, "The warfare against self is the greatest battle that was ever fought. The yielding of self, surrendering all to the will of God, requires a struggle (E. G. White, *Steps to Christ*)," and so it began.

# CHAPTER EIGHTEEN

*For a little while I left you to yourself, to experience the consequences of your unfaithfulness. But with deep love and compassion I will bring you back home. I hid my face from you only for a moment because I refused to approve your behavior. But with everlasting kindness I will show the love and compassion I have for you.*
—Isaiah 53:7-8, Clear Word Bible

It was hard leaving the church completely. I loved the message because it was truth; I loved the church because it really was God's remnant commandment-keeping church of Revelations 14:12. I believed as the writer Ellen White wrote, "The church (i.e. all Christians that are faithfully following Christ with as much knowledge of truth as they have), enfeebled and defective (as it is) . . . is the only object upon the earth upon which Christ bestows His supreme regard (*Testimonies to Ministers*, p.49)." And, "Nothing else in this world is so dear to God as His church and nothing is guarded by Him with such jealous care (*Testimonies to Ministers*, Vol. 6, p.42). I went back to Sabbath services and the afternoon programs less and less often, but my heart was not in it anymore. Knowing what is truth doesn't always make you do right especially when the conviction of the Holy Spirit is silenced.

Eventually, I also left the emergency medical service and got a job with the Maybury Industrial Clinics as a medical technician. One of the supervisors was black, named Herb Terrell; we hit it off just fine from the start and became a good friend. Another supervisor, Rene Seans, a tall dark-haired Anglo, was also great to work with. Later I would meet Rene at another job that would dramatically alter the course of my life. I really liked that job; I stitched and bandaged wounds and did minor surgical procedures, physical therapy, x-rays, and office administration duties. This job allowed me more time to study my undergraduate courses at WSU. My major studies were in the sciences to include biology, chemistry, genetics, physics, and elective courses. These were a struggle from the start since I never really learned how to study and take test effectively. Added to my muted self-esteem was memories of inner city teachers too overwhelmed with their own struggles of ghetto life to teach black kids anything useful and parents too busy rising, feeding, and clothing children to spend much time with any one of us; and so Cs and Bs were better than I expected. Though better than Ds or Fs, the discouragement was like a migraine—always there. I prayed often to memorize long and complicated chemical pathways and tedious biological nomenclatures, but by test time, my mind ran out of gas—overloaded with non-school stuff like, constant money problems, babysitters, standing in food stamp lines, asking relatives for help, pressure to get involved with church again, and my wife's determination to pursue her nursing career.

As I neared the end of my undergraduate years, I walked into the liberal arts counselor's office one day to review my graduation plans. It felt good having completed all my biology major requirements; I was there to simply double-check for any last minutes details about the graduation. The sandy-haired, blue-eyed counselor was less than cordial. As he slowly looked up, he tersely asked, "What do you need?" I told him I wanted to check my degree credits. After a few seconds of scribbling on some paper, he tapped his pencil on the desk and snidely said, "You need eight more hours." With controlled desperation and surprise, I tried to control my quivering voice to assure him there must be a mistake; I had completed all my courses. Looking straight at me, he said, "That's too bad, you're not going to graduate any time soon," then smiled broadly. Hitting him in those shiny white teeth would appease my anger but not help my situation. I turned away quickly and prayed hurriedly as I marched to the dean's officer. Calming myself a bit, I explained what the counselor said, showed him my calculations, and then told him menacingly that I didn't appreciate the counselor's laughing! Picking up the phone, the dean spoke with the counselor briefly. Finishing, he turned to me and said, "You're graduating."

Graduating was fine, but I had no idea what I was going to do afterward. I took the medical school entrance exam and applied to ten medical schools through the central processing company AMCAS. With a C to B—average, I was rejected by all the schools and was hoping against hope to just go anywhere. When I was in Nashville, Tennessee, I spent time at Meharry Medical School meeting people and hoping at least to go there. One such Meharry medical student was Terry Baul who became a dear friend years later. But for all my determination, it was not to be; there were hundreds of equally hopeful applicants with much better grade point averages. Then I remembered that I was a tithe-paying, mission-supporting Seventh-day Adventist. I had donated and ingathered hundreds and maybe thousands of dollars over the years in support of Adventist schools, colleges, printing organizations, and health-disaster relief programs. I was buoyed by the idea that my church would not let me down, that it would give me a chance to prove that I could do well; after all, my church believed in Christian education and helping its young people. I wanted to be a medical missionary, and I knew my church was the best opportunity and hope I had to become one. With that, I applied to Loma Linda Medical School in California. It was the pentacle of Adventist health care and an internationally recognized educational and research institution.

The letter from the Loma Linda dean of admissions trembled in my hands as I quickly opened the letter. "Sorry" was like a dagger in the heart as I read the excuse and betrayal that my grades "did not meet their standards," and it was "unlikely" that I would succeed. Shock turned to anger when the letter ended, suggesting I look elsewhere or pursue another career appropriate to my grades. I fired off a letter to the office of the Lake Region Conference which was predominantly Afro-American; the president contacted Loma Linda without success on my behalf.

God's providence is wonderful! He reads hearts and desires especially if it is to serve Him and bless others. What to do after graduation, what to do with a BA in biology, and what to do about the growing anger and uneasiness I felt toward a divided church; especially the "white half" haunted me. One late afternoon I hurried down the WSU student center hallway on my way home. "Aay, young maan! Hum in here, ya need ta be in dis meetin." The neatly dressed, thin, dark-skinned lady with the huge smile, Jamaican accent, and stylish hat gestured as she stepped from a side room. The lady was Ms. Marjorie Edwards. What timing! I later found out Mrs. Edwards was the director and articulate driving force for Minority Recruitment for the medical school. At first, I thought it was another antiwar or radical black student rally, so tiredly, I said, "No thanks, I got to get home." Ms. Edwards grabbed my arm and pulled me into the meeting. I resisted a little but was too tired to struggle for long. The meeting was about a unique new program called post baccalaureate. It was a special program to help qualified and deserving black and other non-white minority students who wanted to go to medical school but who could not otherwise get in the predominately white medical schools. It was an indirect way of offsetting the injustice and inequity that racism nurtured in the 60s and 70s. Some year's later white students who couldn't get into medical school because of class size limitations felt blacks had taken their deserved spots. Thus, they targeted minority programs like the post baccalaureate program as unfair to them. Pressuring the school's financial contributors and threatening loss of support the unique opportunity to help poor minorities was opened to white students. The program required one year after undergraduate graduation to commit to classes designed to improve success in medical school. They included genetics, biochemistry, anatomy and physiology, other biology courses, along with test-taking skill courses, and off-campus group psychology sessions. The selected group of eight students had to maintain As and Bs in all subjects to continue in the program. Besides a $130 monthly stipend, the best reward was the pride of succeeding on a personal level and earning by hard, dedicated, and focused effort a class position in the first year at WSU Medical School. We all passed!

Medical school was fast and intense. Every hour of the day, most of the night, and weekends were spent taking notes, studying, and quizzing myself. The post baccalaureate program paid off and the eight of us were keeping pace with the large, mostly white and highly competitive freshman class. The black students as a whole tended to hang together, a few light-skinned blacks distanced themselves and sucked up to their white friends. The "light-skins" would not share study aids, notes, or exam tips with other black students for fear of losing their status. Racism poisoned even some of the few black educators and professors who avoided being seen with or talking at length with black students. Academic and collegial status smothered any sense of reaching out and helping minority students. One black professor always spoke with us as if incurably annoyed, but when approached by white students clamoring for information, tutoring, or study helps, his face would light up with giddy florescence and shameless excitement. Like a slave minstrel of the old South, he would nearly brake out in song, dance and voluminous sputters of "yes'ums, whatevers yo'all wunts" to his adoring white fans.

Though it seemed like some of my prayers—especially the ones that centered on passing exams—got lost in the ceiling plaster, I knew God was near, watching, encouraging, and protecting. Such was an incident that happened a few months before I started medical school; it so clearly reminded me once again the grace of God.

The quiet Sunday afternoon was just right for a bicycle ride. The blue patches of sky dancing between brightly lit clouds carried by warm summer winds made such a ride the thing to do. I asked Genora if she wanted to go with little Robert and I riding; she did. Weaving our way through traffic, we were headed toward the grassy parks and fields around Wayne State University. Robert sat on my crossbar, laughing and giggling as our faces filled with the invigorating rush of cool air. Genora paddled hard to keep up with us and was enjoying the ride too. As we crusted a hill and started down, the bicycle began to accelerate faster and faster; Genora was still behind us. Just as I began to squeeze the handbrakes, I heard a clattering noise, then total blackness and silence. When light filtered back into my eyes, I was laying on the street in a daze. The bike was all twisted up, and Robert sat quietly a few feet from me in the middle of the street. I tried to get up and rush to check Robert and immediately felt a heavy, numb drag, then pain in my right shoulder. As I picked up Robert, who didn't have a scratch on him, I said, "Thank you, Lord!" "Robert!" Genora screamed as she staggered toward us, her head was bleeding, and she was crying. "Oh Jesus, oh Jesus!" I tore my shirt and put it on her head. We both thanked God neither of us were seriously hurt. Holding Robert in my left arm, I tried to flag down several cars for help, but they all kept going. I noticed my right arm hung limp and deformed with the collarbone sticking straight out my shoulder. I knew then I had not escape unharmed. Thinking about the accident, I realized that Robert slide forward on the crossbar; and his foot must have caught in the bicycle wheel spokes, causing us to tumble. I didn't know how I landed but was thankful it did not break my neck. Genora, seeing us flip, ran into the curb and was also thrown injuring her head. What a day! What a mess! After about twenty minutes, an ambulance arrived. We were taken to Harper Hospital only three to four blocks away. The emergency staff took care of Genora, stitched her wound, and gave her a tetanus shot. At the same time, they examined little Robert who, as I said "didn't have a scratch on him," not even a bruise. That was a miracle! But for me, the care was quite different; I was between jobs, had not started medical school yet, and had no insurance. "Sorry, there's nothing we can do for you." Tears hovered at the edge of my eyes from the pain and throbbing in my fractured shoulder. I pleaded for someone to just take a look at me. A nurse said, "All the orthopedic doctors are at a conference for the weekend, and there is no one available to help." She offered me some Tylenol and suggested I go somewhere else. I was so angry I took my family home. The Tylenol did nothing. My elbow began to ache along with my shoulder. The swelling and redness increased until tears were my only relief. Genora drove me to the other side of town to Sinai hospital. There the answer was the same—"No insurance, we can't help you, and the orthopedic doctors were all away at a conference." Seeing my predicament, an ER nurse, against rules for treating patients without insurance, secretly got a special sling and put it on me. The pain subsided a little but not the growing anger I felt. At home, the pain worsened, and all night I moaned, tossed, and turned. By morning, I was determined to get help or kill somebody. I went back to the Sinai Hospital ER. The nurses remembered me, and I imagined some felt pity and helplessness but not enough to overcome the calloused apathy often seen in an emergency room. Yes, it may have been pity at first, but it quickly turned to alarm when I growled for all to hear, "I'm not leaving until a doctor sees me!!" I was hastily placed in a small examination room. About twenty or thirty minutes later, the knob twisted slowly, and the door opened. My heart raced, thinking it was hospital security; but thank God, it was a mustached young Jewish doctor named Herbert Mendelson. With my voice at the edge of panic and desperation, I told him my story. He examined me and immediately knew I had an AC separation. The end of my right collarbone had snapped apart from my shoulder. "Do you have any insurance?" he asked. "No," I said and went on to explain I had been an army medic, worked as fire department paramedic, and was about to start medical school in the fall. "That's why I didn't have any insurance or money." He crossed his arms and was silent for a few moments. "Tell you what, Robert, I'm gonna help you, but it is against hospital rules since you don't have any insurance, and so I can't use the operating room either. But I think I can work around that, that is, if you're willing. Are you?" "Yes, whatever you can do to help me." "There is a small procedure room in the basement I can use. I will have a nurse friend to help, and we will need to get some x-rays too." Dr. Mendelson went on to explain another big problem, "Because I'm not in the operating room, I can't give you anything for pain, except a local shot at the fracture site. It's gonna hurt, Robert, really bad."

"Do whatever you have to," I said. We went down stairs amid old dusty boilers and steam pipes to a neatly kept small procedure room. A technician rolled in a portable x-ray, and the nurse cleaned the area on my shoulder. The x-ray showed the separation and also a linear fracture of the right elbow. The local pain shot didn't help just as Dr. Mendelson warned. With a device like a carpenter's hand drill, he drilled through muscle and tendons into the bone at different angles and forcefully pushed in several long stainless steel rods. Blood poured down my arm as I muffled my screams into the generous bosom of the nurse holding me down. "That's it, Robert," Dr. Mendelson said, smiling, "you did good." I tried to return the smile, but it was weak and not pretty. I apologized to the brave nurse for holding her so tight and squeezing her hand blue. Dr. Mendelson's kindness didn't end there; he gave me lots of pain medicine and refills and arranged for me to follow up with him at his officer for the next eight weeks. "How much do I owe you, Doc?" I was determined to pay whatever it took; my gratitude was indescribable. Without hesitating, he said, "Nothing." "I must pay you for all you've done for me." "Robert," he said softly, "I understand what you've gone through. All I want you to do is be a good doctor." That was it—"Be a good doctor." Once more I was speechless at the grace and compassion God showed through this man and in times to follow through so many others.

# CHAPTER NINETEEN

*I have called thee by thy name; thou art mine.*
*When thou passest through the water, I will be with thee;*
*and through the rivers, they shall not overflow thee.*
—Isaiah 43:2

So many nights and days, I felt like quitting. The long hours of frustrating study, memorizing, competing in classes, and struggling with grades was like a dripping faucet—constant, annoying, and destroying.

Genora was pregnant with my second son Andre, and the anxiety continued to build as I thought of child care issues, money, babysitting, time away from study, rearranging and juggling our schedules day after day. The church was another issue. I tried to be as pleasant and positive as possible for the Lord's sake, but the demands of participation in church duties also was taking its toll. My weekend anxiety was as strong as the weekday pressures. My life seemed to be unraveling slowly like a hanging thread the hand of circumstance pulled and pulled until holes began to appear in the garment of your life. The holes suddenly burst at the seams one morning as I dropped Robert off at day care on my way to classes. This was an important week—the week before a major exam—and an important exam I really needed to pass.

I loved my rusted 1968 Boss Mustang. It was black, powerful, and raggedy, but it was mine. The previous Friday, I brought new license plates for both our cars and, in a rush Monday morning, grabbed one of the plates and placed it on my Mustang. Out the door and moments later, I had deposited Robert at the City Temple Daycare a couple of blocks from my home. It was 9 a.m., and I could make a U-turn now. It was 9 a.m. according to the traffic sign and legal; the U-turn could save me ten minutes off my trip. I saw the police car sitting on the side of the wide street, but my concern was getting to class. I checked my watch, then the traffic that was stopped at a red traffic light nearly a block away and preceded with my U-turn on Grand River Avenue. The police car immediately made the U-turn with me and pulled me over. "Let's see your license and insurance," one of the officers asked bluntly. The other policeman was on the sidewalk passenger side with his hand on his gun. I handed the papers to him, and the two walked back to their patrol car. Moments later, they walked back. "Is this your car?" the officer asked more menacingly. "Yes," I responded. "The plates don't match, get out of the car!" he demanded. As I stood getting out the car, I tried to quickly explain what must had happened that morning and that the plates were indeed mine. "Shut up! Put your hands on the car!" As one cop stood by with his gun at the ready, the other searched me. "You're under arrest!" "This is my car, officer," I said as politely as I could with quivering voice. They snatched my arms downward behind my back to handcuff me. "But, officer—"

"Nigger, you're resisting arrest, ain't ya !" one screamed at me. "No! I'm—" "Yeah, you're resisting," the other one said sarcastically. And they started to kick and punch me in the back, side, and butt. A group of people standing at a nearby bus stop saw everything and in unison shouted, "Leave that man alone, he ain't done nothing!" "Mine your own g—damn business!" the officers railed back at them. Each cop gabbed an elbow. "You're still resisting arrest, boy!" they screamed and proceeded with quick steps to ram my head into the front of the police car. As my head swung up, one of them clenched his hand around my throat in a chokehold and squeezed my windpipe until things grayed, and I was passing out. Then with as much violence as they could muster, the back door of the patrol car was opened and I was threw in to the backseat headfirst. With grinning satisfaction, they slide in to the front seat as I struggle through the daze to understand what was happening. I'd been picked up by the police before as a teenager for curfew violations or hanging around on a corner singing with my friends, but that happened to nearly every black kid in my neighborhood. This was different—more vicious and without cause. "Why are you'll doing this to me? I'm not a criminal," I implored. "Nigger, shut your g—damn mouth!" "Sir, could you at least loosen the handcuffs? They're cutting the circulation off in my hands." They looked at each other and started laughing. After a few minutes they got out of the patrol car to check my car and try to start it. While they were gone, I managed to side my arms under me and bring the handcuff in front; my hands were turning blue. I licked my wrist and twisted my wrist to get feeling back in them. "What the hell!" one of the cops shouted as they returned and saw my hands in front. They snatched open the rear door and dragged me on to the sidewalk and started to kick me in the side and back again and again. "Nigger, put those cuffs back where they were!" They kept kicking and plodding me as I slide and scraped my bleeding hands and knuckles along the graveled sidewalk until they were behind me again. Grappling both my arms, I was picked up and slammed against the side door before being thrown back into the car. Linda, a neighbor and best friend of Genora's happened by and rushed over to the partially opened back window. "Robert, what's going on?" "You black bitch! Mind your own business!" one of the cops yelled venomously. "Get away from the car if you don't want some of the same!" I pleaded with Linda, "Go tell Genora," and she hurried off. Another patrol car pulled alongside. In desperation I called to them from the open window, "Officer, can you take me to the police station or to the hospital? These to officers are trying to kill me." They looked at their friends and started to laugh with them as they drove away.

After about another twenty minutes, they arranged for my car to get towed and they drove me to the police station on Livernois Street. As they were bringing me into the back entrance, one of them chuckled, "Let's take the cuffs off this nigger and see how bad he is." Just at that moment, a plainclothes officer walked in from the front desk. In a way, that was a blessing because had they taken off the cuffs, I was going to try and really hurt one of the two before they killed me. "What'd we have here?" the plainclothes lieutenant asked the two cops. "This guy was driving a stolen vehicle, and when we tried to arrest him, he resisted and tried to start a riot down on Grand River." "That's a lie!" I screamed. "These officers beat me up for nothing. I tried to explain to them—" The plainclothes lieutenant, smiling, cut me off. "I can't imagine my two fine officers doing such a thing," he said fatherly. "Put him in the cell back there."

By then, it was two o'clock. Genora had arrived for the second time. The first time she came, she left in tears when one of the cops at the desk, seeing her pregnant, asked, "What do you want, bitch?" When she returned, she had the bail money, and I was let out into the front lobby. As I was leaving, one of the cops remembered, "Didn't you say you wanted to go to the hospital?" My forehead was still aching from cuts and bruises, while my hands and wrist stung from the cuffs and sidewalk scrapping. "That's okay, I'll go myself. I just want to get the hell out of this place!" "Take'um to the hospital," the officer ordered other cops in the lobby. "Just leave me alone!" I demanded as I turned toward the front door. In an instant, about three cops jumped me and wrestled me to the floor, painfully twisted my arms behind my back and handcuffed me. I was dragged to a police paddy wagon and thrown in headfirst. Genora stood by screaming and crying as the van drove off.

I spent the next four hours handcuffed to a hospital bed in the busy, overcrowded Detroit Receiving Hospital in the downtown area. I had been there hundreds of times when I worked for EMS, the emergency medical service. It was always filled with the bleeding, the drunks, the insane, the poor, and the dead. Smells of strong disinfectant could not erase the memory of blood and gun smoke, vomit, urine, burnt flesh, or salted tears that had washed across those floors and seeped into the walls. The smell was permanent. But there I lay, on a gurney, embarrassed, hurt, and angry. Many people who knew me walked over to ask what happened. The black sheriff officers also knew me and were very sympathetic. They removed the handcuffs but had to use the prison-bed handcuffs by procedure. A dark-skinned Indian national doctor came to the edge of the gurney, sneered down at me as he blurted out several medical questions, and then started to walk away. "Aren't you going to examine me?" I asked. He said nothing and hurried nonchalantly away. The American news media, the lure and acceptability of believing and being anything white had poisoned many foreign immigrants' minds, like that Indian. Few will openly admit their feeling about black Americans whom they consider lower than the untouchables of India's Bombay outcast. American and foreign films, books, television, and magazines demonized blacks as dangerous, dirty and ignorant. My caution, resentment, and at times, anger about this matter was heightened when after I finished my residency and returned to my alma mater, Wayne State University, to request practice and admitting privileges. The immigrants who never paid a dollar in taxes, pledged allegiance to America, fought in its wars, or shed one tear for this great country were enthusiastically welcomed, given jobs, privileges, and prestige immediately while most blacks during that time were told there were no openings, and we could not reapply for at least six months.

Eventually, with no explanation except that the Indian doctor said I was O.K, I was put in a small jail in the hospital and later handcuffed and transported back to the Livernois police station. By then, it was dark, and I had missed a full day of medical school work and still had to appear in court the following morning to miss still more classes.

As I walked into the courthouse, I saw the two arresting officers standing against a pillar. They looked at me and started to laugh like two grade school kids after a prank. Hatred burned in my soul that moment, and revenge was born. "It seems the car was yours, case dismissed!" the judge announced as his gavel banged hard on the desk. "Your Honor, can I tell you what the two officers did?" I pleaded. "No! Case dismissed. Get out of my courtroom!" I waited in the hallway an hour or so for the judge to come out. The neatly dressed short man with slick black hair like a mobster walked toward me. "Sir, I need to talk with you about the conduct of the officers." "Sorry, I don't discuss cases outside the court." With that, he hurried pass me and never looked back; as I followed his back down the hall I vowed I would get even with those two fools, especially for thinking it was all a joke, another day of fun with the negroes.

Jokes, ridicule, empty laughter, I hated it, especially when I was the butt end of sarcasm and cruel fun. Memories dredge up embers of long-ago fires I thought were out and cold, but the two laughing cops took me back to the third grade at Smith Elementary School.

The desks were all linked together in rows of twos, and tiny feet dangled from the hard wood seat as I succumbed to the monotony of another boring day. The voice of the thin, gray-headed teacher seemed distant as she walked around the classroom, and my imagination was far away on some wild and curious adventure. *Crack!* The yardstick echoed around the room as the sting on my head and the exploding laughter of my classmates snatched me from my daydream. "Go stand in the corner, Robert." Holding my head, I said, "What did I do?" The class continued to laugh even louder. "Not paying attention. Go stand in the corner and face the wall," she ordered. As I stood totally humiliated and confused with my face in the corner, sequential burst of laughter, like popping corn, turned humiliation into anger. "Robert," the stern-faced frail teacher said, slamming her ruler on her desk, "you're disrupting my class. Go stand out in the hall until class is over!" Outside the class, I looked back through the door window, and everyone started laughing again. A fierce heat rose like a dragon from my stomach, and revenge was turned loose. I opened the lockers and felt a small play set knife in someone's pocket. I could still hear the teacher trying to quiet the spurts of giggles that wouldn't die. I took the tiny dull blade and cut the buttons off every coat I could find. When finished, I felt much better and at the same time much worst for the consequence that would come.

"Mrs. Gardner, would you come to the school, Robert is in trouble," the principal informed my mother. Kneeling next to me, Mom asked, "Bobby, tell Mama what happened? Why did you cut off all the kid's buttons?" Through tears and trembling, I told my mom what happened. She was mad. She called the teacher aside and, with raised finger and fiery language, blasted her for hitting me and punishing me without reason. I beamed a little when her dragon came out, and she warned the teacher to not ever let it happen again. I kind of laughed too when she, with the knowledge only a mother has of her children, added, "Miss, I'm warning you, if you ever hit him again, Robert will attack you." I love my mother to this day with all my heart for rescuing me from the pain of that moment and for the pains in the rest of my life. Mom sat on a bench with needle and thread sewing buttons back on all the coats.

Everyone who heard about the incident of the police beating encouraged me to immediately file an official complaint with the Police Internal Affairs and the Civil Liberty's Law group. After two months of "thorough" investigations, according to the Internal Affairs, the officers "did no wrong," and the Civil Liberty's group dropped the case because it didn't have enough evidence. My two witnesses, one a man at the bus stop who lived in the suburbs and who had initially agreed to testify, suddenly moved and could not be located. The other person, Linda—my wife's friend, who stopped near the police car during the arrest on Grand River—died in a horrific car accident before she could give her testimony.

Needless to say, the stress of everything happening took its toll in my medical schoolwork, my concentration, and general state of mind. I was slowly changing into a stranger even to myself. Half-hearted prayers were spoken less and less. I was becoming a prisoner inside myself—a dangerous, obsessed, vengeful man determined to make those cops pay.

God nevertheless remained in the shadows of my life even as I closed the door of my heart. "Robert, I will never leave you or forsake you, you are written on the palms of my hands," the familiar Voice whispered. It was the same voice that was my constant protector and friend in Vietnam. But the dense anger I felt was stronger than the Voice and my thoughts darkened with resolve hard as steel. It was difficult to imagine things getting much worst, but they did as I held in my trembling hands a letter from the medical school dean's office. "You have been dismissed."

A winter storm settled over my soul with shivering coldness. A pounding pressure like a massive glacier about to explode gripped my head and heart. "All for nothing!" I screamed at the top of my voice; "All this for nothing!" I crumbled the letter in my hand.

Sabbath came, and going to church was the last thing on my mind. Genora and the kids left, and I stayed home alone. I sat for a long time, dazed and utterly distraught about what to do. "Robert," the Voice spoke, "sit down and write". "For what?" I questioned. "It's over." "Robert, just write." I sat down, and the hours passed like only minutes. I don't remember much of any thing happening around me, even whether I stopped to breathe. The words flowed fast and were filled with grammatical errors. "Keep writing, Robert. Don't worry about the spelling," the Voice encouraged. There, it was finished. Nothing in life mattered except getting that letter to the dean's office Monday morning. Monday came. I went to the dean's office and left it with her secretary. Later that day, the telephone rang. It scared me, but I expected the call. The dean spoke softly and hesitantly, "RRRobert, I don't know what to say. I have never read a letter like this before. I didn't realize all this was going on in your life." There was a long silence; then the dean continued, "I want you to come to my officer, and if you don't mind, I would like to share this letter with the board members." A week or two later, I sat in the boardroom with about nine faculty members. Each looked at me like a juror in a murder case, but only a few spoke. "That was an incredible letter and experience," one said. Another asked, "Did anything happen to those police officers?" I almost said, "Not yet". But what I really wanted to hear, I heard. "We feel that due to circumstances and how hard you worked to get to this point in your studies, we want to give you another chance." I felt like a man on death row who just received a stay of execution. "You've missed a lot of classes, and we feel it will be too difficult to catch up. So if you are still determined and want to continue, we recommend you repeat the first year subjects you missed." That part I didn't want to hear but realized they were right; I agreed. Anything else was not important. I was just thankful to be back in school, back in the race. But more importantly as I left the room, stepped outside into a bright sunny day, a flood of gratitude filled my heart that God still worked miracles, He still loved his soldier, and He still wanted me to trust Him.

In my discouragement one prayer meeting night a time ago, I vowed, "I would never come back." But after the wonderful things God continued to do for me, how could I stay away, how could I leave the church I loved so much. Ellen White wrote, "The church, enfeebled and defective . . . is the only object upon the earth upon which Christ bestows His supreme regard (*Testimonies to Ministers*, p.49)." And in another place, she wrote, "Nothing else in this world is so dear to God as His church and nothing is guarded by Him with such jealous care (*Testimonies*, vol. 6, p.42)." Ironically, it was that last statement that ultimately caused me to stop going to church and in the end leaving it all together; I didn't want to bring shame and disgrace to the cause of God. In the months and years that followed, too many things happened at one time; the spiritual meltdown was gradual but steady. In my heart, the song of life became a wail, a whisper, and then a silent dirge. The fire was out. I drifted into neutral, that terrible place where many never return. Neutral, the place where righteous thoughts flow like syrup and the conscience gels, where the will freezes solid, where no good is sort and no evil resisted.

# CHAPTER TWENTY

*I am treading water with no hope of rescue . . .*
*Unless the ocean dries up, I'm gonna drown.*
*Though at times I feel the surge to live, to swim, to dream;*
*My hope fades like the foam at the end of the wave . . .*
*The ocean of life is too vast and I'm too far from shore.*
*Unless the ocean dries up I'm gonna drown.*
—Robert Gardner

The stress of family, church, and medical school was but a ripple on the ocean compared to the tidal wave of trouble spawned by medical internship and residency.

The medical intern is a novice, a short-coat maggot in white, a flurry of tangled knowledge struggling to apply what three years of medical school said was relevant. There were too many patients, too many reports, too many procedures, too many bosses, and too many donuts mixed precariously with too little sleep, too little money, too little time for self, and far too little prayer. My life was unraveling. I was exhausted 90 percent of the time, never fully recovering from one day to the next. Night call was the worst with its nagging summons to check sleepless patients, order meds, dig feces out of constipated old ladies, or pronounce someone dead who died weeks ago when the blood vessel broke in their head. The only sleep I could steal was to go to the basement of the hospital, get on the freight elevator, put my head against the vibrating wall, close my eyes, and ride to the top floor and back down three or four times.

I have a hundred stories about things that happened and some that should not have happened with nurses, clerks and admirers, but the whole of all that happened and how I felt came to a head in the emergency room one evening.

It was flu season, and nearly half the medical staff was sick. At the end of an exceptionally busy day on the medical wards and intensive care units (ICU), the chief medical resident informed me that I had to take night call alone; the other interns went home sick. I knew it was going to be a bad night because the hospital had over two hundred patients, and I was the only intern. As expected, one call after another came from wards all over the hospital throughout the night for medications, evaluations, and minor procedures. Adding to the chaos and misery of the medical wards, I was responsible for ICU calls as well as new admissions in the emergency room (ER). The ER was a strange world—a symphony of sights, sounds, and smells all to itself. It was crowded to capacity nearly every night and, to the intern, looked like a scene from Dante's Inferno. My tired legs wobbled, and red eyes burned from having been up nearly eighteen hours already, and the morning was still eight hours away. "Dr. Gardner," the chief medical resident spoke tersely on the phone, "you have three patients in the ER, get down there!" After a short four-letter curse word, I hurried to the ER. On the way, my beeper sounded from one of the wards and then at the same time the overhead intercom blared for the on-call intern. I was angry and frustrated for a lot of reasons that night, but much of it was directed toward the chief medical resident who slept comfortably in her call room while I struggled alone; it was a right of passage every intern goes through according to tradition. But of all the nights, with so many interns out sick, that was the night she should have helped. Instead, she slept serenely as soft music played, and she dreamed of a perfect tomorrow with her perfect hair in place, her perfect nails manicured, and her perfect smile beaming to brighten the day of all her admirers. Her greatest satisfaction, however, as she stirred slightly in her slumber, was her perfect knowledge that she reined supreme over all the peasant interns.

Forty-five minutes passed quickly, and I managed to answer the ward calls and see two of the three patients in the ER. Suddenly, a side door of the ER flung open, and the chief medical resident barged directly toward me with her neat blond hair bouncing wildly. With one hand tucked in her spotless, pressed lab coat and the other raised pointing at me, she bellowed, "I got called that you haven't seen all the patients yet!" Her Bostonian voice was loud and demeaning and so pitched that everyone could hear. Though irritated, I spoke softly and told her I would see the last patient as soon as I could. "You need to work faster," she snapped. "Make sure you do the urinalysis and Gram stains. And check the blood smears and get the x-rays," she commanded. "And," she added snidely, "I want you to read the chapters in Harrison's textbook by morning on every one of your cases!" That was it! I had had enough! "B—tch!!" I screamed as I raced toward her with clenched fist. Instantly, her sophistication and snobbishness disappeared. Her blue eyes dilated to the size of nickels, and her mouth froze open like a carp. She realized she had gone too far with the wrong intern. She stumbled backward against the wall, and I slide with in inches of her face and shrieked at the top of my voice, "Don't you ever speak to me like that again! Get the hell out of here and don't come back!" She was petrified and ghostly pale. The usually noisy ER was cemetery quiet as the drama unfolded and climaxed with the chief resident running frantically out the ER for her life. Oddly enough as I stood there, I felt a relief as heat rose in my face, and my head throbbed with excitement. From somewhere amid the approving spectators, I heard one or two say, "Right on, brother" and saw on the faces of the ER staff a few smiles and head nods of approval.

As daylight filtered through the windows, and more people appeared in the halls, I realized hell night was almost over, but I still had an eight-hour day ahead of me before I could go home. I glanced at my watch; it was time for morning report. Morning report was in a small-darkened room lined with x-ray view boxes and about thirty chairs in eight rows. It was where the medical staff including surgeons, the senior medical staffers, a few nurses, and other student staff members gathered to listen to the cases and receive teaching tips after each call night. I placed a series of x-rays on the view screens, returned to the podium, and started to describe my cases from the night before. Almost immediately, a familiar voice crackled, "Did you read up on your patients last night?" The chief resident interrupted as she popped up from the back row. Her gesture was clearly grandstanding, and I was too tired and too mad to answer. I gripped the podium tightly, then snatched up all my charts and notes and threw them up into the air toward her. The papers seemed suspended in the air for a moment, and then floated like giant snowflakes all over the room, flittering down on to the heads and desk of the hospital staff. I glared at her coldly and then took my seat. The room was quiet for a long while; nobody moved. "Are there any more cases from anyone?" a senior doctor asked. No one responded. "Well, I guess that's it." With that, everyone left the room without saying another word. I thought for sure I was going to be dismissed from the program, but strangely, no one ever said anything about that morning again. Of course, the chief resident avoided me whenever she could. I actually got good recommendations by the time I finished that first year.

I want to pause to thank a friend for a favor she didn't do. As I said, I was losing it a little each day. The stresses in the hospital and at home were a nightmare. I wanted to quit every day without exception. I envied the patient's in the hospital who could ask the nurses for pain medicine and get it. But I wasn't a patient, and all my pain was inside my head in a place where all my demons lived.

The stress had me panting like an animal as I rushed up and down the halls, wondering what's next. My hands shook, and my legs trembled. "Dorothy, can I get a favor?" Dorothy Norwood was one of my post bac colleagues and dear friend. "Could you write me a prescription for valium?" I asked desperately. "I need it bad, Dorothy." Her eyes started to water. "Robert, I can't do that." "But, Dorothy, I really need something bad," I pleaded as dignified as I could. "Robert, I care about you too much to do that. Please don't ask me. Try and get some rest." She looked long at me, and then walked away. I knew she was right. I never got the pills, nor did I ever get the rest.

I was not the only one to feel the pressure of that first year. One of the interns jumped off a building during the year, some quit, and many other interns asked for transfers to different hospital programs for their remaining two-year residencies. I too had had enough; I transferred to St. Joseph Mercy Hospital, in Pontiac Michigan.

A few months before I transferred, however, darkening clouds gathered around my soul, and the ever-present storm strengthened. I was slipping farther into a neutral state of mind—that place where no righteousness is sought and no evil resisted. I was exhausted physically and my spiritual treasures nearly spent. So it was not hard or even with much thought that I said yes when a beautiful nurse approached me to have dinner with her. My conscience screamed no! But my tiredness said, "What the hell. Do it."

The dinner was as well prepared as you could find in any expensive restaurant. It glistened in the candlelight of the darkened room while sparkling silverware reflected off a silken tablecloth. The music played quietly and seductively as her arms curled around my shoulders. I sat staring into a glass of wine slide into my hand, and I wondered "*what am I doing here?*" I hesitated long, swirling the glass and peering through the crystal into candles that danced with shadows into a place of no return. I sipped slowly and deliberately at first, then faster as the old familiar thirst from my youth returned. My head swayed to her entrancing perfume—sweet, overpowering, and desirable. Blood raced through my body in hot torrents as her hair draped over my shoulder, and her soft wet lips slide around to meet mine.

The cold night air and weaning effects of the alcohol filled my head with disgust and panic at what I had done. "What am I doing?" I berated myself. Over and over, I pounded the steering wheel. The speedometer rose pass ninety miles per hour; light poles and buildings blurred along the expressway. "What am I doing? I screamed. "Just close your eyes and die!" a voice mocked. I pressed the accelerator harder and aimed my car at a concrete pillar. I closed my eyes and waited for the nightmare to end. My eyes relaxed with resignation. Time and sound stood still then like cold water thrown in my face, they flashed opened. I slammed on the brakes evenly to slow the car. The tires screeched violently as I steered away from the pillar at the last second. An invisible line was crossed, and I felt it. I sensed that something had left my body, and a damp stillness curled comfortably into the emptiness like someone returning home from a long trip. The evil was back and real. In its hand was the gift of neutrality. The dark "gift" wrapped in paranoia, scenarios of evil, pictures of death, lies, and a terrible paralysis for which I could do nothing about. I became a prisoner inside myself; I became my worst enemy.

The car rolled to a stop in front of my house. Moments later, I lay staring at the ceiling and wishing that that night had never happened; wishing tomorrow would cleanse the past.

# CHAPTER TWENTY-ONE

*"We are born naked, wet, and hungry.*
*Then things get worst"*
—*Anonymous*

*"One meets his destiny often in the road he takes to avoid it."*
—*French Proverb*

Like spokes in a bicycle wheel, the main streets of Detroit fanned out to the east, north, and west from its origin—the Detroit River. The center street that traveled straight northwesterly like a spear was Woodward Avenue. At the Detroit end, it was filled with happier memories of tall department stores, five—and ten-cent store vendors, holiday shoppers, and Thanksgiving parades. At the other end of the twenty-two-mile spear laid darker memories forged in fire and sharpened by adversity in the economically depressed tip of Pontiac, Michigan. The long handle of the spear that ran through the protected communities of Ferndale, Royal Oak, Berkley, Birmingham, Bloomfield Hills, and Auburn Hills was lined with small expensive boutiques, manicured grass, private schools, million-dollar homes, and the all-pervasive BMWs. The handle of the spear—except for Detroit and the tip, Pontiac—was in the iron grip of white Americans who tolerated no others, except Asians, Pakistanis, Europeans, and Canadians; and these only with selective bias. However, Hispanic, and black Americans were universally rejected, ignored, and actively avoided. A poor white American resident of a trailer park or an illiterate foreigner who never paid a penny in US taxes was deemed a far better neighbor than the wealthiest or most educated Afro American or Hispanic.

At the line where wood met steel, the border of Auburn Hills and Pontiac was the St. Joseph Mercy Hospital where I transferred to complete my medical training. The city of Pontiac was named after the first General Motors car produced there—the Pontiac—and owes much of its economy and employment to GM. The city's population was about sixty-five thousand with a racial makeup of about 35 percent white, 45 percent African American, and the remainder different ethic groups. There were two main hospitals in Pontiac—the General Hospital and Mercy Hospital. The issue of health care across America then as now was always in debate, but in Pontiac, where one received care and the quality of care, often rested heavily and quietly on who you were, your insurance carrier, and your ethic background. Even emergency situations offered little hope for those who didn't measure up to the selective standard of Mercy; quick patient transfers or ambulances redirection elsewhere was the order of the day.

My first few weeks at Mercy were exciting. It felt good to be in a place that was less hectic and chaotic than the Wayne State hospitals in Detroit. I was glad to be away from the pressure of exhausted medical staffers and competitive fellow students. Making it pass that first year internship was the crucible that gave confidence to finish the whole program with pride and accomplishment. I was also glad for a fresh start from the bad choices I made and the chance for Genora and I to do better. My family situation, however, remained tense. Genora was still struggling her way through nursing school, the boys—now three, Robert, Andre and Christopher—vied for attention, while the babysitting and daycare roulette continued. My salary was fifteen hundred dollars per month, but the bills stretched far beyond my salary. The seething memory of the police beating and echoes of their laughter resonated in my mind day and night; I wanted revenge. Like an ugly Caterpillar entangled in a cocoon, the thing immerging was no butterfly. That need for closure took me to Kmart where I brought a BB gun, then later a .22-caliber rifle with a scope. The evil was growing from that beating incident, the guilt of bad choice affairs, and the frustration of the family, the disappointing church life, the racism, and just simply me—I hated me. The voices I heard constantly were ever stranger and overpowering. "You need more power" or "Never again, never again," they would advise and taunt. So it was that I started going to gun show after gun show; in fact, every gun show I was there. I bought a handgrip .30-caliber Enforcer carbine, a twelve-gauged shotgun, two 9 mm handguns (Smith & Wesson and Detonic), a .22-caliber Beretta for backup, a dart blowgun, and books on martial arts, improvised silenced firearms, explosives, and urban terrorism. Out of rage and anger one day, I vented hysterically at my newly purchased white Vega automobile that constantly stopped, wouldn't start, or malfunctioned in a hundred ways. I pulled my 9 mm and shot several large holes into the side of the beast. I wanted the car to die. I was hoping it would explode into brilliant, earth-shattering nothingness. When the blue smoke cleared and the hot barrel steadied, I composed myself and was glad it didn't explode. The car was in the garage, and I was standing next to it. The wound of the police beating was still bright red in my memory; it dredged up childhood defiance—the "I ain't gonna do it" that pledged me beyond my control to death before I let another white police officer or anyone for that matter beat me again. I set about making myself stronger and more confident. I lifted weights and took judo and karate classes of every type, read martial arts books, and tried to master as many killing techniques as I could. When I showed up at Mercy with fresh shirt and tie, neatly pressed pants, and gleaming long doctor's coat, they had no idea how much I was on the edge or yet how desperately I needed things to go well.

I must have made a good impression with the program director, Dr. Daniel, because he appointed me the chief medical resident. Dr. Daniel, a Jewish internal medicine doctor from Pittsburgh, Pennsylvania, was also new to Mercy and as yet had not been tainted by the established undercurrent of racial bias that needed just a stir to awaken. He was a sensitive and compassionate man caught in the middle of loyalty to the porcelain hospital hierarchy and doing what was right. The first year internal medicine residents numbered ten. There were four Afro-Americans, three whites, and three students from Pakistan or India. I think before anyone realized it or considered the precedence or maybe simply because the snide hospital executives was so distracted by golf tallies and self-primping, three Afro-Americans had been appointed as chief surgical resident (Dr. Donald), chief OB/GYN resident (Dr. Jeff), and chief medical resident (me). We were sharp and had shown leadership ability from the start. Personally, I felt good being a doctor. I knew my stuff; my skills were honed in the Wayne State crucible. I was eager to provide the best care I was trained to give.

The first few months, like most honeymoons, were great. We meet the nursing staff, department members, community doctors and all the support staff. We went to medical meetings in the hospital, at the downtown Pontiac hospital, and as far away as the Travis City resort on the West Side of Michigan. Personally, I had very good relationships with most of the staff doctors and administrators; but despite the warmth and fuzziness of the picture, the separation along racial lines still lingered like the sickening odor of cheap perfume. The white staffers, especially the doctors, tended to eat, socialize, and enjoy extended conversation with other white staff members to the exclusion of Afro-Americans. The Indian, Pakistani, and Asians were more tolerated by the white staffers, and they guarded their favored position by not associating too closely with Afro-Americans. This exclusiveness oft times was also directed toward patients of color by the whites and other non-blacks. Nevertheless, the first year was pretty uneventful, and I learned a lot about internal medicine patients.

Things started to deteriorate with one name—Dr. Donald. Dr. Donald was simply brilliant as a surgical resident. His dense eight-inch Afro hairstyle—more reminiscent of an Australian bushman than a Bahamian—wispy black mustache, large dark eyes, and constant half smile shouted confidence and arrogance. He was admired and hated for being right most of the time with difficult diagnostic problems or complicated surgical cases. He was tops in his surgical reviews, examinations, case presentations, and arguments in support of the newest, literature-based surgical or medical discussion. Fellow surgical residents, nurses, and students were in awe of him while the senior surgical house staff loathed his cockiness, smug assuredness, and his taunting of their lack of current surgical insight. To me, he was a friend and colleague. When I had a difficult patient or one who needed an invasive procedure, he was quick to help and back me up. It was this friendship and being associated with the nemesis of the surgical department that dragged me precariously into the crosshairs of racial vindictiveness and conspired revenge.

The friction between the surgical program director Dr. H and Dr. Donald could start a fire at absolute zero temperatures. Dr. H hated Dr. Donald because of his public debates and embarrassing comments about deficient surgical techniques during surgery or while Dr. H lectured on rounds. Dr. Donald's explosive laughter would add insult to injury as he often-watched Dr. H retreat with indignity.

It started with clock-like regularity; the silence and whispered voices that toned down several octaves when Dr. Donald or I entered the staff lunchroom or walked onto the medical/surgical wards to see patients. The good rapport I had with attending physicians changed. They no longer ask me to see their hospitalized patients. Even worst, most of them stopped speaking to me. When I ventured to initiate a greeting they would turn their heads or simply look past me. The worst treachery I experienced was at the end of my four-week infectious disease (ID) rotation. Dr. Mark—the Infectious Disease (ID) attending staff physician—and I had a very good relationship. I learned a lot about antibiotics and teaching pearls on ID patients. Daily, he thanked and praised me for excellent care of his inpatients. One patient who developed a new fever and rising white blood count prompted me to call Dr. Mark. I tried several times to contact him by pager and telephone but was unable to locate him. None of the nurses saw him, and he was not in the hospital or at his office. The next day, he came in shouting at me why I didn't call him and how he tried to contact me, but I didn't respond. This was totally out of character for him. I was bewildered and tried to explain, but he walked off after dismissing me from his ID service. Days later, Dr. Daniel's secretary asked me to come to her office to sign my ID evaluation. Every category was a lie! The report read, "Clinical Judgment, below standard; Patient Management, poor; Reliability, unsatisfactory; and Overall Performance, unsatisfactory." I snatched up the evaluation and scribbled in large letters—BULLSH—T!" Then I threw the paper at the secretary and demanded to see Dr. Daniel. "He's out of town at a meeting," she said nervously. I stormed out the office enraged, shocked, and felt utterly betrayed. I hadn't done anything to anybody, so why were people turning against me?" Eventually, Dr, Daniel returned but was paralyzed to offer any solution to the program meltdown. He was visibly bothered by the racism of his staff colleagues yet choose not to get involve.

Then things got uglier as the whole surgical and medical staff in their private meetings sort ways to terminate Dr. Donald from the residency program. Dr. Donald proved their match. At each turn, he blocked them by referring them to the hospital bylaws and national surgical residency rules and regulations, which weighed heavily in his favor under due process proceedings. He even threatened to sue the hospital and certain individuals. To them, Dr. Donald was an embarrassing problem, a disrupter; and I was his friend, so I too was part of the problem even though I had nothing to do with any of what was going on with Dr. Donald and Mercy Hospital. I soon realized that I also needed to disconnect from Dr. Donald, but he always managed to find and confide in me about the controversy of the day.

One eventful and ordinary day, I sat on the medical ward writing in a chart. I heard Dr. Donald talking jokingly with a patient behind closed curtains in a nearby room. Laughing, he said, "Charlene, I'm not gonna give you any more Stadol [a strong pain medication]. You got to get off that medicine. I'm giving you something else." "I don't want anything else! Give me my medicine!" she demanded. "I want another doctor!" He laughed, then came out the room and went down the hall. The head nurse, tending another patient in the same room, came out the room shortly after Dr. Donald left.

Next day, the hospital was abuzz. Dr. Donald was handcuffed and arrested for trying to molest a patient on the ward yesterday. It turned out the accusation came from the same drug addict black patient, Charlene, who wanted the Stadol. The nurse in the room lied, saying she heard Dr. Donald make inappropriate advances toward the patient. Dr. Donald's credentials were immediately suspended, and after his release from the local policed station, he was barred from the hospital. I went up to the ward to view Charlene's chart, but it was sequestered, and all floor nurses stared at me as if I was a criminal on a spy mission. They watched to see what charts I handled and reported it to the hospital administration. I was eventually told I was not allowed to see any of Dr. Donald's charts nor access any other hospital files without scrutiny.

The drama escalated with lawyers, police surveillance, more lying witnesses, involvement of the NAACP, community activist group, newspaper articles, TV interviews, the hospital picketed by hundreds of black Pontiac residents and supporters from Detroit. There were closed-door hearings at the hospital and public meetings in district courts. The executive board of the hospital voted unanimously to evict Dr. Donald and his family from the Mercy-owned house near the hospital. The story of corporate conspiracy against the black surgeon made national news. This was around the same time black doctors in Detroit were filing lawsuits against the Harper-Grace and Wayne State hospital system for racist practices of white surgeons who refused to let black surgeons use the same operating rooms or use special hospital-owned equipment they hoarded to themselves. I too was caught up in the vortex of racial bitterness of the times and the storm fueled by Dr. Donald's troubles as well as my own. The infectious disease evaluation was the hurricane's eye of my anger. Like Dr. Donald, I also threatened a million-dollar lawsuit against Mercy. Dr. Mark didn't want to talk to me and avoided me at every turn. One day, I managed to corner him in a hospital lounge and asked if I could speak with him for a moment. "Why did you give me a bad evaluation?" I asked pointedly. "That's what I felt you deserved," he responded nervously, not making eye contact. "Every day, all day, I took care of your patients and never once made a mistake, but you said I was unreliable. Every day, you commended me on how well I was doing and appreciated my work. Why did you tell those lies?" His anxiety increased. He said, "You didn't meet my expectations!" His voice grew more irritated. Ice water ran through my veins. Unblinking, I stared straight into his dark eyes and said, "Why did you lie!" His composure vanished. He yelled, "When I was in grade school, the black kids would knock me down, steal my lunch, and take my money. I hated black people then and I hate them now! I hate them! I hate them!" And with that, he jumped up and rushed out the room. I smiled for the essence of truth that filled the room. I smiled because now I knew why he lied. All my life, I chose to believe that people—even white people—are individuals, some good, and some bad. I believed God made all of us, and all of us were subject to evil and wrong choices. Thoughts about the racism at Fort Sam Houston, in Vietnam, in the streets of Detroit with the police and fire department, in medical school and then now gave fertile ground for the demon seeds to sprout. Every day in the winds of the storm the strange voice returned stronger. It came to remind me to "Never trust white people. They are the most dangerous animals on the planet. Under the right circumstances, they will eat their own children." Other voices joined the chorus. "Black people don't make guns and weapons, black people don't explode atomic bombs, black people don't steal billions of dollars from the poor, black people don't own boats or planes that bring crack and heroin into the inner city. Yet they say we are violent, we are animals, stupid, and dirty." I had to stop myself, the voices from the delirium and funnel cloud of hatred I generated was causing the Robert everyone knew to disappear.

Dr. Mark proved that racism, hatred, and bitterness for some ancient wrong could find justification for the hypocrisy that ruined friendships and destroyed trust. The smile that broadened across my face was like sunbeams piecing through the clouds. The smile was satisfying far more than the truth that I learned; I smiled as I stood, reached in my pocket, and turned off the tape recorder. This was the leverage I needed—the leverage to correct the injustice heaped on me.

In the meantime, death threats from whites in the area—maybe Klansmen, Michigan was and still is known for its KKK sentiment—or possibly threats from the police were a frequently and unnerving occurrence. The tension of the fight wore heavily on Dr. Donald and his family. Late one morning, his wife, Sharan, frantically called me, "Robert, please come! He's passed out and is vomiting blood. Hurry, I can't get him up!" I rushed to the house across from Mercy. He was lying semiconscious across the bed with vomited blood all over the room and down the hallway. His wife pleaded for me to take him to the hospital. "Don't take me to Mercy," Dr. Donald slurred as I tried to lift him. "They will kill me over there. Take me to William Beaumont Hospital." He went unconscious. His skin was pale and bloodless, his heart raced, but his pulse was getting weaker. I knew the ruptured stomach ulcer would kill him as surely as a bullet, and I knew I had to get him to surgery fast. I also knew taking him across the street to Mercy was foolish; they would let him bleed to death. I lifted his 215 pounds and struggled to the car with him. He was very heavy. The blood and desperation of that moment reminded me of a gunshot wound to the back of a soldier in Vietnam. His own men accidentally shot the young soldier from Saltlick Kentucky while on night patrol. I remembered lifting him in my arms and running to the helicopter hovering in the dark jungle. I remembered pumping his shattered chest and cracking more ribs to keep his heart going, the mouth-to—mouth breathing, and the vomit of blood, beer, and chest tissue filling my mouth. Over the rushing wind and thudding rotor blades, I screamed, "Don't die! Don't die! Please, Lord, let him live!" I remembered dashing from darkness into the bright lights of the 12th Evac hospital drenched in blood and sweat, raising his shirt and seeing four silver-dollar-sized holes in his lifeless body. The brazen, almost-reckless eight-mile ride weaving through expressway traffic brought us to Beaumont. A black surgeon friend met us and rushed Dr. Donald to surgery and survival.

One evening, shortly after that, a couple from out of town showed up for a meeting with Dr. Donald and me. A dark-skinned tall, heavyset brother who looked like a linebacker for the New York Jets or a very dangerous ex-con was accompanied by a very attractive, curvaceous young lady whose relative was a prominent civil rights figure. They were there to support Dr. Donald's cause and get to the truth about the allegations of rape. Dr. Donald told me later that they went to a rundown part of Pontiac and found Charlene at a party. They dragged her out to a waiting car, and she sat between beauty and the beast. The beauty was the one she feared the most. The ghetto threats from beauty were clear and easily understood. If she didn't tell the truth, the party was over, and no one would miss her. Charlene started to cry and told everything that happened. "Dr. Donald wouldn't give me my pain medicine. This nurse came over and asked what the problem was. I told her, and she said the hospital needed my help. She said if I said Dr. Donald fondled me in bed, the hospital could get rid of him. Also, she said I would get my Stadol, and my grandmother would continue to have a job with the hospital." She started to cry more. "I didn't mean to get him in trouble, but my grandmother told me to do it." Beauty and the beast warned her if she didn't tell the truth during the trial, they would find her. Charlene left town before the hearing and was never heard of again as far as I know. On another night, someone from out of town I never met before asked me, if I was interested in helping blow up the hospital; they learned that I was a soldier at one time and had some skills. My head spun and toyed with the idea. I thought for a moment; then an old, still-familiar Voice broke in, "Robert, considered all the innocent people that would get hurt." I said no.

Everything in my life was crazy by then. Problems and discontentment at home and church were worsening. Genora argued aloud about everything while I usually remained silent and distant. "Why don't you come home early? You got to watch the kids while I study." "Who was that on the phone?" "Is this lipstick on your shirt?" or "Robert, I don't like those guns around the house." The thought of divorce pulsated in my mind constantly. I was unstable. With any given situation, I could not trust anything or even myself, what I would do. I was like nitroglycerin—unpredictable and violently explosive. I couldn't deal with the stress and danger I was putting my family in. Despite her bickering and extravagance, I loved Genora and my sons. The boys, however, were my life. They brought me the only joy I had the only laughter that came from the heart. I carried them everywhere I went the days I kept them. I loved hugging, kissing and playing games with them. In the same vane, the church was also always on my mind. I loved the church and had put my life on the line for my faith many times, especially in Vietnam. How could I bring such shame to the cause of God? The church was full of needless issues having nothing to do with the truth the church taught but rather unconverted personalities. The church, any church, was a hospital for sin-sick and imperfect people. At the Burns Church the leader of the unconverted was the dictator Pastor Little. I lost interest in going and being pressured to listen to a preacher who didn't like me, and for whom I had no confidence in his ministry. The isolation from my medical studies widened with the controversies, likewise the focused patient care I so enjoyed. The one clear fact was that my life and sanity were being destroyed by the bitter vendetta against Dr. Donald. In the beginning, I only wanted things to go well and just finish my training like normal people. But it was not to be. I needed an escape albeit temporary and destructive, so I started going to local bars after work. Over a short period of time, I would leave work during the day to have moments of release in frosted bottles of beer and assorted glasses of liquor. I would drive home in a daze or stagger back to the hospital and go to sleep in a call room for eight to twelve hours. The other residents would sometimes answer my pages or cover for me while on call. To further drown my disappointments, I spent many wasted nights at house parties, nightclubs, movie theaters and private dinners with companions, friends and enemies. The fog in my head mixed daylight and night into one. Who I was and where I was at any given time became increasingly uncertain so to wake up in one strange place or another was not unusual. I was in neutral, out of control, always sorry, but doing nothing about it. Paranoia and suspicion grew like a tumor inside my brain. Some was truly paranoia and hallucinations, but some danger was real. I started carrying my 9 mm semiautomatic everywhere, especially to work. Though I long since stopped believing God heard me anymore, I prayed that no one—police or white hospital staff or trash-talking black person—would bother me or confront me especially when I was in a resentful mood.

One day, I saw a magazine ad for special training. "You can be a RECONDO MERC." RECONDO referred to reconnaissance or military scouting, and MERC stood for mercenary, a hired soldier of fortune. I called and spoke with the instructor Sergeant Franks. Franks assured me I would learn what a real MERC did, get expert training, and maybe a few good contacts for future employment. He boosted that his training camp was one of the best and that I would be welcomed. Since the site was in a southern state, I asked if I had to deal with racism in his course. He gave a definite no and pledged if anyone raised that issue, they were out. I agreed to go for training. With the way things were going in my life, I wanted to be ready for the confrontation that was coming. More about that later.

Amid the turmoil of litigation and polarization of the hospital and community, the hypocrisy continued right up to the end of my second year and graduation. Some months before, I met with the hospital executive committee and their lawyers to discuss my threatened, million-dollar lawsuit. "Dr. Gardner, what grievance do you want to be resolved in the hospital?" the attorney asked politely, expecting the worst. Without hesitation I responded, "I want the appropriate Infection Disease evaluation in my records and want Dr. Mark to apologize." "Is that all?" "Yes," I said. I never wanted to sue the hospital or harm its operations, but they drew the "first blood." I heard later that to avoid the lawsuit, Dr. Mark was asked to change the evaluation after they independently determined it was not correct. He vehemently refused at first, but after the executive staff reminded him of his tenuous membership on the hospital staff and potential loss of admitting privileges, he agreed. His pride and prejudice, however, did not allow him to ever apologize. I didn't care; I got what I wanted.

# CHAPTER TWENTY-TWO

*Watchman! What of the night?*
*The watchman said, the morning cometh,*
*and also the night!"*

—Isaiah 21:11,12

It was finished. I had my diploma in hand and was now ready to work as an internist on my own. My unceremonious departure from Mercy was with a sigh of relief—a sigh from both of the parties involved. I refused to attend the elaborate hoax of a graduation ceremony, as did one other black resident. One resident did attend; however, the fourth black resident had been dropped from the program after missing an examination by one or two points after returning from the funeral of his mother. Dr. Donald was still suspended, pending court hearings, but remained temporarily in the house owned by Mercy near the hospital.

My first order of business was to get a job. A job opening was available a few miles from Mercy with an internal medicine group. I was elated when I went for an initial interview with the director of the group. I was also surprised to see an old friend, Rene, from one of the clinics in Detroit I had worked with many years before. We hugged, and he was also excited that I was being hired. The interview went well. The director and the other six or seven doctors were all white, but he was enthusiastic to have an Afro-American in the group. He asked if I was okay with a starting salary of seventy-five thousand dollars and bonuses totaling another twenty thousand dollars the first year. With my annual resident salary being only $36,000, I smiled and said, "Yes." Before leaving, he asked if I could start the next Monday. Then, he said, "Oh, by the way, Robert, do you know Dr. H, head of surgery at Mercy?" My heart skipped a beat. "Yes." "Playing golf with him this weekend, I'll tell'um I met you."

Monday morning, I was on time. I walked into the waiting area and immediately saw my friend Rene. The previous glow of friendship had vanished; He looked taller then before and paler. "Robert, I don't know how to say this, but Dr. Ski asked me to tell you we won't be hiring you." I was electrified with disbelief. "Why?" I pleaded with Rene. "Let me speak with Dr. Ski." "He said not to let you come in. I'm so sorry, Robert. I'm so sorry." "Was it Dr. H?" I demanded. "I don't know. I'm sorry, Robert."

Stunned, I left the office with pure hatred magnified with the blackness of a hundred nights in my head. "I did everything right! I tried to work hard to be a good doctor! Now this!" "I tried" echoed into the deepest caverns in my head. "How can I pay my bills and feed my kids! All this hell in medical school and residency—for what!" I don't remember what I did immediately, but it ended with a cold can of beer and a deadly resolve to get even.

My depression deepened, as did the split between my wife and the church. I spent hours building scenarios of revenge, reading the *Anarchist Cookbook*, studying sabotage methods, and honing my shooting skill at local gun ranges. I bought new guns and learned to make silenced-weapons and explosive devices. My thirst for this knowledge was insatiable.

One day, I visited Dr. Donald who introduced me to Dr. Edna, one of his medical schoolmates and friend. Dr. Edna was tall for a woman, big-boned, dark complexioned with medium-sized black eyes. She looked like a woman you didn't want to cross until she smiled, and you knew things were okay, sort of. Her smile, though, could not hide the secrets her eyes whispered, like yellow tape at a crime scene—a barrier to keep others out and her buried past hidden.

"Dr. Gardner," Edna spoke. "I heard about all the trouble Mercy caused you. That's some really tough sh—t." She continued, "I have a small clinic in Detroit, and if you want, you can work with me until you find something else." I looked at Dr. Donald, then back at her. "Yeah, I think I would like that. Thanks." I tried to make the "thanks" sound as appreciative as I could, but the fact was, I got cheated out of my training experience and a real job, and nothing else would satisfy until I got even or vindicated.

Gratiot Avenue was another spoke in the wheel of streets that started from downtown Detroit; it ran straight northeasterly for over thirty miles. Unlike the spear that run to Pontiac filled with scenes of opulence, Gratiot Avenue was more like the arm of a crack addict, scared with the needle tracks of self-abuse and dreams long ended. Outstretched like a corpse in the morgue, it reeked of dilapidated storefronts, abandoned gas stations, once brightly lit movie theaters now darkened, and rat-infested, gutted apartments with burnt-out roofs, miles of trash, broken glass, urine-soaked doorways, and barred liquor and food stores ran by Arabs who detested their customers and made them pay beyond their means.

Dr. Edna's office was in the middle of this—an old weather-beaten storefront set between a start-up holy ghost church and another store long out of business. The once sparking plate glass window that showcased a thriving business was now covered with gray paint, and peeling letters that spelled "cleaners." Broken, sagging cement steps adored the entrance along with a dirty green door freshly sprayed with urine each night. People lived upstairs in apartments that ran the length of the block. The always watchful, but reclusive tenants peeked from behind curtains through grimy windows that where glued shut from years of paint layers now dried to an unknown color and cracking.

I met Dr. Edna's niece and cousin. The niece was a nurse assistant, and the cousin served as receptionist. The inside of the "office" was neat with old used furniture, examine tables, and dingy walls, but otherwise, clean. Dr. Edna and I discussed how things would go and what resources we had to improve business. Few things shocked or really bothered me by then, so when she described the patients—mostly poor, Medicaid, drug dependent, and those uninsured—a lump settled in my throat. She continued revealing that her Medicaid and Medicare certifications had been suspended and that she had not passed her medical practice boards yet, and that's why she needed me. "How did you start this place up with all these problems?" I asked. She related how she and another doctor were in practice together until one day, he just tossed her and all her things out on the sidewalk over personal issues. Much later, I found out they were more than colleagues, but lovers, and that the former associate's office was raided by the federal authorities for fraud and pharmacy drug violations. He left the country before being indicted. Anyway, she found this storefront and opened her own business. I didn't ask or want to hear anything else; that was enough for one day. A few days later, we were talking about my salary when she admitted she was literally broke and had trouble paying her office help, rent on the building, her house, and car payments. She had another friend who was helping her with a little money. I was speechless. Before I realized it, I told her I would not take a salary until things started to turn around. I hated the situation I was in, but Dr. Edna was the only one to step forward to help me when I had no other help. I am intensely loyal to my friends and intensely unforgiving to my enemies. So I worked there during the day, and moonlighted at a small community hospital to pay my bills.

Some of my office patients needed to be admitted to a hospital. They had the catalogue of all the diseases common to the black community—hypertension, diabetes, heart disease, infections related to IV drug use, and mental conditions. I went to Detroit Receiving and Harper-Grace hospitals where I went to medical school and trained for nearly ten years to apply for admitting privileges. I was told I had to wait six months before applying and would have to wait an indeterminate time thereafter for approval. "We aren't accepting any more application at this time," the secretary said with total detachment barely making eye contact. What she meant was that they weren't taking any black application. Many of my white, Philippine, Indians, and Pakistani classmates who recently finished residency, like me, were on staff and had admitting privileges without a six-month waiting period. I was furious and left before my presence had taken on infamy. Eventually, with the help of other Afro-American doctors in the area who had similar problems, I got on staff at two small minority-owned community hospitals.

Some weeks later, two important decisions were made: I wanted a divorce, and I wanted military training. Genora was crushed and bewildered at my announcement but continued to nag and play Twenty Questions whenever I came home. Had she stopped to understand my pain instead of attacking things might have been different? I hurt her and hated myself for it. In fact, I hated myself for everything in my life at the time. I hated hurting my sons who looked up to me and needed me. I hated everything I was doing. The only comfort I had was the power to end it when the tiredness and hatred became too great. Many mornings and sometimes in the stillness of a dark room, I'd lay the 9 mm on my lap, then gently pick it up, place it in my mouth and pray, "Lord Jesus, is this the day? Is this the day, Lord Jesus?" My thoughts would flash back to my youthful days in church, singing in the choir, witnessing in the streets, preaching youth sermons; then I'd see the stars over Vietnam and remember the prayers of thanksgiving and the joy of His presence. "Lord Jesus, is this the day?" A reverent quietness would fill the moment as if all heaven stood watching. Demons living inside dared not speak. Another person, more powerful, stood by and spoke, "Robert, one more day. Try it one more day."

I told Dr. Edna I needed time off and would be back in a week or two. I packed my car and drove south to the mercenary training camp deep in a pine and deciduous tree forest. I met Sergeant Franks and immediately liked him. He was much shorter than me, quiet, focused, and without question the expert killer he promised to make all of us.

There were about twenty-five to thirty other men from all over the world; some from Israel, Mexico, Central America, United States, Canada, Asia, and other places. After introductions, safety talks, equipment checks and issuing of weapons we loaded up in pickup trucks and convoyed deeper into the woods. The first task was a long march through forest, over hills, down valleys, walking, crawling, running, and crossing a small river upside down hand-over-hand. We spent the first night chest-deep wading through a stream evading a scout aggressor team. All of us carried unloaded weapons; most were automatic weapons, American, Soviet, and European. I carried a Scorpion submachine gun and my own backup gun, which was hidden and loaded, because I didn't trust this untrustworthy group of students. The concept was to make us a guerilla team, professional and lethal. There was to be no communication with the outside world for two weeks, no radios, no newspapers, no extra food except what we could carry, no baths, no medical help even if we got injured, and no mercy shown for weakness or failing to do our jobs. The incentive for strict discipline was a sniper firing a high-powered scoped pellet rifle. The sniper was camouflaged in a greenish brown rag suit called a ghillie suit. Blending in with the trees and bushes, he was invisible. At night, the sniper used a night vision scope to turn the night into day bathed in a greenish hue to find us. We never saw him except once when Sergeant Frank called to the sniper to move, and he pointed him out to prove he was always there. His job was to watch for training errors and carelessness or to encourage realism. He was ordered to shoot any student in a non-lethal spot anywhere on his body. One student got his kneecap shattered for a mistake. I was shot in the leg when I didn't move fast enough across a rope bridge. The small hole in my leg was a constant reminder the training was serious. We practiced hand-to-hand and stick fighting, bayonet and knife fighting, as well as ambushes, escape and evasion, stalk-and-kill, prisoner snatch techniques, improvised explosives and booby traps. One student had his throat cut accidentally. It wasn't deep but just missed his carotid artery, and another student received a large laceration to his arm. During hand-to-hand fighting, an Israeli soldier picked me up and dropped me over his knee; the pain was excruciating. He apologized, but I was paralyzed for a few moments, unable to move my legs. Only after about ten minutes did the numbness gradually subside, and I could walk again. That was a blessing. We also learned many other things—how to build campfires in the pouring rain and improvise shelters out of anything lying around, how to trap food, and how to find water. One demonstration placed us across a small river, and we were told to keep our heads down and crawl to the escape rope to pull ourselves across the river when the firing started. At that point, we heard a hundred rapid *tit, tit, tit, tit, tit* as trees limbs, leaves, and surrounding dirt exploded from live silenced Mach 10 and Uzi machine gun rounds aimed just over our heads and the ground behind and on either side of us. It was really terrifying not knowing where the fire was coming from. It was like being back in Vietnam during a firefight. Added to that mayhem, the sniper was shooting some of the guys who were not reacting as told, not moving fast enough, or cowering behind logs. Throughout the training, we studied and fired many different weapons—the US AR15, Israeli Uzi, US Mach 10, Mach 11, Chinese AK47, SKS rifles, Soviet Tokarev pistol, German lugers, and an assortment of other third world weapons. Another exercise involved carrying wounded comrades—the heaviest guys (the big Germans)—for two to three miles up hills, across streams, and through woods. We learned the importance of caution and enemy tricks. One day, a truck showed up with a couple of crates of fresh fruit. Most of us were out of food, exhausted, and starving. A number of the guys rushed the truck and snatched up the small crates of fruit as if to hoard all of them. One trainee from New York got about twenty yards before it exploded. It knocked him another five feet, peppering his face, chest, and legs with black power burns and small cuts. Ironically, one night, an aggressor force kidnapped that same New Yorker, who was caught sleeping on guard duty. The next morning, the group was scolded and informed that because the guard was asleep, all of us were dead. As an example, the New Yorker had been blindfolded, roughed up, stripped to his underwear, and tied to a tree all night in the freezing air. We heard him screaming, "You can't do this to me, this is America!" No one felt sorry for him. The point was made, and from that lesson on, he was a model soldier.

Throughout the training, especially at night when the stars seemed to dance amid the branches of swaying pines, the Voice quietly whispered in currents of air, "Robert, what are you doing here? You don't belong." I would ignore the wind and heaven's message and think about Mercy Hospital, think about the police beating. I'd feel the exhaustion and hopelessness that permeated every part of my life. I was determined to finish that training and, even if it killed me, to use it. "Robert, you don't want to hurt anybody." "Stop! Go away!" I scoffed the Voice. The nights seemed so long, so dark as I glazed into the starry heavens, past the glittering planets, past the swirling galaxies, and into endless space, where visions and dreams of indescribable glory lived, but a place I know I would never see. I was getting farther away, farther away from home, my real home.

There were a few dry sunny days, but mostly, the days were cool and wet. After the off-and-on drizzle of rain, the weather cleared and the rain stopped. Then within hours the air turned much colder, and the clouds darkened and moved rapidly as if pushed by a giant hand. We were soaked from the rain nearly the whole time. One night, after being in the stream all evening and up all day soaking wet, we were divided into teams of six and were to attack, escape, and evade other teams throughout the coming night. We were given bottle rockets to fire at each other. Of course, the invisible sniper was always there to increase the tension. After a few firefights with the bottle rockets, most of the teams went into hiding. The north winds started to blow stronger and colder. The tall pine trees clashed and swayed as if in mortal combat with the wind. Then we saw it—snow. Anyone was surprised. The soggy, wet ground was freezing, and ice was forming on pools of water. We were in a tactical training exercise, so we couldn't make a fire, build a shelter, or make any noise because other teams would find us, or the sniper would shoot us. My team of six found a small valley depression and huddled there as we tried to figure out guard rotations. The snow flurries, and winds picked up still stronger, and we were freezing. Our wet clothes began to ice and harden like cardboard. The five other guys put some small tree branches and dead leaves on the ground and huddled themselves more tightly together. I had first watch on guard duty, so I kneeled in the open to keep watch. The others quickly fell asleep or lay still because they were too cold to move. I wore a thin rain parker, but it also was ice cold and wet. As I kneeled, I began to shiver. First, just a little, then uncontrollably. My teeth rattled so hard I thought I was going to break them, but I couldn't stop the spasm. Every time I tried to move or my skin touched a wet spot, I went into a seizure as more heat left my body. I was getting hypothermic and was going to die if I didn't get up and move. My whole body was chilled, but from the waist down, I was paralyzed from the cold. I tried again and again to will my legs to move, but they were dead. I seized over and over again. *I'm gonna died! I'm gonna died!* I thought as the reality sank in. *How ironic to die like this on my knees? I hate the cold!* I didn't remember the last time I was on my knees for prayer, but here I was, forced to kneel and die.

The only way to stop the seizures and muscle spasms was to be perfectly still. "Robert, the lighter," the Voice said. "The lig . . . lighter? W . . . what? Yah, the, the lighter!" Even my brain was beginning to freeze, slowing like a record player winding down. *If I could only reach my shirt pocket,* I thought. Over the next forty-five minutes to an hour, I tried over and over to reach the lighter in my pocket. Inch by inch, my swollen lifeless fingers stretched for the lighter, but every movement hurled me into a violent spasm. "Lord, help me!" my frozen lips muttered. I seized again and again until finally with my last effort, I touched it. "Thank you," I whispered. Slowly and carefully, I curled the lighter in my hand and felt for the lighter snap. I flicked it several times beneath my jacket, but nothing. "Lord, help me," I pleaded. I flicked it again, nothing. "Please, Lord." I tried again, and the blessing came; the heat was wonderful! I cried out, "Thank you, Jesus! Thank you!" Tears filled my eyes, and I knew He had come again to my rescue even when I didn't deserve it. I burned my hands and arms, but the warmth and life was returning to my body. After about an hour, I was able to move and limp to a spot near the group and off the cold ground.

As the wind and clattering pines subsided, a faint orange glow rose over the distant hills. It was morning, and that terrible night was over. The warming rays of the autumn sun gradually pushed the frost and mist from the valley and low places. Sergeant Frank showed up to make sure everyone got through the night; he actually was worried and feared the worst. The freak fall storm caught everyone by surprise. I still was unable to stand steadily and had to use a walking stick to move. Remembering the night and the God who never sleeps, who ever hears the cries of His children, I knew I didn't belong there; I knew I had to leave. But as I thought of the future, I knew that in Detroit, there would be more storms, but I also knew and hoped there would also be more grace.

Over the course of a year, I made many trips south. Two events are worth mentioning. Interstate 65 ran the north-south length of mid-America and cut through the heart of Nashville, Tennessee. The green-and-white highway sign reflecting the setting sun took me back to wonderful memories of Riverside Adventist Hospital. I saw the campus church with its steep gray stairs, the well-manicured grounds with carpet grass and beautiful flowers, the hospital, Betty (the nurse I almost asked to marry), Mrs. Florence Kimbro (Elder E. E. Cleveland's mother), brother Lane Todd, Ted Brown, and so many others; I smiled. The Nashville skyline faded as my driving trance resumed. Then a thought came from deep inside—not my brain but from my heart, where the prisoner lived. *Why don't you stop by Oakwood College?* Before long, I arrived on campus near Huntsville,

Alabama. It was dark, and cars were parked all over, especially near the church. I saw a sign that announced the week of prayer services. Oakwood College was the mecca of education for Afro American Adventist and many others, including different racial groups and even some nonmembers. It was the powerhouse for training ministers, gospel workers, and professional careers of all types. The Oakwood College choirs were world famous and thrilled millions with a repertoire rich in classical excellence and harmonious gospels and spirituals capturing the legacy of black heritage.

"What are you doing?" a dark sensation asked. "Go, Robert," the Voice said. I removed the combat knife and black metal automatic I carried, laid them on the floor, stepped into the dark, then into the light of the church. The church was packed. Every head was turned toward a popular and dynamic young minister with a short Afro haircut. I immediately recognized him. I once saw him at Andrews University in Michigan and again at the Burns church in Detroit. I slide into a back row seat off to one side. I felt drugged from the long ride but also strangely revived and safe there, close to God's people. The familiar music, seeing people I loved, hearing the "amen's," shouts of praise, and joyful outbursts caused me to say softly, "Thank you, Lord."

"Let's bow our heads." The young evangelist raised his hands for the appeal. "The Holy Spirit is working. Keep your heads bowed and pray, saints." A tingling sensation swept over my body; I felt like I was in a vise. Something was lifting me and pulling me forward, up out of my seat. Inside, the prisoner clenched his bars and cried for help. Before I realized it, I was walking toward the speaker. I wanted special prayer. My heart was breaking; I wanted to be free of the curse I was under and the demons that ruled my life. I was almost there when "STOP! Sit down!" the preacher commanded as he snapped his head toward me and pointed an accusing finger. "Don't you see the Holy Spirit working? Go sit down!" I froze as if electrocuted. My eyes narrowed. *What?* I thought in unbelief. "Go back. Sit down! God's people are praying in here." I glared at him and said to myself, *Man, don't you know I can take your life? Right now!* I turned and left the building, going to get my 9 mm. The spirit of rage returned with the shriek of a hundred demons. "No, Robert! Just leave. It's gonna be all right," the Voice spoke, halting the storm that was building inside me. Still seething, I thought to myself, *That fool didn't know how close he was to dying.* It didn't matter if his smiled was bright enough to melt snow or cause leaves to fall off trees when he spoke; were it not for the grace of God, he was surely going to die that night.

The other event worth mentioning occurred as I traveled back to Michigan. I had decided to detour to North Carolina for sniper training. My new high powered hurting rifle was well suited for the skill I planned to master. I called ahead and informed them I was coming. As usual, my thoughts were numerous and filled with confused imagery and scenarios for revenge. The hum of the tires and alternating white-and-black lines of the highway put me again into a trance. For no apparent reason, my thoughts, as they often did, reached into the past.

It was my sister Beverly's thirteenth birthday, and she wanted a yard party. As his custom was, my father said yes to his little princes. And, of course, my brother Billy and I were the "peasants" if the analogy were to continue; we were told to watch over things. The party started, and the throbbing rhythms of Motown drifted throughout the neighborhood. Many of my sister's friends showed up, milled around, or danced under strings of colored red, blue, and yellow lights. Before long, a gang of thugs showed up to crash the party. They were cursing and pushing people around. The party moved into the house, but before anyone knew it, the thugs rushed in too and started rampaging throughout the house. Some went upstairs into the bedrooms, looking for things to steal. My aunt Mildred chased them downstairs. The house had thirty to forty people jammed together. The gang members were still cursing and threatening people and vowing to tear the house up. Beverly started to cry, pleading with them to leave. They laughed at her and continued trash talking and pushing guest. I had had enough. I went and got my father's .22-caliber rifle, pushed my way through the crowd, and hopped up on the mantle shelf over the fireplace. The whole place went quiet as I pointed the rifle up in the air. The leader of the group with slick processed black hair stepped forward and said, "Who in da' hell do you think you are?" His homeboys encouraged him with "right on!" I looked long at him before speaking. "You got to the count of three to get the hell out of my house." Our eyes were locked on each other. My voice was clear and steady as was my resolve to kill him. He looked around for support. "One . . . two . . ." There was a sudden mass push in the crowd, and he and his gang started to leave. "I'm comin' back!" he shouted and cursed as he rushed out the front door. Some cheered, but I began to shake because I wanted to shoot him anyway.

It started to rain, the highway turned to glass, and I switched on the windshield wipers. The rain pounded the roof harder and harder. The windows fogged over, and then the whole car shook from the vibrations of horrific lighting and thunder. I couldn't see pass the hood and got nervous as eighteen wheelers roared inches away from my side. My car shook and seemed lost in a sea of noise and torrents of water. I tried desperately to pull off the road, but the deep, piercing blare of truck horns warned me I was in the way. I didn't know where the side of the road was; it was pitch dark except for the lighting and blurred truck lights. Taking a chance, I eased over till I felt gravel under my tires. Trucks continued to zoom close by and continue to shake the car, as did the shock waves of thunder. The storm seemed to hang around my car and lasted for over an hour or more before I heard the Voice. "Don't go to North Carolina." A strange sensation of dread filled my head. I dozed off to sleep and awakened to stillness. The storm was gone, the highway vacant. Without saying anything mentally or otherwise, I turned the car around and went home.

# CHAPTER TWENTY-THREE

*To every thing there is a season,*
*and a time to every purpose under the heaven:*
*A time to be born and a time to die.*
—Ecclesiastes 3:1

Shortly before starting to work with Dr. Edna, I moved out of my home in Southfield, Michigan, and moved into an apartment in Madison Heights just north of Detroit some fifteen miles. The neat small apartment didn't last long; I ran out of money and had to move back to Detroit. The new apartment on Detroit's eastside was a dump. I didn't know the ceiling leaked, and the carpet was always damp and moldy. Worst, the apartment building either contained or was surrounded by prostitutes, thugs, thieves, and people on street drugs. I knew better than to be there, but the place was near Dr. Edna's office. I paid the down payment of $350 but never got a chance to sleep there. I stayed at many places, mostly in the call room at the small hospital where I moonlighted. After coming home one evening, I found a lot of my stuff soaked from the rain. I was furious and demanded my money back. The landlord—a crusty, unkempt-looking thin man—refused to give the money back and said the company had to make that decision since I signed the lease. The next day, Dr. Edna offered me a very small room in a rental house she owned near her home. Reluctantly, I accepted it and further obligated myself to her.

When I returned from the south, Dr. Edna had good news; our office was moving from the broken-down storefront to a dingy yellow brick building just across the street. Though it was small, it looked like a real medical office. There was a lobby, front desk area, two examination rooms, and a break room in the back.

So many crazy things started to happen it was hard to keep track, but none of it was good. The patients continued to be mostly drug-addicted young people with bad arm, leg, or neck infections from injecting street drugs. Most of the drug cocktails were combinations of heroin and prescription pain pills, like Darvon, Darvocet, Stadol, Codeine, or Demerol. A single pill could get about $40-60 on the street. One black lady, about twenty years old, was a regular at the clinic. Shania always came asking for pain pills and was quick to show the trembling

Medicaid card she held in her skeletal hands. She was emaciated with a potbelly and looked more like a python who'd swallowed a pig than a human. Dr. Edna tried to talk to her about her drug habits; she laughed and promised she had or would stop. Dr. Edna had a gift for talking to the addicts, so we were saddened but not surprised when we heard that Shania was dead. She'd gotten a prescription from some other doctor, made a cocktail, and walked home one freezing January night. She opened the front gate to her house, stopped, fell asleep standing up, and froze to death. They found her standing with the gate open, frozen solid. The fire department had to saw the steel gate loose with her attached.

Patients along the Gratiot corridor often went to four or five, sometimes many more, area clinics to get pain pills to make cocktails. Most pharmacies—as were the price-gouging grocery stores, liquor stores, and gas stations—were run by Middle Eastern, Indian, Pakistani and Oriental people who lived in expensive secluded suburbs far from the misery they helped create. They knew what the prescriptions were for but didn't seem to ask any questions, even when patients returned two or three times a day for the same quantity of drugs. One honest pharmacist called me to inform me one of our patients had stolen a prescription pad and was selling them with my forged signature. Police questioned Dr. Edna and me after drug enforcement officers raided a number of pharmacies for drug trafficking.

One day, a local drug dealer, whose brother was a patient at the clinic, walked in. I was in the back room with another patient, and I could hear Dr. Edna talking with someone with a loud voice and her trying to quiet him. "You tell him from now on, he works for me," the dealer threatened. I only heard part of his offer. "You better get out of here," Dr. Edna told him in a hushed voice. I left the patient in the back, felt the 9 mm I carried in a back holster, and went to the lobby. Dr. Edna was closing the door behind the dealer. "What was he saying, Dr. Edna?" "Don't worry about him. He was just talkin' foolishness." "What did he say?" I demanded. She told me. My first rule of confrontation is that if an enemy threatens you, kill him on the spot without conversation. "Wait, Robert." Dr. Edna stepped in front of me. "I'll talk to his brother." She did, and his brother came over to the clinic to apologize. Dr. Edna knew how stressed I was and would have found and killed him. "You tell your brother don't ever come into this clinic and threaten the doc," she advised sternly. The brother clearly understood.

On another occasion, I heard a big commotion in the lobby. When I rushed to the front with my 9 mm in hand under my white coat, I saw a man and a woman handcuffing a young thug on the sidewalk in front of the clinic. Dr. Edna explained that the guy came in, drew a gun, and demanded drugs. The man and woman who tackled the man on the sidewalk were undercover police officers posing as patients. They just happened to be there to see if I was doing something illegal. It was a blessing since I was coming from the back to take care of business.

Dr. Donald continued to cause problems for me. I received a call from him one evening, asking if I could do him a favor. He moonlighted in a small mostly black community downriver from Detroit and could not go there anymore but didn't tell me why. "The pay is good, and all you have to do is see some patients for a couple of hours. They're looking for a replacement doctor. Just do me this favor, the clinic director is a friend of mine." As always, sensing dread, I said, "Okay." I drove some twenty-five miles to the small town. It really was a place where angels and police feared to be, and what was I doing there? It doesn't matter where you go—Detroit, Chicago, New York, anywhere in America or the world—drug addicts, homeless beggars, prostitutes, pimps, drunkards, and thugs all look the same, like they're a union or something. But here their numbers were concentrated. Both sides of the street, starting two blocks from the small clinic, they sat, glared, and searched for prey. As I got out my car, I adjusted the knife I carried strapped to my leg and both 9 mm pistols I carried. I tucked one in my belt in front so everyone could see it as I walked the short distance to the clinic entrance. All along the way, as people saw my black medical bag and white coat slung over my arm, low whispers rose like incense. "It's the new doc, it's the doctor. Hey, we got another one." The clinic director was a sharply dressed, slightly overweight lady with short pressed black hair and large jewelry handing like Christmas ornaments. She looked more like a madam in a whorehouse than a medical director. Despite her appearance, she was very nice and quick to thank me for coming. She then went on to describe what I would be doing, which mostly involved seeing Medicaid patients and writing their prescriptions. "Prescription" went off in my head like an air raid siren on Saturday morning. Before I could respond, she said, "You only need to be here two hours, and I'll pay you $500 per hour." I was broke and needed the money, else I would have left immediately. My comfort level slumped another notch when I asked where the examination room was. She said, "You don't have to examine them, just rewrite their prescriptions for pain pills." I said, "I'm sorry, I can't do that unless I examine them and look at their medical records." "Okay," she said with hesitation. I examined three or four ladies, looked at their medical records, and tried to talk to them about getting off the drugs. It was like talking to zombies. They didn't want my advice or didn't care about changing anything in their lives; they were walking dead. I left there with $500 cash since no more patients came in, and I vowed to myself not to return. Again, my anger brewed toward Dr. Donald for the mess he continued to pull me into.

A month or two later, I read that that clinic was raided by police, and everyone was jailed or sent to prison for drug trafficking, forgery, and practicing outside medical standards. No one ever confronted me about being there, and I'm sure the street had many undercover agents who saw me, gun and all.

As I said, things inside me were bad. I was tormented by what I was doing to my family, the racism that caused me to practice third world medicine in the inner city, the feelings of revenge, the tension of the weapons I hated, and the uncertainty of tomorrow. Every day, I awoke with a racing heart and rapid breathing, wondering what would happen that day. On some especially nerve-racking days, I came to work, saw a few people, went across the street to the liquor store, brought a six pack of 16 oz beers, malt liquor or wine coolers, retreated to my office, locked the door, swallowed 20, 40, or 60 milligrams of Valium, drank my alcohol, fell asleep across my desk for one or two hours, and then drove home to my cluttered lonely eight by ten room.

Dr. Edna still worried over bills and lamented not being able to pay me much. I received about $600 over six months, or $3 a day if calculated that way. One day, she told me about a friend opening a small clinic in Inkster, Michigan. Inkster was about thirty miles west of Detroit. It too was predominantly a socio-economically depressed area with Afro American poor and big city problems of drugs and crime. But the little brick building was a real clinic that folded a year prior due to bad management. Now, under new management, I was asked to come and see patients. It was Dr. Edna's way of "helping" me again. The boss was handsome, smooth talking, and a person who got what he wanted, mostly by intimidation. He was middle-aged, brown skinned, and muscular like he once played football. He always dressed in a business suit and tie, wore the best cologne, and sported a large jeweled ring like the player he was. His name was Harris. His girlfriend, Silvia, was drop-dead gorgeous, tall, and curvaceous. They lived together sometimes and rarely were apart when at the clinic. To me, she loved and feared Harris. She knew he wasn't the right man she needed in her life. I admit, at times, I wished I were in a position to be that man; she was really beautiful inside and out and deserved better things in life. I sensed at times she was a spiritual person, sensitive and seemed to be looking for something that only heaven could give—peace. But Harris caused her to look in all the wrong places. I was just as bad because I was too ashamed of my own life to point her in the right direction.

After working there for about two months, I asked Harris when was I going to get paid. Like the first month, he leaned back in his leather chair and said, "Be patient, Robert, I'll fix you up as soon as more money comes in." "I need my money soon!" I said without trying to sound desperate even though I was. "Come back next Friday," he said. Later, I found out that money was flowing into the clinic. Dr. Edna got paid for getting me there, his girlfriend got paid for being a part-time receptionist, and the folk at the racetrack got paid. On next Friday, as the sun began to set, I arrived at the office. I was in no mood for excuses. I chambered a round in my 9mm, took the safety off, and placed the weapon where I could draw it fast. I knew that Harris also carried a gun, and he would use it. I also knew I was not going to leave that office until he paid me. Harris sat regally behind his walnut desk as cigarette smoke drifted lazily toward the ceiling. "Hey, sit down, Robert." He took a long drag off his cigarette. "I can't pay you anything yet." He looked at me with a slight downward smirked of his lips. "Why?" I said dully with obvious tension. "We just don't have the money." Our eyes watched each other carefully. It was like a Gary Cooper movie at High Noon, but this was no movie, and one, or both of us, was about to die. Harris's forehead wrinkled, his eyes narrowed. Clearly, the tone in my voice made him angry. My thoughts and hand was set on my 9mm. I didn't know where his gun was, but it was somewhere close. "I'm not leaving here until you pay me." "I told you we ain't got no money!" He raised his voice. "Draw, Robert!" a voice said. Something else seemed to hold me. Moments passed without either of us saying anything. We stared at each other, expecting the madness of exploding nines to settle the matter. My right arm tensed, about to pull my weapon, when Harris spoke. "Okay. Let me write you a check, and you can cash it tomorrow." My right arm and hand eased as I sat watching him write a check for three hundred dollars. I took the check without saying anything and backed out of the room.

Next day, I tried to cash the check, and there were insufficient funds. I told Dr. Edna, who calmed me down and offered to give me three hundred dollars. I never went back to the clinic. It closed a short time after that. Well, Harris lived another year and died of a heart attack.

Probably, the closest I came to the electric chair or the grave started with my pager ringing. "Hello, this is Dr. Gardner. You called?" The telephone booth was off a busy main street. I pulled over to answer the unfamiliar page number. It was about ten o'clock at night. "Dr. Gardner, this is Agent Brown with the Michigan Attorney General's Office." It was the voice of an Afro-American who spoke with authority and professional poise. "Don't be alarm, but I want to advise you that our agency will be at your office to confiscate all records, medical and account, tomorrow." A deep-seated anger was starting to build. *What now?* I thought. The agent continued, "It has nothing to do with you, Dr. Gardner. We are investigating your partner, Dr. Edna. Please be advised, do not tell her what I am telling you. Understand?" "Yah, Go ahead." His voice changed somewhat, and I could detect a hinted of sarcasm and disgust toward his ethnic brothers as though he held a divine superiority. "We have had your clinic under surveillance for over six months as part of drug operations to catch medical fraud and illegal pharmacy activity in your area. We've been following you, but we have nothing on you. We know you are honest and trying to practice good medicine. But Dr. Edna has filed questionable insurance claims. We will contact you later." The phone went silent as I held it to my ear. Car horns blared and traffic noise rushed by, as waves of depression weld up in me. "Now what?" I sighed. Dr. Edna was my friend, and I am loyal to my friends. I called her immediately and told her everything the agent said. She was quiet until I interrupted her silence. "What's going on, Dr. Edna?" "Robert, I'll tell you when I see you." I went by her house, and we talked. She denied any wrongdoing, but I sensed she wasn't telling me everything. When I pressed her firmly for the truth, she revealed that there might have been some minor errors but nothing of significance. I later learned that there was more money coming into the clinic than she admitted, and a large part of the money, maybe several thousands that should have been my salary, was sent to her former business partner, close friend or most probably lover for legal fees after he fled the country.

So with that news and the rest of my life in shambles, I had had enough, especially from law enforcement and the white power structure that controlled it. The harder I tried, the worst things got. It was time to end it all.

The next morning, I drove toward the clinic. There was a line of black unmarked, official-looking cars on both sides of the busy street. I keep going as if in a trance. I drove to my parents' house some blocks away. I moved as if controlled by an overwhelming force I was powerless to turn off. I couldn't stop what I had programmed myself to do. I looked for my mother, but she was gone. My father was home but in one of his moods that always upsets me. I wanted to hug him and say good-bye but left without saying anything. I was dressed for death. I wore green camouflaged pants, a waist-length solid green jacket, and an unshaven face devoid of expression or feeling. "This was the day." The sun was bright, and life never noticed the darkness about to come. Beneath my uniform, I carried two 9 mm automatics, a silenced .22-caliber pistol, a serrated hunting knife, a pipe bomb, and nothing to live for. I was tired of everything in my life. Tired of the struggle of medicine, social injustice, a ruined life, a useless church, and being an all-around failure. The demons rehearsed what I was to do. I would walk to the back of the clinic and cut the throats of those there and, if any alarm arose, shoot all others, then detonate the pipe bomb in a way to rupture gas lines and magnify the explosion. I didn't expect to live; I just didn't care anymore. The first person I would shoot would be the black agent with the nasty attitude. He represented the worst of the bunch because contempt was expected from the white officers but not from the black officer. It was sad how often Afro—Americans belittled their brothers to impress white colleagues. He would be the first to die. "Yes," the demon voices agreed. "That's how it will go." I opened the office door and walked in. "Go to the back," they said. The office had about six people gathering files in boxes. There were another three or four in the back as I looked down the short hallway. Just as I started to move to the back, my head full of death scenarios, a tall broad-shouldered white officer stepped forward. "Oh, Dr. Gardner. I am so sorry about this. I know this a terrible thing, and it disrupts your business". The agent held both his hand out as if in supplication. "I just want you to know we will quickly get these records back to you. Again, I apologize." I was startled by his kindness and soft-spoken voice. Police don't talk to black people like that in Detroit. They simply don't apologize or express regret. I didn't say anything back; I was confounded and dazed. I walked to the back of the clinic, looked at the people who stared back uneasily, turned, and left the building. As I drove off to somewhere, I don't remember, I started to cry. I never saw that officer again or knew who he was. But I believe he was an angel sent by my Heavenly Father. He saved the lives of all those people, especially the mean-spirited black officer, and undeservedly, mine.

# CHAPTER TWENTY-FOUR

*In the night I see the rain and wonder*
*if it is not all the tears since time began.*
*Tears of sorrow, tears of love, of joy, of pain.*
*Rain? Maybe it's the only way God can let us touch*
*The moisture in His eyes.*
*Maybe it's only rain? Maybe tears?*
*In my heart I know tomorrow will come,*
*The darkness will fade,*
*The sun will shine and He will smile.*
*But for now, I see the rain, and wonder.*

—Robert Gardner

We never got the medical records back, and so we were out of business. Somehow, Dr. Edna escaped any criminal charges but was censored by the medical board and not allowed to practice medicine. From that point on, she realized she needed to be totally honest with me because I was now her main source of income. I was upset about the lies and money she embezzled; I tried to put that behind me. The other point was that I needed her too. I still stayed in the room she let me use as a favor, and as deadly as I was to my enemies; I was intensely loyal to my friends. Dr. Edna was the only helping hand extended when I was down and out, so life together went on.

The Gratiot office closed. I continued to moonlight at the Park Community Hospital while Dr. Edna stayed home or went to the racetrack. One day, she called and said she found a new building on Wyoming Street, Detroit's west side. The neighborhood was much nicer, cleaner, and had one or two fewer drug-addicted clients than the east side. The dingy tan brick building was the office of a family practice doctor who recently passed away. It had all the amenities of a real office including a small laboratory, a dusty, unusable x-ray area, adequate exam rooms, and a very nice waiting area. The place was overall clean and ideal for the practice I wanted to have. But if omens are real, then the rushing into the office that first afternoon of a seven-year-old boy, son of the butcher a few doors down from the office was a bad one. The wide-eyed skinny black boy clutched a bloody towel around one of his hands as he looked up at me with tear-filled eyes. His father knelt beside him, sobbing, "I told him not to touch nothing!" Over and over, he moaned as he shook his head back and forth. I peeled the soaked towel away to see only mangled pieces of flesh where his fingers once were. "He stuck his hand in the meat grinder. I told him not to . . ." His father wailed. Dr. Edna quickly replaced the towel as I ran to the shop to see if I could retrieve any of the severed fingers; I couldn't. All were too badly mutilated to reattach. Our next big huddle was to try and borrow money—get a small business loan from a local Afro—American bank. We knew the white bankers were not likely to approve a loan. While the loan application was being processed and negotiations with the doctor's widow continued about the rent, Dr. Edna called me one night to say the alarm at the office was going off. I was on call at the small community hospital and couldn't leave until the next morning. People in the neighbor said they saw several men put a door jack into the office front door, noisily rip off the whole door frame, walked in, and carted off typewriters, a fax machine, and many other items in a matter of minutes. The police never came, and no one thought it was their business to do anything. Needless to say, clouds of depression and anger settled in once more. I wished, just for a moment, just a second, that I could think of something good, and it come true. I felt like I was suffocating. My heart raced all the time. I drank too many beers and swallowed too much Valium, but nothing else eased the pain that weld up in my soul. I was lost in a storm of desperation that was dark and as endless as that freezing night at the mercenary school. Driving often helped me sort out things; it allowed me to escape the quandary of the moment. With no certainty, I often drove around not knowing where I was going, where I had been, and in the fog of my situation, where I was. The only thing certain was that I was alone, angry, broke, and spiritually bankrupt. The new office was a wreck, the house mortgage was due, and the kids needed clothes and food. And on my other list of things I hated, I knew I couldn't stay at Dr. Edna's house much longer. I needed money and needed it then. The glare from passing cars transported me into scenes deep in my mind. One after another pictures and plans raced by with clarity and precision. One scene took me back to an idea I considered many times, breaking into a National Guard armory. I planned to steal automatic weapons, like the ones we trained with in the South—AR15s, M60s, and .45 calibers. Maybe there would be some M79 grenade launchers or hand grenades, I hoped. The scenes paused though as I thought of what I would do or had to do if caught or an alarm went off. What if I had to shoot someone? If it were a cop, then it would be no problem. As smooth as a Hollywood film, other visions played out scene after scene of how I could do them. Then the vision faded as the danger of my plans became apparent without help. Who could I get to help? Maybe those people who wanted me to blow up the hospital? I was startled when a voice from the shadows of my mind spoke, "There are a lot of rich white folk you can get money from. You don't have to hurt anybody, just be careful. It'll be easier than the armory." I pulled over into a dark section of a large parking lot. I turned off the engine. Silence filled the space where time should have been. I sat still and waited. It whispered again, "It'll be easy, be patient, and you'll have all the money you need." I never saw them coming. Out of nowhere, the shadowed black sedan slammed to a stop in front of me. I was blocked in. A pain, a venomous heat gripped my stomach and curled along familiar paths through my chest to its lair deep within my head; an ancient rage born of hatred and revenge slithered to life again. It was not a rage of simple anger or mindless passion but of cold, deadly resolve programmed to come alive at such a time as this. I don't remember opening my car door in the darkened parking lot nor how smoothly I drew the 9 mm Smith & Wesson. Time slowed, then halted with the barrel inches away from the security officer's forehead. The young white patrolman was slow getting out the passenger side; I wasn't. They had been driving around and noticed my lone car in the parking lot. The cop looked up in nervous surprise into the steady nightmare of the 9 mm and an even colder set of eyes buried behind a full beard. Half out the car, his voice quivered. "Saaay, pal, we just want to talk." "Get back into the car," I spoke evenly and quietly. "I just—," he started to speak. "Get back into the car," I interrupted unhurriedly as my finger tightened on the hair-triggered nine. The sound of the nearby traffic seemed distant and the night air cool and lifeless. The young officer inched toward me. I squeezed the trigger. "Dammit, man!" the black officer behind the steering wheel screamed as he grabbed the belt of the young white officer, pulling him back into the car. "Didn't the man say 'get back in the car'?" The black cop slammed his foot on the accelerator and took off with tires burning. I spun around, throw my gun on the seat next to me, raced my engine, and sped off in the opposite direction. I bounced across several lanes of traffic, then around a corner headed for the freeway. "Take the old road," the Voice said. I swerved away from the expressway and headed down a two-lane dark back road. The adrenaline was at full throttle. More scenarios. If they put up a roadblock, I'll ram it and shoot it out with them. "Maybe I should get out this car and take my chances on foot." I pulled out my short-barreled shotgun and a pipe bomb. "I hope no one tries to stop me." I drove the speed limit so not to attract attention. Forty minutes later, I was back in Detroit. The adrenaline rush left me exhausted and trembling. *Why didn't the gun go off?* I began to revisit the scene in my head. *What were you going to do to the other young officer, the black one, Robert?* My program answered affirmatively, "Kill him too." I started to sweat again. I didn't want to kill anybody and especially those innocent men who had nothing to do with my situation except being in the wrong place at the wrong time. I started to shake more as tears crested the edge of my eyes. "Thank you, Lord," I spoke quietly. "Thank you for sparing their lives." More tears came, and I was unable to control the deep longing I felt. "Lord, help me! Please help me!" I stuttered. The minutes passed in silence, and glaring headlights from oncoming cars were interrupted by the Voice, "You're near Sharon's, go there." Sharon was a student nurse I met at the Pontiac Hospital. She was short, bubbly, and very attractive in so many ways. When she laughed or smiled, you had to join her. She was also fiery, feisty, and a lady you didn't want to upset. Yet she was gentle, generous, and genuine in her love and loyalty to family and close friends. She wasn't sure it was me peering through a crack in the chained-door. "Robert, what's wrong?" as she cautiously opened her apartment door wider. "What happened to you?" Sharon had never seen me so disfigured or so hideous with a full dirty beard, sweat-drenched camouflaged clothes, and tears in my eyes. "I'm sorry to bother you, Sharon, but—" "Robert," she interrupted, "you don't have to say anything, you look tired. Come in and get some rest. We can talk tomorrow." She brought blankets and made a bed for me on the couch. Without saying a word, she handed me a washcloth, showed me the bathroom, then disappeared into her bedroom. I lay down, closed my eyes as the darkness of the day blended to hide the darkness inside me. As sleep placed a comforting hand over my eyes, a final tear course its way down my cheek and from deep within, my heart thanked God for such a friend.

The apartment was bright and quiet. Sharon was gone. It was nearly noon. A note on the kitchen table said, "Make yourself at home, I'll fix dinner when I get back." Hours later, I heard the key in the door. Her smile was dazzling and unhurried, as always, and it made me feel good and safe. After dinner, we talked a long time; she was stunned. She put her arms around me and gave me a hug of assurance that things were starting to change, and she was there to help. "You need money, Robert?" she asked. "I'm okay," I answered, not looking at her. There was a long silence. "I'll be back," she said, and then she left the apartment. A short time later, she returned. "Here, take this for the kids. And don't say nothing else to me about 'I'm okay." I stared at the two thousand dollars; then she walked toward the kitchen. "Let's eat," she said turning with a big smile. The weeks that followed strengthened our friendship, as she made sure I got cleaned up and went back to work. She was an angel, and to this day, I love her for the gift she was from God. Despite efforts, however, to make things work in my practice, Detroit's blighted urban economics, the pervasive racial tension, the depressing neighborhoods, the low income, the predator drug-addicted patients, the turmoil in my family, and the estrangement from the church, it was clear I had to do something different. The daily fear of killing every one that had ever done me wrong, the fear of embarrassing the cause of God, and even more, the fear that sat quietly inside me each morning as I held the 9 mm and wondered if this was "the Day it all ended," I had to leave. I knew no one would understand, especially my sons—Robert, Andre, and Christopher. I loved them so much, more than life itself, but I knew if I didn't leave I was going to die. Dying by the hands of the police or my own would have been more painful than leaving. At least by leaving, I would live; and somehow and somewhere, I would always be there when they needed me. The rickety wooden trailer was old and splintered, but it was all I could afford. The sixty-four dollars and gas card in my pocket was the last money I had in the world. When the money ran out, that was it. I loaded all my books, clothes, odds and ends into the trailer and hooked it to the borrowed dark blue Ford. The Ford was leased through the medical corporation Dr. Edna and I formed. She agreed to make the payments until I found a job. That Ford had a history of hardship all its own; it had already been involved in two accidents requiring major repairs. I didn't know that sometime later I would almost be killed in it and again see the watchful hand of God at work.

# CHAPTER TWENTY-FIVE

*The steps of a good man are ordered by the Lord:*
*and he delighteth in his way*
*Though he fall, he shall not be utterly cast down;*
*for the Lord upholdeth him with his hand.*
—Psalms 37:23, 24

It's funny how time seems to slow down and speed up. Sometimes it just disappears. That's how my drive toward the Mexican border was—unmemorable. I had only two specific plans—cross the Mexican border at Laredo Texas or drive into the mountains of the desert southwest, find a dark cave, and kill myself. The Mexican plan was to go to Central America and join with rebel leader Daniel Ortega and his Sandinista guerillas. I had been training and practicing mercenary skills for over two years, and now it was time to go to work. The second plan was in the event I couldn't get across the border; there wasn't anything left to live for.

San Antonio, Texas, was two and a half hours north of Laredo. Interstate 35 connected Mexico with Texas and was one of the busiest roadways in American commerce, illegal immigrant smuggling, and drug trafficking.

I was in San Antonio ten years ago and despite the hardship of basic training and the disappointment of losing training honors because of racial jealousy, I was glad to be back there. I didn't know what I was going to do in San Antonio. I had no clear plan how to get across the border with my guns and, worst, no money. I thought about the large wooden Adventist church on Hackberry Street, the Ephesus church, and if any of those wonderful people were still around. I thought about Albert Marks, my prayer partner in Vietnam who I met at the Ephesus church in 1966. Then I remembered Elwood Clay. Elwood was tall, thin, and wore a neat short Afro hairstyle. Above his full lips was a stubby tangled moustache that seemed to match perfectly his thick black-rimmed glasses. Elwood was an enigma. He was a fiery preacher of righteousness, spoke rapidly mastered Spanish, roamed the country as a self-supporting missionary, was a jack of all trades, an intimidator, and at times, just plain scary if you crossed him. I met Elwood at the Adventist serviceman's center on Ashby Street near downtown San Antonio. He had not long returned from missionary work with the Chamula Indians in

Chiappas, Mexico. He was living and working at the serviceman's center and on Sabbaths was around preaching and talking with the servicemen from Fort Sam Houston. We hit it off right away and became good friends. Years later, we met again in Detroit where by then he had married a beautiful Hispanic Christian lady, Rebecca, and had three wonderful children. While in Detroit, I was a frequent visitor to his home; and to me, it was like heaven. We often prayed together, sang, preached, passed out Christian literature, and witnessed in the streets together. I loved my brother and his family even to this day and miss them dearly.

As I drove closer to old, familiar streets, I wondered if Elwood was still in San Antonio. I lost contact with him and many others as my life during and after medical school began to unravel. I remembered that he sent me a card or a letter telling me he was moving back to San Antonio. I pulled to the side of the street and thumbed through a small worn phone book I kept in my pocket. There it was—his phone number and address. I found a telephone and called. My pulse quickened at the hope of hearing his voice. He was home! Elwood was just as excited and hurriedly gave me directions to his house. His joyous hug was strong and genuine as were the tears in our eyes. Rebecca and the kids were equally jubilant to see me again. When the dinner was over and the kids and Rebecca went off to bed, Elwood and I sat and talked. He was silent as I recounted some of the darkness that had swallowed my life. I spoke until my voice trailed into a whisper. Tears again filled my eyes; I couldn't stop them as I stared at the floor. Elwood's hand slid crossed my shoulder, and he started praying for me. He asked me to stay the night and rest, but I told him I had to go but would call again before I left town. I was lying; I didn't know where I was going that night or any other night for that matter. Maybe a quiet street somewhere to sleep in the car as I had done a hundred times before. I felt too dangerous and guilt ridden to stay with my friend, so I left. The night was star studded and dark, but the darkness I felt inside was darker; it offered neither stars of hope nor even the hope of a new morning.

"Robert," the Voice interrupted the noise in my head. "Remember Leo Edwards," He said, "call him." *Leo Edwards?* I said to myself. I'd almost forgotten about him. *He probably won't remember me.* I turned on the light, picked up the phone book and searched. I found his number and called.

Dr. Leo King Edwards Jr. was a slim, quiet, fast moving, shorthaired, happy-go-lucky medical resident at Detroit Receiving Hospital (DRH). DRH was the primary training hospital for Wayne State School of Medicine. Leo and I met several times, mostly in the lunchroom or on the wards. Being Afro-American in an academic environment of people who didn't want us to be doctors, we connected right away and became friends. I wondered if he was still in Texas or even if he had graduated. *Of course, he graduated. He was smart, determined, and focused.* Again, I wondered if he would remember me.

Leo was as I remembered him; he was heavier, lot more hair on his face and head, but his smile was as big and generous as ever. Without hesitation or lost of years, we hugged as if time was yesterday. He had changed only a little, but as he stood back, I could tell he noticed a terrible tale in my eyes. He saw weariness deep and hard, an emptiness that shadowed that brief moment of joy. His voiced stammered, "Robert, what's going on?" I wanted to blurt out my whole miserable life as fast as I could to rid my soul of demons. I wanted to ask for help, to ask for something to save me from me. I don't know why I felt that way, I hardly knew him, yet he was the person I was drawn to—the person the Voice told me to find.

It could have been a minute or an hour, maybe two, or three; I don't remember time. Leo sat motionless, not knowing what to say after listening to me. "Got a place to stay?" he said quietly. "No, not yet," I whispered. "Stay here for a few days until you get rested, then we can talk some more and figure out something, okay?" I was too exhausted to say anything but okay. He showed me one of six or seven rooms in the old convent building on Polaris Street. All the rooms were empty except an end room where he stayed. I brought my camouflage backpack, a couple small guns, a pipe bomb, a laundry bag of balled-up clothes, and a rolled sleeping bag and placed them on the cold linoleum floor. "Sorry, I don't have a bed, Robert, but you are welcome to stay here." This will be fine." I thanked him as he turned to leave. I unrolled the sleeping bag, slide the 9 mm under me as I had done a thousand nights, and waited for the darkness of the room to quiet. Unlike most nights when my senses sharpened to the slightest noise or moment, I felt safe and quickly fell into a dreamless sleep.

The sun shown weakly through crumpled metal blinds, and like a bear emerging from a winter's sleep, I squinted through matted eyes, trying to figure out where I was. I looked out into the branches of a large pecan tree and watched the last rays of the sun flitter between the green leaves twisting gently in the wind. It was getting night again. I had slept a night and a day, but it felt so good.

I was still in my crumpled camouflage pants and shirt when I took the wooden steps to the first floor. The first floor near the front entrance had a large commercial type kitchen. A door off the kitchen let into the front office and business section of Dr. Edwards's office practice. On the other side of the frosted receptionist window was a small very comfortable waiting room with sofas, large cloth chairs, a few wooden ones, and a large big screen TV. In the patient examination rooms, there were medical charts, exam equipment, and tables. The back office was beautifully highlighted by a stained glass window and plush carpeted floor. The room was adorned with certificates, trophies, awards, and artworks that Leo brought or received as gifts. Dr. Edward's office was partly a gift from the Catholic dioceses, which he belonged to and a way to get medical care into the poor east side of San Antonio near the church. The diocese allowed him to rent at a low cost and gave permission for him to renovate the old nun convent into an office and living quarters for him.

I soon learned how popular and loved he was. Everyone knew the Edwards family. Neighbors often brought lunch of casseroles, meats, pies, cakes, Mexican and soul food, and a hundred other expressions of appreciation. Leo told his family all about me, or as much as he felt safe to tell them; and within a week of being there, I was adopted by the Edwards. I was surprised to go back to my "bear cave" and find a single iron spring bed, mattress, and pillow. "I'm not letting any of my sons sleep on the floor," Mom Edwards chided with hands on her hips. Michelle, Leo's sister and nurse, was a diamond. Not only was she beautiful from her smile to her shoelaces, she was just a wonderfully beautiful person inside like her brother and the rest of her family. I came to love Dad Edwards for his venerable wisdom. He looked like the great Afro-American leader Fredrick Douglas with his silver Afro-style hair and long ragged beard. His old truck, his farm animals, and riveting stories from his past were his joy. Anthony or Toni, Leo's younger brother, was simply full of fun and talented beyond measure. He painted, played several instruments, sang, reveled in professional photography, and just enjoyed life and living. Virginia, the little Hispanic lady with the sunburst smile, was the office manager, receptionist, and administration person. I grew to love and cherish her for the hundred and one things she did to help me feel comfortable.

I had been at Dr. Edward's office-home for about a week. "Robert," Leo said as I sat on my iron bed, "would you like to come downstairs and see some patients with me?" *Patients?* I thought to myself. "I'm not a doctor anymore." "Come on. Just a few," Leo urged. More out of respect for his kindness than really wanting to see patients, I agreed. Of course, I had brought a few new clothes with the $500 Leo gave me when he ask if I had any money, and so I no longer wore my camouflage, but other habits were harder to let go—my 9 mm was never far from me.

Among the many other things Dr. Edwards did was to actually hire me to work with him. He gave me a salary of $1,500 every two weeks, paid my Michigan child support, introduced me to all the area doctors, assisted me in getting admitting privileges to area hospitals and nursing homes, set me up in an office of my own, asked Michelle to also be my nurse, hired an additional nurse to work with me, asked Virginia to do my billing, and gave me all the new patients to the practice for several months. He never asked for anything in return. He never asked anything about my past; he never wanted to know. He only wanted to help. His heart was like that.

The Edwards family was a gift from God; they were the "life raft" sent just when I needed it, just when the last threads of hope had slipped from my gasp.

# CHAPTER TWENTY-SIX

*"A man that hath friends must shew*
*himself friendly; and there is a friend*
*that sticketh closer than a brother"*
—Proverbs 18:24

Despite the glow of hope Dr. Edwards's kindness ignited, the prison cell inside me was bleak as ever. Guilt and anger guarded the door of my heart, and weighted chains of a wounded conscience rattled day and night. I continued to drink, take sedatives, and on occasion, found uneasy comfort in the arms of strangers. I continued ever more deadly scenarios of revenge against any unfortunate police officer that would confront me. I further honed my sniper skills at the gun ranges in the Texas countryside on weekends. I felt best, however, when I was alone. Alone, I could allow my mind to drift. It was like waiting for a phone call from someone who would solve all your problems or make them worst. Maybe I was waiting for God to speak to me long distance or something. But I knew at any given moment, I could explode or sink deeper into another situation. My heart raced, my pulse quickened, breathing became deep and frantic until I reached for a cold beer or two or six; and then I was calm.

Over time I had little desire to visit my friends, Elwood and Rebecca, or even drive by the local Adventist church. On many Sundays, I attended the Holy Redeemer Catholic Church where the Edwards attended. It was an Afro-American Baptist-style Catholic Church—the kind of congregation that rocked and swayed to rhythmic inner city gospel music and promenaded with fashion elegance I enjoyed. Nevertheless, at church I was only a spectator, a bystander without religious feelings or purpose. After church I returned to partying at clubs, dancing, movies going, attending plays, or sitting around watching sports with a can of beer in my hand. During the week though, I worked hard, like Dr. Edwards being the best doctor I could be. In a typical week I cared for fifty to seventy-five office patients, ten to thirty hospitalized patients, and made rounds at seven nursing homes. That was my life, as fragile as it was.

My popularity with neighbors and patients began to heighten by my association with the Edwards. This seemed to bother Leo some when his patients asked more and more about me or lavished me with gifts and food as they had done him. All in all, we got along well, but I knew I couldn't let or depend on Leo's support forever or in anyway directly or indirectly cause offense to my friend. My love and respect for him meant things had to change.

First, I painted the dark blue leased Ford to a light blue, then fixed the dented front fender—scars from earlier neglect and accidents in Detroit. The car belonged to Medical Services of Detroit, my business name, with Dr. Edna and Dr. Donald as partners. I think that car was cursed from the start, not because it was a Ford but because of who drove it. Dr. Donald left for Nassau, Bahamas, suddenly to escape mounting legal problems, leaving the car in the Miami airport without telling Dr. Edna and me where it was. After learning where it was I flew to Miami and drove the filthy car back to Detroit. The dust-covered car truly was filthy. Garbage and bags of urine-soaked, feces-filled diapers, dead flies, and maggots had baked for three months in the hot Florida sun. The car had a dented front fender from an accident during one of Dr. Donald's drunken nights on the town. Dr. Edna kept that secret from me too.

A week or so after returning to Detroit, I parked the car in front of my office on busy Gratiot Avenue. Moments after going inside, I heard a loud crash. A black limousine hit the rear of the Ford, sending it into a telephone pole. The back and front of the car crumpled to the tune of $4,000 in damages.

On afternoon in San Antonio, the Ford Leasing Company called from Detroit, asking to renew the lease or return the car. I decided to return the now light blue car to Michigan and buy a new Ford Mustang in San Antonio. In order to drive the new Mustang off the lot, I had to show poof of insurance, so I transferred the insurance from the old Ford to the Mustang. Bad idea, and I felt it. At the moment, it seemed the only choice, so I proceeded to drive the lease car back to Detroit by way of Texas, Oklahoma, Kansas, Missouri, and Indiana into Michigan without insurance.

Again, the monotony of night driving settled into the doldrums of static-filled am music, rushes of cool air from the rolled-down window, silent wandering thoughts, and adjusting the mirror from blinding headlights.

*City Limits, St. Louis, Missouri*, the green highway sign flashed. The darkness of the countryside turned into the spaced streetlights and warm glow of the city expressway. Behind me, two eighteen-wheeler semi-tractor trailers raced side by side. I turned slightly toward the passenger side catching the glint of reflected light high up the grassy slope. I took a second quick look and saw a pickup truck. Out of control, the grayish Ford F-150 with pipe railings fixed to its rear bed bounced high over the curb of the expressway ramp one hundred feet up the grassy slope. I knew there was going to be a terrible accident as the pickup truck careened wildly toward the traffic-filled highway below. I slammed the gas pedal from sixty-five up to ninety miles per hour to get out of the catastrophe about to happen. I took a quick glance in the mirror; the two tractor-trailer's brakes and horns screamed, as smoke billowed from burning rubber tires clawing at the pavement. Chaotic headlights jetted crisscrossing beams all over the highway. The trucks twisted back and forth like giant pythons locked in battle trying to avoid the onrushing pickup. I quickly changed lanes, anticipating I might have to stop to help the injured when *BAM!* The back window of my car exploded, and the blue Ford jolted violently like an animal caught in the jaws of a monster. I gripped the steering wheel with all my strength to keep from flipping over. I stared straight ahead tensed, too intoxicated with adrenaline to look back. Frantically, I chanced a look side to side searching the highway for an escape. I knew I had been hit by one of the tractor-trailer weaving out of control and was about to be crushed. Then as if the monster was through toying with me, it suddenly let go. It was the pickup truck and its drunk driver that had somehow missed the tractor-trailers and found me. After releasing me from its grip the pickup truck swerved on two wheels from one side of the expressway to the other. Then, as if summoned back by its hellish master the pickup growled as it accelerated like a demon down the highway, up a distant off ramp, and out of sight. I slowed enough to make it to the shoulder of the highway. One of the tractor-trailer drivers quickly drove up behind me and got out to see if I had been hurt. He was surprised I had not been killed. "Did you see that!" the driver screamed. "Need help, buddy," he offered. My legs were too shaky to get out of the car at first. "No. I'm okay," I said. "I'll call the police. Do you need an ambulance," the driver asked. "No, I'm okay," I said flatly. When I finally did get out the car, I saw why he was so amazed that I was just okay. The whole left side of the back of the car was caved in inches from the tires and gas tank. Thankfully, the rear window exploded outward instead of inward and showered my head with sharp glass missiles.

After the initial shock, anger sat in at the fool who nearly killed me; then another realization set in—I had no insurance on the car. Now I knew for sure that car was cursed.

When the state police left, I checked out the car; it was still drivable. Cursed or not, I think the demolished car was a blessing to many holiday travelers who saw it and pulled away from me. Many adjusted their driving and slowed down after seeing me. Children pressed their faces and fingers against windows of passing cars. "Look, Daddy, at the raggedy car!" It really was an advertisement for highway safety.

Whatever I did unknowingly to help others on the highway didn't help me. The gnawing pain of no insurance on that leased car for which I had to pay for was indescribably depressing. "What else is gonna happen!" I pounded the steering wheel. And before I knew it, I said, "Lord, please help me." I surprised myself. Then I said it again, "Lord, please help me get out of this mess."

I arrived in Detroit late in the afternoon. I called the insurance company to tell them about the accident and that I had cancelled the insurance a few days before. There was a long silence on the phone. "Mr. Gardner," the agents finally spoke,

"I'm not sure we can do anything to help. You should have kept the insurance until you returned the car. I'm sorry." "You got to do something to help!" I appealed in desperation, almost to the point of panic. "Send us the police report. That's all I can say," the agent responded sympathetically before hanging up.

I was in a daze. The world had suddenly gotten darker and colder. The one thing I wanted to do was to get rid of that cursed car as fast as I could. In Detroit, it wasn't unusual to see old beat-up and new cars—some rusted out from the winter's salt and others rattling from jarring encounters with potholes—but my car was different; it scared people. I imagined they wondered what fool would drive a wreck like that on any street anywhere.

It was after five o'clock in the afternoon when I slowly eased the battered car into the lot behind the Ford Leasing Office building. Most employees had gone for the day, and no guards were in sight to stop and ask where I was going with that piece of junk. I looked cautiously to make sure no one was watching from the windows; then I put the keys over the visor, opened and eased closed the door, then walked away as fast as I could. I admit it was wrong, but it felt good. It was like ending a relationship with an old girlfriend who had too many issues, too many secrets, and too many ties to the past. The next day, I phoned the Ford leasers and told them I had left the car in the lot and that I had a little accident. The person on the line just said, "Okay, we'll wait to hear from the insurance company." I didn't tell them I had cancelled the insurance.

I returned to San Antonio and waited every day to hear from the amazed person who found the demolished parked car in the lease lot or the insurance company. But I heard nothing. After about a month, I called the insurance company. "We paid the bill," the agent said. *Thank you, God!* I shouted in my head. In my head I also heard the Voice breathe, "I saw the truck before you did. I heard your cry for help. I'm still here."

Michelle, my nurse was working late in the office. "Robert," she spoke, handing me the phone. "One of Leo's patients is having an allergic reaction to her medicine." I spoke to Ms. Brown, and she described her rash and itching that had gotten worst throughout the afternoon. I asked if she had trouble breathing or swallowing. In a trembling voice, she said, "No". I told her I would make a house call to give her an injection that would help.

Just a week or so earlier, Ms. Brown sat patiently with others in the office waiting area. She wore a loose, colorful skirt, a fitted blouse and stylish tan sandals that wrapped eloquently around her shapely thin ankles. Her legs were crossed, and one hand was under her chin as she pretended to be watching television. Even from a distance as I came in through the lobby door, I saw her cream-colored skin—soft and silky—and those catlike eyes that were seductive, dark, and in that brief moment, so exciting.

"Where do you want the shot?" I offered with a smile. The Benadryl, a strong antihistamine, was often used for mild allergic reactions. "Is it gonna hurt?" she said, looking through swollen eyes and trembling like a kid at the dentist office. "Depends on where you want it," I said, trying to look more serious. She turned her shoulder toward me and slid her sleeve back. "It might hurt less if I put it in your hip," I suggested. Cautiously, she pulled up her dress, exposed a tiny area of hip, and never flinched as the Benadryl quickly went in. I rubbed the area with alcohol much slower than usual and was interrupted by, "Are you finished? That was wonderful," she said with relief. I didn't feel a thing." She smiled, turning toward me. Even with swollen eyes, she was beautiful. In that brief moment of attraction, I was breathless, I felt a little dizzy, and knew I liked her. "Well, Ms. Brown, I hope you feel better. Call the office if you need something." My heart restarted after I left and wouldn't stop racing until I saw her again.

A week later, I received a thank you card and an invitation to dinner. Over the next few months, we enjoyed more dinners, movies, and conversation. I loved doing things for her and buying surprise gifts. We were great company for each other, and I didn't spoil it with too many details of my past. I learned that she was recently divorced and had a twelve-year-old son. She was very bitter toward her ex-husband who had remarried and had little if any contact with his son. That resentment grew into a fortress of protection, distrust of others, and a defense for self-preservation that would eventually dismantle our relationship. The relationship between her and her mother was another drama; it was always tense. Ms. Brown was her father's favorite, so her mother felt the breakup of the family was due in a strange way to her. Budd, her father, was an old-school playboy. He abandoned the family for life in the fast lane of honky-tonks, sultry women and smooth alcohol. He left Alma, his wife to raise and struggle with three small children. Thus, the legacy of bitter distrust and suspicion passed from mother to daughter and to a future with Ms. Brown I'd wish had turned out different.

Ms. Brown was somewhat religious. She was a member of the Methodist Church, the one she and her family had gone to for years. I was not inclined to go to any church for the right reasons, but when she asked if I would go with her, I agreed. Far from feeling anything spiritual, I simply wanted to please her and was willing to do any and everything to win her heart—a heart that was well guarded.

Some years later, we got married in a small ceremony of Las Vegas strangers. Up to the last few minute before the limousine arrived, she flipped a yes-no coin in her head. "Do you want to get married or not?" I asked with finality. Hardly looking at me, she stood transfixed, staring at the bright diamond ring on her finger. If Ms. Brown loved anything in life more than life itself, it was diamonds—diamonds, ease of life, and the evasive approval of her mother was all there was to life. I was frustrated by then and was willing to walk out of her life forever. I was just going to walk away. "Okay," she said, and we got married.

I was working in the office and hospitals it seemed almost every day, including weekends. On occasions, there were some friction between Leo and I over work schedules and probably some personal things having to do with mutual friends and acquaintances. I knew I had to find my own way soon in order not to dampen the kindness and love extended to me by Leo and his family. Inside, I still felt numb, nervous, empty, and breathless. I trembled almost constantly for the next calamity to come crashing into my life. Financial crisis was Genora's specialty. I wondered what situation she was creating in Michigan to suck me into with last minute pleads ending in "They're your kids too, you got to do something!" I loved my sons more then anything else worth loving, more then myself for sure. Never did they ask or need something that I did not provide it. I wanted to keep and raise them but Genora was adamant and hostile when it came to that suggestion. She was their mother and for that alone I loved her.

One evening, I called an old friend—Leonard Johnson. I'm not sure why; I just needed to talk to someone I trusted, someone real and someone who would listen. Leonard was fifty-four years old, a physician, pilot, and colonel in the United States Air Force. Although he had traveled the world, it was my good fortune he was stationed at Kelly AFB in San Antonio, Texas, and was the command surgeon for the Electronic Security Command. I met Leonard before I went to Vietnam in 1966 and greatly admired him. He was a military officer and a tremendous Christian. All his life, he wanted to be a pilot and a doctor in the air force; he was both. Although he loved his career, his first love was God. He never missed an opportunity to be an ambassador for heaven. When his duties required him to attend official military meetings, he would fly small private airplanes or borrowed military jets to meetings but along the way, always found time to visit the local Adventist churches and camp meetings. He was smooth, handsome, and articulate. As a speaker, he captured attentions, harnessed enthusiasm, and gave flight to the dreams and hopes of young and old. His friends and acquaintances numbered in the thousands. Above all his gifts, he was easy to talk to; that's why I called him.

On a few desperate occasions when I spoke with him, he sensed right away the conflict raging in my heart. He reminded me in gentle tones of how I use to be, my dedication, faithfulness, and love for things spiritual. He always listened with quiet compassion and offered practical advice ending in "let's pray."

"Robert, what you need is some time to relax," Leonard said. "If you join the air force, you get time off, vacations, malpractice paid for, travel, and a bonus." It was the bonus of twenty thousand dollars I so badly needed that I said, "I'll look into it." Some days later after talking it over with Dr. Edwards, I contacted a recruiter, completed the paper work, and was accepted as a captain in the US Air Force in September 1986.

A number of female friends were very unhappy, especially Ms. Brown. But Ms. Brown was the one I was most interested in and promised I would come back to visit.

I was excited to make the phone call to tell Leonard the good news. And, indeed, he was just as excited to hear that my life was changing for the better. He himself was about to retire after a long distinguished air force career. He knew that the air force would give me structure, challenge my military skills, and bring out the best in me. He wanted to celebrate the occasion for my decision and come to Eglin Air Force Base in Northeast Florida to visit me once I got settled in.

My first year in the air force went fast. I was a staff internal medicine doctor and enjoyed my work very much. In the back of my mind I looked forward to seeing Leonard again. I wanted him to see what his gentle words and fervent prayers had done in my life. I don't remember the day or the hour or even how the news came. I only felt a hole where my heart once beat. "Leonard died in a fiery airplane crash over the weekend," the August 6, 1987, *San Antonio Register* newspaper said. Leonard's penetrating eyes looked through the newsprint's black-and-white photo of him. The small Comanche Piper Cub airplane was making its way from Nashville, Tennessee, where Leonard had visited his daughter and was going to his tenth reunion at Elkhart High School, in Elkhart, Indiana. His trip was nearly over when, as so often happens in late summer in the Midwest, a thunderstorm rose quickly; and with it, terrible winds, lighting, and thunder torn angrily at everything in the sky and on the ground; a pilot's worst nightmare. Leonard tried to make an emergency landing at the Glendale Airport in Kokomo, Indiana; but that day it was not to be, Leonard closed his eyes to await the life's given call to rise.

# CHAPTER TWENTY-SEVEN

*Deep calleth unto deep . . .*

—Psalms 42:7

The lost of my friend stayed with me for a long time. I even visited the local Adventist church a couple of times out of a sense of debt to Leonard. I felt I owed my friend the effort to straighten out my life. The people in the small Florida church were cordial but not warm. My feelings toward many of the white churches, Adventist and others I visited left me emptier then when I arrived. It was painful to think and worst to believe that little had changed in human nature that even Christianity was hard press to make a difference.

My experience with the drug dealers, prostitutes, conmen, cops and some black folk in three-piece suits affirmed the problem was universal and not just our problem or their problem. Nevertheless, my disaffection and caution of whites was born of experience, not bigotry or prejudice. I had been arrested many times by the police, ostracized at the church's premier university, cheated for promotion by the army, dehumanized by the medical school, defamed by a hospital system, economically snubbed by employers, and even jealously ignored for my accomplishments and rank in the air force at times—all by Anglos. I've seen the mistreatment and well-rehearsed animosity unjustly heaped upon some of the most loving black Americans you could imagine. Sadly it seems, as a fact of life the attitude and feelings of many, even among so-called Christians toward Afro-Americans, is one of distain and avoidance. Like a toothache in the night that finds no relief till morning, we've endured this long night of pain only by the providence of the Almighty. There is a terrible verdict waiting in the celestial courts against all those in government, news, communications, legal, medical, business, religious, and a thousand others who pledged *"one nation, under God with liberty and justice for all"* and have defaulted. America has been creative in her proselytizing of ethnic hatred and exportation of black negativity. The irony of all of this is that the more America changes the more it remains the same. The human heart is a battlefield from which none leaves without wounds or leave at all by the grace of God. Enough venting, except for one final thought; some of the most loving, generous and sincere people I have met have been white and I loved them for their unique kindness and special friendships.

To get away from the stress of work, I created other stresses for myself. Something was missing in my life for which I had no energy or willingness to find; like a turtle I crawled back into my protective shell of neutrality. I resisted no evil, denied myself no pleasure in food, drink, and hanging out on weekends. I was in neutral and what ever happened, happened. There were times, however at Eglin AFB, when I just had to get out of the area; so on Friday afternoons, I'd clear my patient schedule, get in my silver Ford Mustang, and drive twelve hours to see Ms. Brown in San Antonio. Before I realized it, I fell in love with her and endured constant restlessness until I saw and touched her again. She became everything to me. My life had been a mess, my divorce from Genora agonizing, and my secret military training a perennial nightmare. And now for the first time in eons, I felt a pulse in my heart that was not fear. I drove the seven hundred miles to San Antonio and back to the AF Base in Florida nearly thirty times during the three years at Eglin. Ms. Brown symbolized hope of normalcy to my life; I was willing to do anything to have her—anything.

One day, we were walking in the mall. "Robert"—Ms. Brown pulled my arm—"let me show you something!" She led me into a jewelry store. "I love this ring. Will you buy it for me?" Queasiness came over me, like eating at a greasy spoon. "What was she doing?" I said to myself. But since I was in neutral, I bought the $900 "friendship-I-think-it's-an-engagement" ring stupid. She was thrilled. I was numb and still quit queasy. *What the hell did I just do?* I thought. Anyway, it made her happy, so I was happy, I guessed.

During the three-plus years at Eglin, I was fortunate to receive training as a flight surgeon while on temporary duty assignment at Brooks AFB in San Antonio. My friend Leonard was a flight surgeon, and I remembered him telling me this was the best of both worlds—being a military doctor and learning to fly.

In 1989, I was transferred to Bergstrom AFB in Austin, Texas—one hour north of San Antonio. This was great since now I was closer to Ms. Brown. I had an apartment off base but spent most of my weekends in San Antonio. By then, I had been promoted to rank of major and shortly thereafter transferred to Brooks AFB in San Antonio. At Brooks, I was an internal medicine consultant to the worldwide US Air Force and in particular aircrew members who had developed medical problems. Over the four years I was there, I accomplished three important things. First, I learned to fly the Cessna airplane, then jet trainers and helicopters. Second, I helped finished a thirty-year AF research project on abnormal heart rhythms—ventricular tachycardia—that particular malady had grounded and ended the careers of many pilots and crewmembers. Dr. William Kruyer and I went to Washington DC to brief the AF surgeon general. Our efforts helped to reinstate many pilots back to flying status. The training of each pilot cost over a million dollars, and so this was a big deal and welcome news to all. We were given a standing ovation, and I received a medal. The last important thing I did was to marry Ms. Brown.

My tenure at Brooks was nearly over when I was promoted to lieutenant colonel. I asked to be transferred to Randolph AFB across town in San Antonio, and surprisingly, my request was granted. I had made a lot of friends in high places by then, and a phone call was all it took to get what I wanted.

Although things seemed to be getting better and more stable in my life, I was in a spiritual coma. Patients in comas sometimes hear the monotonous beeping of monitors, see wavy images of people peering over the bed rail, or smell pungent odors of alcohol and anesthetics. At times, people in comas recount simple dreams; and at times, they have nightmares. I had two nightmares worth recalling because it reminded me that Jesus was the great physician who specialized in comas.

I sat at my desk one afternoon and opened my LES (leave and earning statement). "What!" I shouted. "This can't be!" My pay was reduced from $3,700 to only $100 dollars. Every LES has a section at the bottom that explain changes to member accounts. "Due to accounting errors, you have been overpaid $43,000, and your current pay schedules has been adjusted to correct this deficient until all amounts are settled." My head was swirling. "I can't live on $100 every two weeks! Something is wrong!" I raced over to the military accounting office. The finance officer affirmed the information and said there was nothing that he could do. I went back to my office deeply depressed. Before I knew it, I buried my head in my hands and asked God to help me. "Robert," the Voice said, "write what I place in your remembrance." So I did. I wrote for an hour or more, I don't remember. When the letter was finished, the Voice spoke again. "Take the letter to the general." So I did. This was totally out of protocol. The general usually was not available, an appointment was always needed, and this was a trivial matter handled by lower-ranking officers. In fact, as I stepped into the plush waiting area, the secretary looked up at me, then the clock. The general was about to leave for a meeting and would be gone out of town for a while. As I stood at the door, the general came to his door. Our eyes met in recognition. "Hi, Colonel Gardner, what you need?" The secretary's mouth hung open because he didn't have time to tell me the general couldn't see me today. I apologized for the interruption and asked to speak with him for just a moment about a personal matter. Without hesitation, he said, "Sit down." I quickly told him the problem, showed him the letter, and waited for his response. "Lieutenant, get the finance colonel on the phone." "Charlie, want you to do me a favor. I got one of my officers I want you to help. He got a letter I want you to look at, okay." Then the general smiled at me and said, "Go on over to finance, they'll straighten this out. Let me know if you have any problems." I went quickly over to finance, pass the finance officer who said, "Nothing could be done," then right to Charlie. Within ten minutes, Charlie said it's all taken care of, and in fact, "we owe you $2,000 back pay." My heart sung praises to God that afternoon, and I felt a change occurring in me.

The other nightmare occurred earlier before I left Florida. I had just spent the weekend with Ms. Brown and had to get back to the base by Sunday evening. Usually, I drove; but this time, I wanted to spend the twenty-four hours with Ms. Brown instead of driving, so I took the plane to San Antonio. As I left San Antonio under threatening gray skies, the darkness had deepened, and the rain and winds picked up as we landed in New Orleans. By then, lighting, strong winds, large raindrops and dime-sized hail plummeted the airport. Most of the larger airplanes were grounded, and incoming flights were delayed or cancelled. I had to get back to the base because I had no orders to be in Texas. It wasn't illegal, but the rule was to be back in time for normal duty hours; I was frantic. The only flight to Pensacola, Florida—forty miles from the base—was a small commuter jet that carried about twenty passengers. Besides being frantic, a fear settled over me that I couldn't explain. It seemed like something invisible and ominous was all around me as I made my way to the plane. Passengers were given umbrellas as they raced across the tarmac to the waiting jet that sat in ghostly outline behind a curtain of horizontal rain. The jets shivered as it gained altitude. The rain and hail pounded the aircraft as everyone sat hard against the seats until the plane leveled off. Jolts and air pockets tossed the small jet like a wrestler flinging a tiny opponent across the ring. As we careened through boiling dark skies, the lighting grew fiercer and lit the blackness almost continuously. Tail winds pushed the plane so it felt like we were traveling at sonic speed. As we neared Pensacola, the winds became hurricane in force. The baggage door over the seats flung open, passengers' gasped, some screamed, and even the flight attendant shrieked and started crying as she clung to her seat. Up and down, rolling side to side, the plane wings seemed about to be ripped apart in the air. "Ladies and gentlemen, I will try to make a landing at Pensacola." The pilot tried to sound calm, but his voice quivered. With each ten-foot jerk upward and horrific twenty feet drop downward, I grunted, "Oh Jesus! Oh Jesus!"

Suddenly, the jet jolted almost vertically straight down. More people started screaming and crying as seat belts strained to hold us in place. Rain and hail raced parallel past the windows as lighting flashed like disco strobe lights. The plane swayed back and forth vibrating as it raced straight down like a missile headed for its target. From the angle of the landing, I knew the pilot had lost control of the jet, and we were going to crash at more than three hundred miles per hour. "Oh Jesus, have mercy on us!" I prayed over and over as I gripped the armrest and braced my foot against the bulkhead. The jet shot through altitude, and as suddenly as it nose-dived, it slowly began to level somewhat, but we were still pointing head down. I looked out the window and saw building in the lighting flash and knew we were only seconds away from crashing. I closed my eyes and said, "Jesus!" once more. At that moment, the jet arched upward as if being lifted, the buildings and runway swooped by at a blur, and the plane struggled and violently shook as it climbed back into the ink sky. "Ladies and gentlemen, we will have to go out in to the Gulf of Mexico to burn off fuel. The storm is all around us. After a while, I will attempt to get us down. Thank you for your patience." As the plane bounced its way into the darkness over the Gulf, I thanked God for hearing the cry of a sinner. The jet descended rough but more normally the next time. I left the plane weak and shaken. My heart pounded as if coming through my chest, I knew I couldn't ignore God's mercy and grace much longer. I knew He was doing all he could to save me and tell me how much He still loved me.

# CHAPTER TWENTY-EIGHT

*If it seem evil unto you to serve the Lord,*
*choose you this day whom ye will serve . . . .*
—Joshua 24:15

I enjoyed being stationed in San Antonio. It was my new home and where all my newly acquired dreams were. Randolph AFB was only eight minutes away from the fresh two-story tan brick house Ms. Brown and I had built. A beautiful home, a beautiful wife, a great job, and many new friends but still, a vacancy in my heart that was as hollow and empty as ever. Going to the Methodist Church with Ms. Brown was good, but it was not the Adventist family. It was like being with relatives at Thanksgiving dinner and having nothing in common but wanting turkey and dressing.

Once at the Methodist church I was asked to teach an early-teen Sunday school class mostly of girls. Ms. Brown was actually a third-grade teacher in the public school, but these rambunctious and precocious ladies were intimidating, so she asked me to give the lesson. Their regular teacher was ill, and after a few minutes of watching them zone-out the adults in the room and huddle to talk about boys, I could understand why. It felt strange, but I was relaxed and managed a few smiles and to eventually get their attention. Ms. Brown sat next to me as I taught and seemed to really enjoy the lesson too.

Pastor Fenton was tall, very dark skinned, medium built, and slightly balding. Although his preaching style was classic Methodist, there were many stirring moments generously flavored with old-time Baptist rhythm and rhyme. What I liked most was the appeal songs; his clear baritone voice vibrated emotions like few I've heard before. Even the usually unimpressed pew warmers tapped their toes and in finality would jump to their feet, waving hands and shouting, "Amen! Halleluiah! Praise God!" Man, he could sing! Pastor Fenton was also a seasoned minister, a mentor, and a counselor. It was his sermons that began to remind me of my rich heritage in the Advent church. In fact, our shared roots stemmed from the Great 1844 Awakening, which heralded the Second Coming of Christ based on the Bible prophecies found in the books of Daniel and Revelation. It was a worldwide moment, starting spontaneously and touching nearly every continent. The unbelievable news caused mass revivals, heart searching, and in some cases, fear and fanaticism. The faithful events of the 1840's was largely spearheaded by prominent Methodist and Baptist preachers who went from town to town holding meetings attended by thousands. When Christ did not appear, many became disillusioned, despondent, anti-Christian, and backsliders. Still, others believed the prophecies true and restudied the Scriptures. Among those was a small group who later became known as Seventh-day Adventist. They believed in the certainty of a literal visible return of Christ and that the Seventh-day Sabbath of the Bible was never changed. The events of the 1844 period did have meaning and answers were divinely given as a result of earnest prayer, fasting, and Spirit-guided Bible study. They searched the scriptures night and day until the truth became clearer. The Adventist discovered in the ancient Jewish sanctuary service that the Day of Atonement, a time of soul-searching among the Jewish people had its counterpart in the heavenly sanctuary as a Great Investigative Judgment. The Great Awakening then was the clarion call to that awesome event. The key point was not that Christ was coming back, but that judgment against the human family had began in heavenly courts. (Revelation 14:7, Daniel 7: 9-10, Hebrews 9-10).

When the Methodist pastor learned that I used to be a Baptist but now a Seventh-day Adventist, his warm openness changed to caution and reservation. Maybe I bothered his conscience some. I know in my heart he really was a man of God who loved the Lord and truly looked to heaven for his final reward. It wasn't long, however, before he started aiming Sunday sermons toward me to show the error of Saturday Sabbath, the belief in death till resurrection morning, and the Ten Commandments that were nailed to the cross according to him and many other churches. I had no comments. Ms. Brown at my side would steal a glance to see my reaction. I only made mental notes and remembered that God loved him and all who desired, looked for, and followed truth. The irony of going to the Methodist Church had two unexpected results—it was drawing me back to God and separating me from Ms. Brown who was the love of my life.

Like so many defining moments in life, the details of time are lost. What was clear, however, was that my years of marriage to Ms. Brown were difficult. Our ideas about generosity, communication, trust, loyalty, and belief in God were as different as two people could be. Inside, my self-esteem, my insane love for her and my awakening conscience torn me apart day and night. To please Ms. Brown, I compromised every ideal I had to the point of considering giving up religion, God, and ever communicating with my sons and family; it was her wants and wishes or nothing. The lost of my identity was almost unbearable. I even gave pause to end it all with a piece of cold steel wedged in my mouth as I had considered so many times in Detroit. Only once had I been so madly in love with someone to the point of hurting myself or clearing the field of anyone who came between my lady and me. Ms.J looked like Ms. Brown in size and shapeliness. Her large eyes, explosive laugh and zest for life and fun was intoxicating. She was the proto-type for all who followed. When my foolishness hurt her she returned to an old boyfriend. I went to his house one evening and found her there staring out the window dressed in a shear nightgown. My rage was immediate. I had been betrayed. Ms. J stood behind the half-open curtain frozen in fear because she knew my temper and my capacity for destruction. She also knew how much I loved her and she loved me. I was her everything and she was mine. I stormed to my car, slammed the accelerator and left a cloud of burning rubber as I sped away. With love and tenderness she found me later and apologized. But it was never the same after that defining moment. Then I couldn't forget the boyfriend who snuggled behind her standing at the curtain with a big, in-your-face smile. That smile, like the police officers would not go unanswered. A few days later I went back to his house to ask, and then beg him to leave her along. He was handsome, smooth talking and flashed that nauseating, self-assured smile like a game show host. He carried the smile, but I carried a 9mm and a silenced-22 caliber automatic and was there to erase that smile, forever. He let me in and I sat across from him never blinking, focused and clear about why I was there. I was waiting for him to jump bad or be sarcastic; that's all I needed to waste him. There was an invisible force or pressure in the room; I could feel it. The scene was like a deadly drama with unseen spectators edging me on to do it. When he looked into my eyes a mix of tears and fire he stopped smiling; he realized how much I loved her. "Well man", he said, "You should get your act together. She ran to me because of you." He was right; I was the fool as always. The 9mm in the small of my back was poised for a fast draw; I eased it deeper into my belt as I stood up. "I'm sorry I bothered you", I said walking pass him out the door and into a cold starless night. Looking back on that night I trembled for the thousands of times that scene played out in the lives of others and ended in crimson tragedy, yet I was spared once more. Oh the grace of God!

Each day and each memory brought me closer to the realization I was trapped beyond my power to change. I didn't know the person everyone called Robert. He and I were two different people living uneasily in the same body. We talked and argued, laughed and cried, prayed and cursed; one wanted to live, the other wanted to die. Then there was that day; like no other day.

The day was ordinary, and driving through afternoon traffic was bumper-to-bumper, hot, and slow. The sunlight danced passed dried raindrops, spattered insects as heat rose lazily from the car's hood. The radio seemed monotonous and distant as my thoughts dwelled on ramblings of no particular importance. Then the song came on, "Choose you this day whom you will serve, will it be God or man the choice is yours." The harmony of the Winans—the singing gospel brothers from Detroit—was pure, and the message was clear. A voice in my head growled, "Turn it off!" But my hand would not move to turn the knob. I stared outward through the windshield as my mind stared inward. I was back in Vietnam. I saw the faces, the sweat, the laughter, and tears of those who died. I saw those I pleaded with to accept Christ and the Bible studies in the mess hall, in the foxholes, inside the bunkers. I saw the long lonely nights of terror and the fear that seized me, and yet the quiet courage God gave me so far from home. Behind the steering wheel, I flinched as long-ago bombs and bullets whizzed passed my ears. I saw the jungle green and napalm fires leaping from burning villages and rice fields. I remembered the Voice that warned of danger and the angels that surrounded me. I heard the sirens of ambulances, the gunfire, and wailing in the streets of Detroit. I smelled the brains dripping from dashboards and scattered over bathroom stalls, I saw the weakness and depression that robbed my family of my presence and cast my soul into years of hell and hate. And then there was the Voice. I remembered the Voice—the Voice that always spoke gently to my wounded heart, the Voice that would not leave even at my worst. I saw Leonard Johnson, his smile, and his gentle words of encouragement. I saw the Fultons, my first parents in Christ, who taught me the love of Jesus when I was only seventeen. How I wanted to reach out and touch them, hold them, and feel safe again. "Choose you this day whom you will serve, will it be God or man, the choice is yours," the Winan's melody echoed. The sunlight no longer danced off the windshield; it glistened like diamond facets through fountains of cascading tears. "Oh Lord, I remember," I spoke softly. "Father, please forgive me, forgive me for my sins." More tears, more memories. "Father, help me. I miss you so much!" And I cried until the fountains became deep oceans and swirling seas of remorse and shame that one so blessed had wandered so far.

The storm that raged for so many years and the dark clouds that had shrouded my life lifted in that moment. The bright rays of grace transformed my long night into a sunlit day. It was just an ordinary day that became an extraordinary moment. My heart was finally set free, and on that day I promised I would never enter the darkness again, never leave the Voice who loved me as no other. Never, would I leave the presence of such marvelous light, such wonderful grace.

Though the battles continued and storms crested the horizon day after day, my trust stood firm. I found peace and found joy I thought forever lost. When the Voice said, "*Come*" I was re-baptized and now live in service to the Eternal God! Praise Him! The great storm was over!

# EPILOGUE

**Psalm 103:1-14**

*Bless the Lord, O my soul: and all that is within me, bless His holy name.*
*Bless the Lord, O my soul, and forget not all His benefits:*
*Who forgiveth all thine iniquities; who healeth all thy diseases;*
*Who redeemeth thy life from destruction;*
*Who crowneth thee with lovingkindness and tender mercies;*
*Who satisfieth thy mouth with good things; so thy youth is renewed like the eagle's.*
*The Lord is merciful and gracious slow to anger, and plenteous in mercy.*
*He will not always chide: neither will He keep His anger forever.*
*He hath not dealt with us after our sins; nor rewarded us according to our iniquities.*
*For as the heaven is high above the earth, so great is His mercy toward them that fear Him.*
*As far as the east is from the west, so far hath He removed our transgressions from us.*
*Like as a father pitieth his children, so the Lord pitieth them that fear Him.*
*For He knoweth our frame; He remembereth that we are dust.*

**Mark 4: 39**

*And He arose, and rebuked the wind, and said unto the sea, PEACE, BE STILL.*
*And the (Storm) ceased, and there was a great calm.*

**Amen.**

**Robert A. Gardner**